W. Schuchman, Lith.

John Wallace.

THE

PRACTICAL ENGINEER:

A TREATISE ON THE SUBJECT OF

MODELING, CONSTRUCTING AND RUNNING STEAM ENGINES.

CONTAINING, ALSO,

DIRECTIONS IN REGARD TO THE VARIOUS KINDS OF MACHINERY CONNECTED WITH STEAM POWER.

PREPARED WITH SPECIAL REFERENCE TO THE NEED OF

STEAMBOAT OWNERS, CAPTAINS, PILOTS AND ENGINEERS,

AND ALSO ALL CONNECTED WITH STATIONARY STEAM ENGINES, ON LAND OR WATER.

SECOND EDITION, IMPROVED AND ENLARGED.

BY JOHN WALLACE,

PRACTICAL ENGINEER.

Orders, with the money inclosed, sent to W. W. and John Wallace, No. 319 Liberty Street, Pittsburgh, will receive immediate attention. The books will be sent by Express or by Mail, as persons ordering them may direct.

PRICE, FIVE DOLLARS PER COPY.

Postage or freight to be paid by the purchaser.

PITTSBURGH:

PRINTED BY W. S. HAVEN, CORNER OF WOOD AND THIRD STREETS.

1865.

PREFACE TO THE FIRST EDITION.

The author presents to the public this volume on "Practical engineering," in the full confidence that such a work has long been desired, and is very much needed by the practical engineer, as well as those who have had little or no experience in this department of science, but whose business requires the aid of steam power. There have been many scientific works published upon the subject of steam, and various other matters connected therewith, altogether foreign from the object sought to be explained; if they were, indeed, intended to assist and instruct the practical engineer. We venture the assertion that there are a hundred things, aye, a thousand, the knowledge of which would be beneficial to the practical engineer, which have not been alluded to nor mentioned in the books hitherto published on this important subject. The reason of this may be attributed to the fact that men of *mere theory* have undertaken to put forth books for the purpose of instructing *practical* men in matters which the authors have never learned, and about which they are totally ignorant. So far as the theory is correct, they are entitled to credit for its promulgation.

But abstract theory can never meet the wants of the practical engineer, and instruct and assist him in working steam engines. In other words, it is folly to assume that a theorist alone can be possessed of such a correct and practical knowledge of steam engines as will meet the hearty response and approbation of that class of persons for whose benefit this treatise is published. It will readily be conceded, then, that a work, in order to be useful, must issue from one who is acquainted not only with the *theory* but with *practical* engineering; and it must exhibit in every page evidence of the author's practical experience. When such is the case, practical men will not only at once perceive the author's capability to explain and elucidate the different branches of the subject upon which he writes, but will be much pleased and instructed by a perusal of the work. Such a book is now presented.

The author of this work has had experience in practical engineering, extending through many years, in various places, and with almost every description of engines. His sources of knowledge are therefore extensive, and the results of his information are given in the pages of this work in a plain, concise and practical style. He has been employed in constructing and working at engines of various kinds, in Pittsburgh, Wheeling, Cincinnati, Louisville, and New Albany, Ind.; and was for some length of time a practical engineer in running the Ohio and Tennessee rivers.

His knowledge of land and stationary engines is quite as extensive as that of most other persons, and he feels therefore confident of the utility of the present work to practical men.

The author has had in contemplation to publish a work of this character, for some eight or ten years, thinking that the public would be benefitted from its perusal; but hoping to be anticipated by some one of merit and usefulness, the project was time after time abandoned. After having perused many works from which engineers (himself among them) expected to derive benefit and information, and finding them wide off the point sought to be obtained, he was persuaded to enter on the task of compiling a book suited to the wants of the practical engineer.

This volume, therefore, has been written and compiled especially for the practical man ; but its pages will be found both interesting and instructive to engine builders. They would do well to consult its pages previously to modeling machinery for steam engines. It is entitled "The Practical Engineer," and should be in the hands of every steamboat captain, as well as engineer. It will not only instruct him in many things of which he is ignorant respecting the machinery and workings of the engine, but will be of great use in enabling him to draw up an order for an engine, with so much clearness and accuracy as to enable the builders to perfectly understand what is required, and upon what terms it can be filled. This is an important consideration, and one which, unfortunately, captains have been heretofore too little acquainted with. It will also be found of interest and profit to the pilot to read this work, as it may lead him to the discovery of danger from the working of the engine, and excite him to greater care in the discharge of his duty.

The second volume will be devoted to marine, factory, and other stationary engines.

In conclusion, I would say to the practical engineer, engine builder, captain and pilot of boats, make this book your study, so far as duty requires, and you will find that your time has not been lost; but, on the contrary, you will be possessed of such a general knowledge of steam engines, as you little thought of previous to its perusal; and upon the strength of which you can each embark upon your respective duties with confidence, knowledge, and a certainty of greater success.

JOHN WALLACE.

Pittsburgh, July 1, 1853.

PREFACE TO THE SECOND EDITION.

In place of a second volume of the "Practical Engineer," which the author in the above preface proposed to publish, he now presents to the public a second edition, improved and enlarged, of the work itself. The additional experience of eleven years in making all kinds of machinery connected with steam engines, enables him to add much to the utility of the book. The many testimonials that he has received of the benefit derived from perusing the "Practical Engineer," and the fact that the demand for it was urgent after the edition was exhausted, were both gratifying to him, and afforded a stimulus to exert himself to make the book still more worthy of public patronage.

In preparing this work the author has drawn chiefly on his own experience and observation. There are a few selections and tables from Brunton, Scribner, &c.; but in giving information on subjects so intimately connected with property and life as those which relate to steam machinery, he was not willing to put forward any thing the reality of which he had not tested.

JOHN WALLACE.

Pittsburgh, 1864.

CONTENTS.

INDEX OF PLATES.

THE

PRACTICAL ENGINEER.

BOILERS.

Boilers are of almost every kind and description, shape and size, for the purpose of generating steam, for running low and high pressure engines, and may be classed under the names of upright, horizontal, revolving, circular, flat, elliptic, cylinder, slide, tubular and flued boilers.

UPRIGHT BOILERS.

Upright boilers stand on end perpendicularly, having the fire-box within the second shell of the boiler. Between their inner and outer shells there is generally left a space of from 2 to 3 inches (more or less, according to circumstances), which is filled with water about 6 or 8 inches above the low water line. In Wallace's upright boiler there is a *boiler within a boiler*, coming down from the top of the fire surface to within 2 or 3 feet of the grate bars, the depth depending altogether on the size of the boiler and the kind of fuel used. If wood, saw dust or shavings, &c., be used, the fire-box ought to be made deep, but shallower for coal. For particulars of John

Wallace's upright boiler, &c. see description of plates of the same; by referring to the index for upright boilers, see page of same. There are also in use *tubular* upright boilers, with the fire passing up through the flues, out of the tops of the boilers. These boilers, on account of the fire passing above the water line, are liable to be *overheated;* and there is *danger of leaking* on the tops of the boilers around the tops of the flues, where they are turned over and caulked. I saw a boiler of this kind thrown away for that reason. When steam was up, and the fire passing through the flues above the water line, it caused the flues to expand more than the boiler, and the steam would leak out round the tops of the flues nearly as fast as it could be made—partly owing to the flues having been made of rather heavy iron.

There is another kind of upright boilers, that I saw made in Angelica, New York, altogether different from any made in this part of the country. The outside boiler shell is wrought iron; the inner shell is four-square, made of cast iron, bolted together on the opposite or angle corners, by screw bolts and flanges, and cemented, having from about 90 to nearly 200 copper flues passing through the cast iron sides; one tier with about 1 inch space between the outside of the flues, then another tier on top of this, running crosswise, and each successive tier at right angles with the preceding. The water passes through the inside of these flues, and the fire operates all around on the outside of them, and also within that part of the square box which is not taken up by the ends of the flues. But there are *serious objections to this kind of boiler.* It is almost impossible to clean them out, especially if lime water is used; and they are very expensive to build, as well as to clean, if they should get out of order inside or around the flues. In such a case a large portion of the boiler would have to be taken apart, and that perhaps only in order to make some trifling repairs, A job of this kind may take as many weeks as a cylinder or flued boiler would require days, and cost as much more in proportion to the time lost. Accordingly, boilers of this construction should be dispensed with, excepting in some particular cases, where room would be an indispensable object.

HORIZONTAL BOILERS.

Horizontal boilers are always laid nearly level, say 1 inch to 20 feet, leaving the ends where the blow-off valve is, a little low, so as to run the water entirely out of the boiler. Most of the boilers now in use are of this description, as it is the best position to attain the greatest amount of fire-surface, and to apply the heat from the furnace to the boiler to the best possible advantage. When used for stationary engines, these boilers are generally enclosed in bricks; a few are enclosed in a sheet iron fire-bed, lined with fire bricks all around the front end of the furnace; the other part is filled in with soft common bricks, and sometimes between the boilers covered with fire brick tile, made to order, to fit the circles of the boilers; also if the boilers be not too far apart, they are frequently filled in with common bricks. The back ends of flued boilers are sometimes covered with tile made for the purpose, and sometimes with cast iron plates. I prefer the latter.

LOW PRESSURE BOILERS.

Low pressure boilers are generally not capable of carrying high steam, as they have a large diameter, and the fire-box or furnace is within; and very frequently have return flues, for the purpose of using up the heat, and economizing the fuel to the best possible advantage. These boilers vary from 6 to 14 feet diameter, more or less. I saw two on board the Northern steamer *Indiana*, on Lake Erie, at Cleveland, that were 10½ feet diameter, and used two tiers of 4 feet grate-bar, making a length of 8 feet, the cylinder being 74 inches diameter and 10 feet stroke. I was in the hold when they were drawing the fires; they were white with heat, hot enough to melt pig metal in a few minutes after being thrown in. The fires were, if I recollect right, blown up with a fan, as they generally are in the East when the boilers are down in the hold, and have little draft under the grate bars, different from boats that have their boilers set up on deck—and when running at a fast speed will produce a very strong draft, especially when running against a strong head wind.

Two of the largest low pressure boilers I ever heard of were used at a blast furnace in Staffordshire, England. They were 14 feet diameter, 36 or 40 feet long, and with two 36 inch flues in each boiler, the fire passing out under the boiler, then in through one flue and back out at the other into the stack. They consumed about 18 tons of coal in 12 hours. The cylinders were about 54 inches diameter, 10 or 12 feet stroke. They carried steam 14 lbs. per square inch. The blast cylinder was about 10 feet diameter, 10 or 12 feet stroke; each tier of grate-bars was 6 feet long, making the fire bed 12 feet long and 12 feet wide in the furnace, or altogether 144 square feet. In proportion as the diameter of the boiler is increased, the strength is diminished, and in proportion as the diameter is reduced, of course the strength will be increased.

Large low pressure boilers for the ocean used to be made in early days of *sheet copper*, and cost about 50 cents per pound. The objection to iron boilers then was their corroding by the salt water; but this objection is overcome at the present day, by means of some chemical process, and iron boilers are now coming into general use, as they are believed to be stronger than copper and only cost one-sixth or one-seventh part of the price of copper boilers.

I have traveled frequently on the steamer *Mary Washington*, in Chesapeake Bay, from Baltimore, and also on the Rappahannock, from Fredericksburg, Virginia, to Baltimore. This steamer had a large low pressure boiler made of copper, and the fire-box and ash-bed within the same. The fuel used in this part of the South is mostly pine wood, brought to Baltimore by sailing vessels. The inside of the air pump was lined with brass, the main shafts were wrought iron, and the walking beam cast iron. The heads of these large boilers, and many other parts, must be well braced with a large number of bolts to make them sufficiently strong. The boilers, cylinder and air pump are down in the hold of the boat, and the walking beam up on deck.

As a general thing, I believe it is customary to carry not more than from 14 to 28 lbs. of steam on low pressure engines. Frequently double-flued boilers, such as we use on our western rivers for high pressure engines, have been used on the same waters for running low pressure engines, with the only difference, that the boilers used for low pressure do not require to be so strong as those for high. I have known steam to be carried about 60 lbs. per square inch for low pressure engines on our western waters, with double flue boilers. They would require a large amount of cylinder in order to cut the steam off and give it room for expansion.

HIGH PRESSURE BOILERS.

High pressure boilers are generally made of smaller diameters than those used for low pressure, in order to be sufficiently strong for carrying high steam. Very few of them are made over 4 feet diameter; the sizes generally used are from 42 down to 30 inches diameter, varying 2 inches in each diameter, making seven different diameters. A great many for smaller engines may be found with smaller diameters, but when made of less than 30 inches diameter it will be found difficult to clean them out, especially if that cleaning should be required often, as when muddy or limestone water is used. These boilers are usually from $\frac{3}{16}$ to $\frac{1}{4}$ of an inch in thickness; some few are made $\frac{5}{16}$ inch, and even $\frac{3}{8}$ inch thick, with about 6 feet diameter, but they are seldom used so large. Our steamboat boilers are now nearly all made $\frac{1}{4}$ inch thick. The height of steam carried on our high pressure boilers varies greatly, from 20 lbs. up to 200 lbs. per square inch—the general average height, varying from 60 lbs. to 120 lbs. per square inch, altogether owing to the thickness of boilers and amount of work to be done; and the medium height between the two would be about 90 lbs. per square inch. The boilers should be made of good quality ¼ inch iron, where a tolerably high pressure is wanted, as in our rolling mills, blast furnaces, grist mills, &c.

There is a great variety of boilers made for the purpose of raising steam for high pressure engines. The two kinds now in general use for running stationary engines are the *cylinder* and the *flued* boilers. In earlier days the cylinder boilers were preferred, for the reasons that they were a great deal cheaper, and considered safer in case the water would get low—there being no danger from collapsing when water was scarce, as in the case with flued boilers when the flues become bare and red hot, particularly in short boilers, and so are very likely to collapse. Another great advantage of cylinder boilers is, they are much easier to be cleaned out. This is important, especially if the water should be impregnated with lime and make astrong scale. In these boilers there is no difficulty in removing the scale by using a sharp pick made for the purpose; only great care must be taken in working about the rivet heads, as there would be danger of their becoming loose and flying off. Another great advantage of the cylinder boilers is their being more easily and cheaply repaired, as they generally may be repaired in their beds, without being removed, by taking out the grate-bars or a portion of the furnace walls, as the case may require.

Another reason why cylinder boilers were generally used was, that fuel formerly was very cheap here. We could get the best of stone coal hauled to any part of our city for 3 cents per bushel, this being the retail price by the single load, and I think, probably about $2\frac{3}{4}$ cents wholesale for foundries and factories; and those whose establishments were near the pits, could get it for little more than the price of digging, which, I think, was then, $\frac{1}{2}$, $\frac{5}{8}$ and $\frac{3}{4}$ of a cent per bushel, slack being in those days scarcely considered worth hauling, Sometimes it was used for the purpose of making coke. But at the present time labor is worth nearly three times as much as it was thirty years ago, and the price of coal has risen to 10 and 12 cents per bushel.

CYLINDER BOILERS AND THEIR ADVANTAGES.

Cylinder boilers are the simplest, cheapest, safest and best boilers that can be made; they are equal in strength to the flued boilers. Some perhaps will say the heads of flued boilers are much stronger and stiffer than those of cylinder boilers, owing to their being braced length ways by riveting the flues to the boiler heads. The part around and below the flues, indeed, is very strong, and no doubt would bear a greater pressure than the boiler hull. But the head above the boiler flues, which is nearly half of the diameter, receives bnt little or no benefit from the flues. Sometimes this part of the head has no braces at all. I have often seen flued boilers which were braced and supposed to be very strong; but above the top of the flues they would bag out, sometimes a half inch, more or less. This is a proof of their not being sufficiently braced. These braces ought to be made of the toughest and best iron, to prevent their breaking or cracking in expansion and contraction. They should be made of iron one-third part heavier than that formerly used, and at least two or three braces instead of one. I know some boiler makers will object to this as a deviation from their common mode of making them; but the secret of the whole matter is, they do not like to be troubled about making alterations. A wrought iron boiler head, if well braced, ought to be about as strong, when the boiler is worn out, as when it was first put in, and since boilers are very frequently made by the pound, the extra-expenses will be only a trifle more, and the work be stronger and safer. You should know and understand what you are ordering, and in drawing up an article, state precisely what you want, and never yield to please those whom you employ and afterwards have to pay. Always bear in mind, "a thing well done is twice done."

But to return to cylinder boilers. *Their heads, if well braced, may be made as strong as flued boiler heads*, and they can easily be braced so as to carry as much pressure as the hull will stand, and this is all that is necessary. Cylinder boilers are much *lighter* than flued boilers, and are *much easier cleaned out*, as mentioned before. Another advantage is: in case they should give out on the bottom or outsides, they can be very frequently mended in the furnace, without moving the boilers out of their place, by taking the grate bars out or removing a part of the side wall. Another advantage is, as there is a greater body of water in these boilers, they do not require to be watched as closely as the flued boilers. Of course, they must be attended to —I will not advocate carelessness; but as these boilers are without flues, there is no need for you to be uneasy about the tops of the flues becoming red hot for want of water, and on this account being liable to collapse. It is true, if the brick work outside and between the cylinder boilers should be 2, 3 or 4 inches above the low water gauge cock, the boiler iron might become red hot, if the water should be suffered to get below the brick work, at any time; but the damage done in this case would not be so great as in the heating of the top parts of the flues, because the flues will more likely collapse when getting hot than the boiler will burst when overheated. The iron on the flue is easily pressed together, the pressure coming from the outside, notwithstanding the good quality of the iron used; sometimes it will give way without tearing or breaking. Not so with the boiler hull; to give way it must explode, and burst or rupture, and then the iron is generally rent in sundry places, more or less as the case may be. I have frequently seen boilers give out on the sides where the brick work was enclosed, at the low water line, in consequence of the water being suffered to get below the low water gauge cock. Often the boiler iron would be cracked from one rivet hole to the other for one sheet or more, then it was crystallized and brittle at the low water line, owing to having been suffered to get dry and suddenly cooled by the water coming in. Another advantage is, you will not be troubled with sweeping out the flues every week, or at least every day. Another, and not the least advantage is, there being in them a much larger body of water in proportion to the heating surface of boiler iron, they do not require to be examined so often at the gauge cocks, since the water will boil away much slower than in flued boilers. The reason is obvious, when taken in consideration that the flued boilers have a much larger amount of fire surface in proportion to the quantity of water used.

It is the opinion of some that there is but very little steam made by the heat passing through large flues in boilers, say from 10 to 20 inches in diameter, as it is the nature of heat to ascend. It will be taken for granted that a greater quantity of steam will be made on the upper parts of the flues than on the lower ; since the ashes are constantly more or less carried off with the draft every time the fire is stirred up, they are continually settling in the bottom of the flues, and become a non-conductor. The extra quantity of steam made by flued boilers over that produced in cylinder boilers is not so great as is imagined by some. This extra quantity is, no doubt, attributable to another cause generally overlooked, viz. to the fact of having the quantity of water reduced to about one-half, owing to its being displaced by the flues, so that only one-half of the water is to be heated by the same amount of fire used under the cylinder boilers. With the aid of the flues the water being heated so much sooner, say in about one-third of the time, steam can be got up more rapidly with the flued boilers.

This being admitted, I will describe a new cylinder boiler, made and patented by Washington Irwin, formerly boiler maker in Pittsburgh, but for the last twelve years in Nashville, Tennessee. Having made a large cylinder boiler for Mr. Bell, of Tennessee, for a blast furnace—42 inches diameter, and 80 feet long—which was heated by gas, Mr. Bell found it failing to make as much steam as he expected according to the size of the boiler and the quantity of iron and water contained within the same. He came back to the boiler maker, saying: "Mr. Irwin, I am afraid of having overdone my boiler, as it does not produce steam in proportion to the quantity of water used." "Very well," replied Mr. Irwin, "I can easily cure that." And he undertook the job by placing what may be called a steam drum inside of the boiler, which I will now describe: First, suppose you have a cylinder boiler, 40 inches in diameter and 20 feet long, made of ¼ inch iron, then you make the inner steam drum of thin sheet iron, for the purpose of displacing the large amount of water usually carried in cylinder boilers. This inner drum may be 20 or 24 inches in diameter, one end of it being riveted to the inner head of the boiler, 2 inches from the bottom of the boiler, to allow sufficient room for cleaning. The drum is made from 1 to 3 inches shorter than the boiler inside, and is closed steam-tight with a head, to allow room for the outer boiler to expand freely independent of the inner drum—it being heated first, of course it will be the first to expand. To make the drum safe, it is made clear of the boiler at one end, and fastened at the other to accommodate itself. Thus one end is made independent of the other, to prevent the breaking of a joint and springing a leak. Inside of the boiler, and on top of the drum within the same, there are several pipes or tubes, say about 6 inches in diameter, reaching to about 4 inches of the top of the inside of the boiler. The steam then will pass freely down these pipes into the drum, and is taken out from the drum to the engine by means of a steam pipe.

This cylinder boiler is said to produce about the same amount of steam that a flued boiler of the same size does; it costs much less, and is much safer. You can carry this boiler about three-fourths full of water, and in this way increase the fire surface in comparison with that in a common cylinder boiler. There is another advantage in the inner steam drum over that commonly used on top of boilers, viz. the steam, not being exposed to the atmosphere, is not liable to condense, and dry steam is worked.

The iron used for the inner drums may be made very light, just heavy enough to bear caulking; the pressure within and without being equal, the drum is in a state of equilibrium, and on this account the steam drum will not require more than from one-third to one-half the thickness of the boiler hull.

SINGLE AND DOUBLE FLUED BOILERS.

We are opposed to the use of single flued boilers, believing it to be bad economy on the part of those who get them made. No doubt it is generally done with a view to save cost; for one flue costs more than two. But there are other things to be taken into consideration. There will be more openings in two flues than in one, and of course a much better draft, and the flues being less in diameter, will be much stronger; and being lower down in the boiler, there will be room for a sufficient quantity of water to cover the flues. In addition to this, there will be more room in the boilers for steam, and more steam can be produced in a shorter time with two flues than with one.

We had once an application to make two flues for a boiler that had but one. It would not work as it was. The fuel would not burn for want of a draft. After two flues were put in there was no more complaint. With less fuel there would be a stronger fire and more steam.

It is always a saving of fuel to have plenty of boiler. Besides, it is pleasanter for the fireman, and easier on the grate bars and fire fronts, and the fire has time to consume entirely the fuel; whereas, when there is too little boiler the fire requires to be stirred up frequently until it is sometimes almost at a white heat. This is hard on the bars, the fire fronts and boilers, as well as on the walls, which are liable to be soon made useless; while the continual stirring of the fire sends large quantities of the fuel through the grates before it is consumed.

FLUED BOILERS.

Quarter circle flued boilers are quite as dangerous as elbow flues. They work on the same principle, but differ a little in their construction. They take up about 2 feet less room in the length of the fire bed, and absorb most of the heat returning into the flue; but they are unsafe for high pressure engines, and therefore unfit for use, on account of the pressure at the end being on only one side of the flue.

ELBOW-FLUED BOILERS.

Formerly elbow-flued boilers were much used on board of steamboats, but are now dispensed with altogether.

The elbow flue joins the bottom of the boiler about 3 inches from its end, and by this arrangement a great amount of heat (which in the present boilers is lost on the back of the fire bed and back plates,) is applied to the raising of the steam. The principal advantage to be gained by the use of elbow-flued boilers is the power they have of generating more steam than those now in use, but this advantage is of no practical account, from the fact that the pressure of steam is unequal on the elbows of the flue; and although they are braced up with bolts, yet they cannot be made sufficiently strong, but are apt to collapse in the elbow, which is the weakest part of the flue. This makes it unsafe and of course unfit for use. One reason for using them was, they took about 24 inches less room in length on the back end.

OBJECTIONS TO FLUED BOILERS.

Flued boilers for stationary engines have been objected to by many for a great variety of reasons, some of which I will mention. *First.* They have been considered as very dangerous on account of the tops of the flues being liable to become red hot, in case the water, from neglect or some other unforeseen cause, might be suffered to become low in the boilers. *Secondly.* Many, particularly country people, are of the opinion that when a flued boiler is used it is indispensably necessary to have what is called a regular engineer, and for higher wages, too, than they are willing or even able to give. *Thirdly.* The cost of this kind of boiler is much greater than that of the cylinder boilers, the difference of the price being just in proportion to the difference of the weight of the boilers, to which you may add the expense for the brick work, and the back plate for the boiler flues. *Fourthly*. The flues require constant scraping out, to keep them clean, otherwise they would be of very little use. *Fifthly*. You may be obliged to place your boiler in so small a space as not to have any room left at either end of the boiler, for sweeping out the flues. *Sixthly*. Another objection is the great difficulty found in cleaning out the boilers around and under the flues, especially if lime water should be used; and *Lastly*, the difficulty and expense of repairing the boilers and flues.

ROTARY BOILERS.

In about the year 1825, during my apprenticeship, I assisted in getting up the patterns for a rotary boiler at the establishment in which I was employed, for the inventor, whose name I do not recollect. The object he had in view was to generate steam a great deal faster than could be done with the present stationary boilers. The boiler, being altogether immersed in fire, turned round on a gudgeon at each end in a pillar block. The journals were cast hollow, and bored out so as to supply the boiler with water through one of the gudgeons, which was made tight by means of a stuffing box, and the steam was to be taken out the same way. It was the calculation to carry very little water in this boiler, and by immersing the same in the fire and revolving it, to generate steam very rapidly. I stood by when steam was up, and saw them experimenting with it, but as it was not found to be of great use, it was abandoned. I will state one of the objections to it. As the boiler was a revolving one, it was intended to be turned by the engine when it was running, but while steam was raising it would have to be turned by hand or some other means, to prevent the boiler from burning and becoming red hot, which would cause it to leak. Another difficulty presents itself, namely, with respect to the trying of the gauge cocks. As it was the intention to carry but a few inches of water in the boiler, the gauge cocks would be near the outer surface of the boiler, and in order to try them you would have to stop the boiler, which would require to stop the engine too—a loss of time not be overlooked.

BOTTLE BOILERS.

Bottle boilers are upright boilers, and have been frequently used for marine engines. One advantage of this kind of boilers on sea is, when the boat is as it were on the beam's end, there would be no danger of the flues being exposed to fire, as is the case in horizontal boilers; they take up less room and require less castings, and, no doubt, answer the purpose for low pressure engines. Not having possession of a particular description, I pass on to

STEEL BOILERS.

Steel boilers are being introduced on locomotives. This is, of course, one of the latest experiments of the age, and it will take time to test them fully. I suppose the sheets might be somewhat thinner than those made of iron, as the material is stronger, and there would be a double advantage in using them on locomotives and light water steamers, as the boilers would weigh considerably less, and being thinner they would raise steam proportionably quicker; besides, they would be a great deal less likely to burn or spring in the seams at the caulking, than the heavy boilers. A boiler of $\frac{5}{16}$ iron, double thickness, would be at the seams $\frac{5}{8}$ inches thick, and on that account, unless kept extra clean, it is very apt to spring over the fire at the rivets, and leak, and also about the rivet heads, on account of the water being so far from the outer surface of the iron.

SHORT BOILERS.

A large portion of heat is lost in using short boilers, and we have frequently seen the blaze issuing from the tops of the chimneys of both river and land engines. To prevent this, the grate bars should be shorter and in proportion to the length of the boiler. Where this cannot be done without the loss of the bars in use, the remedy is to build a temporary bridge wall on the top of the bars next the existing wall. In this way the proper length of the bars can be ascertained when new ones are made. It is a common error to make the bars for short boilers too long, and for long boilers too short, and thus the disproportion between the two sizes of boilers is greater than between the length of the bars respectively for them. The rule should be, 1 foot of bars to a certain number of feet of boiler, the quality of fuel being taken to the account.

LONG BOILERS.

The error referred to is more frequent in the case of long boilers. It is not uncommon for boilers 40 feet long to be put up with 4 feet grate bars. This is altogether out of proportion. As an approximation to definiteness, I would say that when fuel is cheap, the proportion might be 1 foot to 6; where economy in fuel is an object, the difference might be increased to 1 to 7.

For flued boilers, 1 foot to 6 is the right proportion, unless fuel be plenty, and then it might be 1 to 5. In 24 feet boilers the flame would travel 48 feet, which I am confident is a much better arrangement in every respect than 30 feet boilers and 4 feet bars.

Long boilers are now coming into general use. They have used them on our rivers 40 feet in length, aud cylinder boilers have been made 42 feet long for land use. This, we think, is going to the opposite extreme; 40 feet is too long for a steam boat boiler. Such a boiler can hardly stand nnder its own weight without a centre bearing, and under a steamboat boiler we do not approve of this. We believe that 40 feet is too great a distance to carry the heat for making steam, and beyond the point where a boiler ceases to do this it is worse than useless. It adds unnecessary weight, takes up room, and acts as a condenser to cool what steam has already been made. It is better that the boiler be too short than too long, for several reasons: long boilers require much more time to raise steam, they will spring easier than if they were shorter, and by being too long they condense the steam at one end of the flue while you are making it at the other end of the boiler. Besides, they will not bear their own weight in hauling, or rolling, without being materially dinged, unless they are handled by skillful persons with the greatest care and precaution. The medium length of boilers is generally the best. Never choose either of the two extremes. We would say, for general use, from 24 to 34 feet in length will be about the best size, varying the length from the one to the other to suit the different diameters of boilers and sizes of boats on which they are to go.

BOILERS IMMERSED IN FIRE.

I recollect of an extensive iron manufacturer speaking about the cost of six boilers for a blast furnace. His idea was to have three boilers abreast on the furnace and the other three placed on top of the lower, connected with large water pipes, the three lower boilers full of water and the upper three about half full. The three lower boilers were to be immersed in the flame, and the flame also to reach up to the centre of the upper boilers; the object of which was, by giving more fire surface in the same furnace, to use up the heat and make more steam than is ordinarily done. I think it not unlikely this kind of boiler will answer the purpose.

THICKNESS OF BOILER IRON.

No steamboat boiler less than ¼ inch thick should be allowed to be put on boats made for high pressure engines having boilers 24 inches and upwards in diameter, and all boilers over 42 and up to 48 inches in diameter, should be made of $\frac{5}{16}$ iron. We would here suggest for the consideration of those who are ordering engines to be built, the propriety of having four sheets or more of the boiler iron that is over the fire $\frac{1}{16}$ of an inch thicker than the balance of the boiler, as that part of the boiler is the most exposed to the heat or action of the fire, and is more likely to burn or bag than any other part of the boiler. We think it would be econmy to make boilers in this way. In addition to this, we would suggest another idea, and feel fully satisfied on this subject that we are right. It is this: that the last sheet of iron in the bottom of each of the boilers should be made $\frac{1}{8}$ of an inch thicker than the iron in the boiler hull. This is the sheet to which the boiler stand is to be fastened. The object of this sheet being thicker is, that the boïler will stand more firm and secure, and the stand pipe have a larger and stiffer bearing upon the body of the boiler than it now has upon a sheet of the usual thickness.

The sheets of iron on top of the boiler to which the steam pipe is fastened, we would have the same way; and all boilers fastened together with screw bolts should be $\frac{1}{8}$ inch thicker than the boiler hull iron, because $\frac{1}{4}$ inch iron would spring between the bolts, and would be liable to leak. The iron is not sufficiently strong to be screwed up tight and hold large boilers together.

We are aware that wrought iron steam and stand pipes are now used, and that they are riveted on to the boilers and hold the iron close together between the rivets; but still that does not prevent the boiler from springing up and down on the boiler stand, owing to the great weight on such a small surface of thin iron. To remedy this, we would recommend a heavy sheet of iron to which the boiler stand pipes should be fastened, with thick flanges on them.

If you could bring your boiler stand, like a land engine, to rest on the boiler head, then it might do—but this cannot be done. Had the plan which we now speak of been adopted when the cast iron steam pipes were in general use, the use of the extra flanges inside the boilers under each steam pipe branch, with six holes in it, for the purpose of making the boiler iron stiff enough to be screwed up tightly, and help to stiffen the iron between the bolt holes, could have been entirely dispensed with. This method of strengthening the boiler iron is frequently adopted, and we deem it *patching up something that was not sufficiently strong in the first place.*

If boilers were made stiffer, as we have proposed, there would be less danger of the joints breaking, or of them leaking whenever exposed to stormy weather, or any ill-usage caused by the motion of the boat.

We think that our Government should not allow any steamboat boilers to be used of less than $\frac{1}{4}$ inch iron, of good quality and warranted. Boilers over 42 inches in diameter, $\frac{5}{16}$ of an inch thick, and the extra $\frac{3}{8}$ sheets we have alluded to for the boiler connections and the steam pipes, you may not at present be disposed to adopt; but the last sheet of iron on the bottom of the boiler that rests upon the top of the boiler stand and bears up the whole weight of the boiler, should be made $\frac{1}{8}$ of an inch thicker than the boiler hull. Let every one who is interested in the welfare of the community, and especially the traveling public, see to it. We have no doubt but that the time will soon arrive when this plan will be generally adopted.

Small boilers 32 inches diameter and less, having $\frac{3}{16}$ iron, should have less steam in the same proportion that the iron is reduced from the usual thickness, which is $\frac{1}{4}$ inch.

THICKNESS OF FLUE IRON.

The iron used for making boiler flues should be full as thick as the iron used for the boiler hull, for three reasons:

1st. It is much easier to collapse a flue than to burst a boiler.

2d. We very frequently hear of flues collapsing where it is stated that there was a sufficient quantity of water in the boilers; and we believe it, from the fact that they frequently collapse when about starting out. We recollect once seeing a boat, below the Falls on the Ohio river, that had collapsed her flue, and which, we believe, was under way at the time the accident happened. When we saw her she was in the middle of the river, and they were endeavoring to bring her to shore. The bow was covered with steam.

3d. If the water gets a little low in the boiler, the tops of the flues become bare and are liable to get red hot; and by being heated more on the top they become weaker just in proportion as they are heated, and under the pressure of the steam, flatten or press together.

Abstract reasoning is of no weight against experience and demonstration of the fact, that the flue iron made of the same thickness of the boiler is weaker than the boilers, and for this reason they should be made proportionably thicker, say $\frac{1}{16}$ inch, than the boiler hull. Another point requires particular attention in the construction of flues: that they be exactly round,—not having any flat places,—for this materially destroys the strength of the flue; and if any part is more likely to give way than another, it is that part which is out of round. Great care should be taken to see that every sheet of iron is perfectly sound, clear of blisters, flaws and scales. For want of this, much unnecessary trouble is caused, that might otherwise be avoided were every sheet thoroughly inspected by the boiler maker before putting it in.

THICKNESS OF BOILER HEADS.

Steamboat boiler heads should always be made of wrought iron. The time was when they were almost universally made of cast iron. There are two objections to cast iron heads on steamboat boilers: they often break between the flues, and they are too heavy. Wrought iron heads for 34 inch boilers should not be less than $\frac{1}{2}$ inch thick; 36 inch boilers, $\frac{9}{16}$; 38 and 40 inch boilers, $\frac{5}{8}$ thick; 42, $\frac{11}{16}$; and up to 48 inches in diameter, $\frac{3}{4}$ inch thick. Both front and back boiler heads should have at least two strong braces in each head, and large boilers more. The back head in which the man hole plate goes, should have a large band riveted inside of the boiler head, around it, to make the boiler head stiff so as to stand screwing up tight. The ring should be 1 to $1\frac{1}{2}$ inches thick by 2 or $2\frac{1}{2}$ inches wide, owing to the size of the boiler, planed up on both sides. Sometimes these heads are made of a solid sheet, and flanged for riveting to the boiler; others are made of gunnel iron, with a flat piece riveted inside. This, we believe, is the stiffest head of the two, but either of them are good enough if they are well made, and of good material. The gunnel iron ought to be from $\frac{5}{8}$ to $\frac{3}{4}$ inch thick—twice the usual thickness.

DIAMETER OF BOILERS.

For the use of steamers in general we are not in favor of small boilers—nothing less than 34 inches in diameter. This is as small as a man can properly clean out, and small enough for raising steam. Nor do we think it would be good policy to go over 4 feet in diameter for our high pressure engines. 40 and 42 inch boilers are as large as they are generally made, but we believe large boilers make much more steam, in proportion to the amount of fuel used, than small ones. They require, however, a larger furnace, a greater body of water, and longer time to raise the steam. In small steamers, 30 and 32 inch flued boilers are sometimes used, but it is with difficulty that a man can get in to clean them.

COMPARATIVE FIRE SURFACE OF BOILER HULLS AND FLUES.

There is a greater amount of fire surface in the two flues of a boiler than in the boiler hull. In a 40 inch boiler, 20 feet long, with two flues of 15 inches each, the boiler hull will have 5 feet 6 inches fire surface, even with the top of flues, and the flues 47¼ inches each; now if we expose 7 feet of the boiler hull circumference to the fire, by carrying the water high and using a large steam drum, which will make 140 square feet, the flues have 42 inches clear fire surface, or 7 feet circumference in the two flues, making 140 feet fire surface,—which is precisely the same as in the boiler. But the amount of steam raised in the flues will be less than in the boiler, decreasing in the same proportion that the heat diminishes as it passes off from the furnace.

It is said by some, that a double flued boiler makes twice the amount of steam that a cylinder boiler of the same size does. This is not correct, according to the foregoing calculation. It is shown, that there is about as much fire surface in the two flues of a boiler as in the boiler shell up to the water line; but a great difference exists in the heat after being partly exhausted and spent on the boiler before entering the flues. The flame in short boilers may come through the flues, but it is for a very short period, whilst the fire is hot under the boiler. A flued boiler will make fully 50 per cent. more steam than a cylinder boiler of same size.

CROSS BOILER AND BRIDGE WALL.

The splendid four boiler low pressure steamer *Mexico* had a cross boiler at the end of the grate bars, which answered for the bridge wall, and was connected to the main boilers with pipes. The object no doubt was to make more steam, and to save the constant repairing of the brick work, which was frequently thrown down by heaving in the wood. I was about to put one in our shop, and had it partly made, when I learned from a man who had tried one, that it was difficult to keep it tight, and of no real advantage ; I then abandoned it.

UPRIGHT BOILERS A FAILURE FOR PROPELLING STEAMBOATS.

Upright boilers were tried on the steamer *Lafourche*, which was built at Cincinnati about thirty-five years ago. I was informed that on her way to New Orleans, she either burst her boiler or collapsed her flues, and had to be towed back to Cincinnati, to be overhauled. She could not stem the current to any advantage, and on this account, the upright boilers were thrown out, and others put in their place.

The steamer *Nebraska*, when she first came out, had an upright tubular boiler, having the fire box and ash pit within it, but not having a sufficiency of power, her engine and boilers were thrown out, and a horizontal double-flued boiler, and new engine, put in their place, when she gave entire satisfaction.

The steamer *Advance No.* 1 had one upright tubular boiler, but it would not make a sufficiency of steam to run the boat against the current. Another boiler of a similar kind was put in alongside. I went on her up the Allegheny river seven or eight miles, on her trial trip, but the water was too low; she came back to Pittsburgh, and started up again the next high water; when about one hundred miles up the boiler gave out at the bottom of the flues in the fire box. A hole was then drilled in the bottom of the boiler, between the flues, and the mud was found to be 1½ inches or more thick in the bottom, and owing to this, the boiler was burnt, which was the cause of its springing a leak around the tubes at the bottom and putting out the fires. As we made the castings for the two engines, I told them at the beginning that the upright boilers would not do for the river, that they would fill up with mud, and it would be impossible to clean them out, but they thought to keep them clean with a blow-off, which could not be done, as there were nearly two hundred small flues in one boiler, and they were quite close together. They then brought the boat down and put in two small double flue boilers, and had no trouble afterwards.

N. B. Where upright boilers are used the water should be soft and clear.

PORTABLE BOILERS.

A portable boiler has the furnace within the boiler to avoid the necessity of brick walls and stone foundations, which cannot conveniently be got in some sections of the country, and they can be moved from one place to another in a short time and with less expense than the common boilers with brick walls and stone foundations. This kind of boilers is preferred by many in the oil regions for the reason that in boring oil wells they have to move from one place to another.

They are also used for portable mills throughout various parts of the country. They cost more than flued boilers, and require great care and attention in keeping the water in its proper place.

SMALL TOP BOILERS,

ABOUT FIFTEEN INCHES IN DIAMETER, USED INSTEAD OF TILE.

The steamer *Eclipse* had eight large size boilers. In place of fire brick tile, between the boilers at the low water line, they put in seven small boilers, making in all, fifteen boilers, the object of which was to generate more steam, by having the fire to act on them instead of on the tile, which was almost red hot. I was informed that they were soon taken out, failing to answer the desired purpose. She was one of the largest class of lower trade boats, having two cylinders 36 inches in diameter, 11 feet stroke, puppet valve. Her piston rods, in the rough, were 8 inches in diameter, and 15½ feet long.

WATER FIRE FRONTS.

I have seen cast iron boiler heads made for high pressure boilers, having the fire front cast on the boiler heads, a double thickness, leaving 2 or 3 inches of water space between them, with room in the centre for fire doors, and extending down even with the top of the grate bars. The object of this was to generate more steam, save the fire brick lining, and keep a cool front. It was tried for a short time, but never came into general use. The cost in all these experiments was more than the profits. These extra boilers were very difficult to clean out, and liable to burn on account of dirt and lime settling in them. They have all been abandoned long ago as useless, with the exceptions of those used on low pressure boilers for ocean steamers, &c.

VARIOUS KINDS OF PATENT BOILERS.

There have been a great many kinds of boilers patented, but I have never seen or known any of them to come into general use. They are mostly weighty, costly, and very hard to clean out, and if they should be overheated or get out of order so as to require repairs, they in many cases have to be taken to pieces, besides requiring a considerable length of time, and to repair them would cost almost as much as a plain double-flued boiler.

AUXILIARY BOILERS.

There have been a great many experiments tried for the purpose of assisting the main boiler or boilers to generate more steam with less fuel than could be done without, of which I will mention some that I have seen, such as outside flat boilers, cross boiler and bridge wall, hollow grate bars made of copper, hollow fire fronts cast to the boiler head, top boilers, &c.

I will give you the particulars respecting flat outside boilers. We had in our shop one 32 inch cylinder boiler in use for a considerable length of time, and by request we put in two additional flat outside boilers on each side of the cylinder boiler, connected with water and steam pipes to the main boiler, for the purpose of raising more steam with the same furnace, by using up the heat that was in the side walls, which were white with heat. We expected on trying them to have more steam than we could use with less fuel than we formerly used, but we were sadly disappointed. We will admit that they made some little additional steam, but not in proportion to the additional extra amount of fire surface, for the following reason: the fire close to the sides of the flat boilers did not burn so well, for want of air; it was with the fire here as it was with the old Franklin grates that had cast iron back plates, it would never burn well close up to these plates but would be black and dingy, and brick was preferred on that account, then the fire would burn bright, making the walls white with heat. Just so with the side boilers, they were of no account; the cost far overrun the profit, and being flat, only 6 inches wide, they were full of braces. They were about 30 inches high and ran back 12 feet. The centre boiler was 20 feet long. They were not so strong as round boilers. It is a wrong notion to suppose that because the walls are red hot the heat is lost; the heat still remains in the furnace, and reacts on the boiler, and also causes the fuel thrown in to burn much better than it would do on flat sides of boilers kept black by being filled with water. After using them for some time we took them out to connect with a larger boiler on the other side of the house for a larger engine, and then we filled up the holes in the cylinder boiler where the steam and water connections were, and tried the same boiler again without them, and got along very well. Now I will speak from experience. These boilers are never worth putting in a stationary or river engine. The cost far exceeds the profit. The conclusion that I have come to is, that they are of no particular advantage for rasing steam even in low pressure engines. I mean the fire operating inside of the boiler, on the sides of the same, amounts to little or nothing. The only place that these low pressure boilers would be profitable and safe, is on lake and ocean steamers, for the following reason: in steamers on those waters the boilers are down in the hold, and are pretty close to the hull. When the fire-bed is lined with brick they are often in great danger. These boats are subject to be caught out in storms and driven and rolled from side to side, and very frequently the freight is tumbled about, and in such cases the brick work would be thrown down and the fire-bed would become red hot, and burn up the boat and all on board. In such cases this is the only kind of boilers that will stand the test, for when caught in a storm, they being filled with water between the inner and outer shell of the fire-box, there is no danger.

CYLINDER BOILERS FOR STEAMBOATS.

Cylinder boilers, from 18 to 30 inches in diameter have frequently been tried for propelling light steamers, ferry and tow boats, &c. Those who used them no doubt thought they would answer a good purpose, but a few trials soon proved the contrary. We recollect of two steamers, the *Harlem* and the *Franklin*, that used them for a short time. The *Harlem* had five of these small boilers, 18 inches in diameter, and the *Franklin* four of the same size; but after giving them a fair trial, they were taken out and replaced by double-flued boilers.

There are many objections to these small cylinder boilers; they are too small to be properly cleaned out, and a great deal of the heat is lost in the chimney. The heat from the chimneys, in warm weather, is a great annoyance, and the boat at all times is liable to take fire from it. They always require much more fuel than flued boilers.

The small cylinder boilers at best, are but poorly calculated for generating steam, and as a general thing should not be used on steamboats. They consume a much larger amount of fuel in proportion to the quantity of steam raised, than flued boilers.

DISTANCE BETWEEN BOILERS.

It has been the custom to set boilers but 2 inches apart between the boiler heads, leaving where the iron was not more than ¼ inch thick, but 1½ inch between the hulls of the boilers; but at present it is quite common to have them 6 and 8 inches apart. This gives more fire front under the boilers, allows the flame and heat of the fire to get between the boilers to better advantage, and makes steam much sooner than if they were closer together. For proof of this, examine two boilers that are close together, and they will be found black and sooty; then examine two that are from 6 to 8 inches apart, and they will be clean and white like a well-heated oven. The distance between being greater, the fire has a better opportunity to operate on the boilers, and by so doing necessarily generates more steam.

As a general rule, the space between the boilers and between the outside boilers and the walls, should not be less than 3 nor more than 4 inches. The objections to wider spaces are, they have to be covered with tile, which in some places it is difficult to get, and involves an increase of expense; more room is occupied, and more fuel consumed; the brick or tile in such wide spaces is liable to be broken and fall down, and then the fire will act on the boiler above the water line, causing the iron to crystallize and crack. But where the spaces are but 3 or 4 inches, fire brick can be used, and these should be set on their edge, especially between the boilers, as they will take firmer hold and be less likely to fall down. The boilers should be so constructed as to have from 6 to 8 inches water above the centre, in order that the brick fitted in between them may be longer on the upper than on the lower side, and so be prevented from falling through.

CAUSES OF BOILERS EXPLODING AND FLUES COLLAPSING.

The explosion of boilers and collapsing of flues proceed from various causes, a few of which we will endeavor to show. First, we will speak of the explosions of former years, and then refer to some of modern days, and compare them together.

In former times boilers were seldom made more than half the length of those in present use. The common length for steamboat boilers was 16, 18 and 20 feet, and being so short, they were sooner filled with water than the present large boilers can be, and also much sooner boiled dry or emptied of water by the blowing off of steam. As soon as the engine stopped the steam would be blowing off, carrying more or less of the water in the boiler with it, and consequently required more regular attention to the water than the boilers of the present day, owing to the additional length. The extra length of the boilers of the present day allows about double the room for steam, and by opening the furnace doors and flue caps, there is but little necessity for blowing off steam compared to that of former days.

We would also state that, although the long boilers generate more steam in the same length of time, in proportion to the amount of fuel used, than the short ones, yet when either of the engines are stopped, the short boilers will commence blowing off steam almost instantly, and that with the furnace doors and flue caps open. The reason of this is, that the heat is much greater on the short than it is on the long boilers. Hence we believe the principal cause of explosions in former times to have been the small amount of water that was carried on the top of the flues in the boiler. The lower gauge cock, which was also the water gauge, was placed at about 1½ or 2 inches above the top of the flues, and the upper cock was about 2½ or 3 inches above this. Now while long boilers generally carried from 5 to 6 inches of water on the top of the flues they had scarcely any occasion to blow off steam; and if it is considered necessary at the present day to carry a greater amount of water than formerly for safety, this proves that the lower water gauge cock carried water too low for safety, and had it been carried in short boilers in proportion as it is now carried in long ones, the lower gauge cocks instead of being 1½ or 2 inches, would have been 8 or 10 inches above the top of the flues, and this would have prevented many of the short boilers from blowing up, and the same amount of steam blown off as soon as the engine was stopped would have made them nearly as safe as the long boilers.

Taking all things into consideration, it is a wonder that explosions have not been of more frequent occurrence. There was something radically wrong in the former construction of engines. No doubt many good boats have been blown up for want of doctors to keep up a regular supply of water during long stoppages at wood yards, landing passengers, &c. It was formerly customary to stop boats in the channel of the river, and send or receive passengers from the shore in a yawl. During these stoppages more or less steam would be blown off, and it was impossible to pump any water into the boilers until the boat could be got under way again. Sometimes, in receiving or discharging passengers, where the width of the river would admit, the boat would run around in a large circle to keep the engines in motion for the purpose of supplying the boilers with water; and at wood-yards, the wheels were unshipped for the same purpose.

Very soon, however, single engines were succeeded by double, which proved of no advantage, for it was more difficult than ever to supply the boilers with water when the engine was stopped. If the boilers were supplied at all, the water wheel must be kept in motion, and often the shore engine could not be run at all. To run the outside wheel to pump up water would probably take as much steam as it would require to run the boat, and to supply the boilers at such an expense would have been bad policy. This shows that there was something wanting in the machinery to make it complete.

Not having had time to ascertain the particulars, or to make any inquiries whether there were any doctors used previous to this, we cannot, therefore, give any definite information on the subject. The first doctor we heard of was used on a small steamer called the *Orleans*, and some four years elapsed after this before they were deemed so important as to become general. It was about this time that engines were changed from single to double, and this plan was adopted upon the steamer *Missouri*, a large seven-boiler boat. Immediately after this the doctors came into general use, and are now considered indispensable, especially on large steamers. We can now stop our steamers when and where we please, and as long as may be required, without any fear of want of water from not running the engines, for the doctor is ready at all times independent of the main engine.

We will here state some particulars in relation to the explosion of boilers, and also mention the kind of boilers used, and where they exploded. The first was the *Moselle*, a small three-boiler boat, that exploded while putting out from Cincinnati, and killed about one hundred and fifty persons. We were well acquainted with both the engineers, the principal one having worked at a shop in Wheeling in which we were a partner. The *Moselle* made use of the short boilers, and had no doctor. She exploded when about putting out, immediately after starting the engines. The *Ben Franklin* had started just ahead, and we understand the captain of the *Moselle* boasted that he would beat her. I have no doubt that the steam was held in as long as possible to make a display, and to enable her to pass the boat ahead, and all to get a name. But the experiment cost too much. It was paying too dear for the whistle.

I ask attention to this case, as she was in the act of rounding out and was small and heavily laden. When a boat is rounding out it usually lists to the one side. Might not the water in the boilers have been low and the flues on the high side of the boat bare? In the meantime, the flues thus exposed to the fire would become red hot, and so soon as the boat straightened up what else could be expected than an explosion by the water coming in contact with them? And here we would earnestly recommend to the captains and engineers of boats, in all cases of rounding, both in landing and departing, or in any other position in which the boat is likely to list, to keep the steam low and the water in the boilers high. Too much attention cannot be given to this, as we are confident that to neglect of this important matter more than to any other cause, explosions of boilers on steamboats should be ascribed.

The *Gen. Brown*, a four-boiler steamer running between Louisville and New Orleans, burst her boiler while putting out from a wood-yard when about making her second revolution. We were acquainted with both her engineers, one of whom was instantly killed. The other survived, but had both arms broken. The latter worked under the same firm while we were principal foreman, at New Albany, Ind. Some forty persons were killed by this explosion. We were but little surprised at the blowing up of this boat, as she was in the habit of making "*brag trips*" from New Orleans to Louisville. The *Brown's* boilers were short, and she had no doctor, and no doubt there was too much steam and too little water in the boilers, which was the cause of the explosion.

The *Tri-Color* burst her low pressure boiler while lying at the Wheeling wharf, and killed seven or eight persons. I was engaged by the captain to take charge of this engine while the boat was in process of building. The boiler and engine were second-hand, having formerly been on the steamer *Velocipede*, built at Cincinnati. The boiler had the fire box and ash bed within it. The cylinder was, I believe, 24 inches in diameter, upright, worked with a walking beam. Fortunately for me, I was prevented from taking charge of this engine. The name of the engineer who was on at the time of the explosion was Hunt. He was said to be a first rate engineer. Whether the explosion was caused by want of water, defect in the boiler, or too high steam, I am unable to say. The boiler was large in diameter and fired within.

The *Wyoming*, *Kanawha*, *Kate Fleming*, *Lucy Walker*, *Louisiana*, *Car of Commerce*, *Metropolis*, and many other boats, have burst their boilers, though we cannot say whether they were all lying to or not when the explosions took place, but we are inclined to think they were making ready to put out when the accidents occurred.

We will now make some remarks with regard to the collapsing of flues. We saw a steamer called the *Chochuma*, that was said to have collapsed her flues while under way just below the Falls of the Ohio, on her trip downward. She was in the river, and we noticed the steam flying around her bow. At that time they were trying to get her to shore on the Indiana side. Although it may seem strange to some that a boat could burst her boiler or collapse her flues while under way, yet it does not surprise us, so long as the steam is kept back by checking it off in the throttle-valve, in order to keep up high steam in the boilers. If the engineer should happen to have his throttle-valve a little too close, so as to work off less steam than he makes, the boiler must blow off steam; and should this be the case, the steam being throttled off so close as to be the cause of its blowing off, they no doubt thoughtlessly hang a wrench or two on the safety-valve lever, and in this way overload it, and explode the boiler or collapse the flues while the boat is under way.

We have frequently heard of explosions when there was plenty of water in the boilers, and the engines running at the same time. This may be easily accounted for in the manner we have referred to; but we do not think this has ever happened on the river while working off steam on the engine with an open throttle-valve. It is bad policy to throttle the steam off too closely, as it causes the engine to labor more, and of course the boat to run slower.

A boat collapsed her flue as she was putting out from the Pittsburgh wharf. One of her engineers was instantly killed and the other died next day. We saw both of them. Several other persons were scalded.

The steamer *Fashion* collapsed her flue while passing through the lock. She had a doctor on board, and no doubt there was a sufficient quantity of water in the boilers when the explosion took place, but she had too much weight on the safety-valve.

To this, we believe, may be attributed the explosion

of all the boilers heretofore alluded to. Of all the flues that have collapsed on the steamers above referred to, but one of them, that we are aware of, had a doctor for supplying the boilers with water in case of an emergency. And all the boilers (we except the *Louisiana*—never having seen her, we are not positive as to the length of her boilers—however, we are inclined to think they were short,) were shorter than those used on large steamers of the present day.

Now, when we compare the long boilers with the short ones, we find that there is not one-fourth the danger of them exploding; but as much steam cannot be made, in proportion to the amount of iron used, with the long as with the short boilers.

As a general thing, the flues are not made as strong as the boiler hull. The flues of large boilers, 40 and 42 inches in diameter, should be $\frac{1}{16}$ of an inch thicker than the boiler hull iron; that is, all flues 14, 16 and 17 inches in diameter, should be $\frac{5}{16}$ inch thick, and for 18 inches and upwards in diameter, the thickness of the iron should be increased in proportion to the increased diameter of the flues. The reason of this is the pressure is always on the outside of the flue, and on the inside of the boiler. Now it is plain that any cylinder will bear far more pressure from within than from without. Consequently that which is subjected to the greater pressure should have the greater strength. A 40 inch boiler, carrying 120 lbs. steam, inside pressure, I would consider safer than the same boiler converted into a flue with 60 lbs. steam, outside pressure. The pressure from the inside is resisted by the adhesiveness of the iron, which offers but little resistance to pressure from the outside. A 34 inch boiler, ¼ inch thick, is allowed 135 lbs. steam to the square inch, a 40 inch boiler is allowed 115 lbs., a 46 inch boiler is allowed 100 lbs. According to this proportion, 180 lbs. would be allowed to an 18 inch boiler. Now, I consider the 46 inch boiler safer with 100 lbs. inside pressure, than the 18 inch boiler converted into a flue for the same boiler with 100 lbs. outside pressure.

Another cause of collapsing of flues is, the water being suffered to get too low in the boilers, the dry part of the flue being exposed to the fire becomes weakened and gives way under pressure of the steam. And still another cause is, the carrying of steam too high in boilers. Flues should be made as round as possible, for if they have flat places in them they are much more liable to collapse.

We have never heard of long boilers, say from 30 to 40 feet, blowing up. But we do not wish it to be inferred from this that they cannot be blown up. Now, when a boat is detained, for the purpose of discharging or receiving passengers, although the furnace doors and flue caps are thrown open, the fire remaining in the furnace is quite sufficient to explode or collapse the flues of the short boilers; yet the same fire under the long boilers would not, and could not do any harm, and if let alone, would burn out. To explode them at all would require additional fuel. A double length boiler, 40 feet, as we have already shown, will not generate as much steam as two 20 feet boilers, and the amount of steam less will be just in proportion to the difference of heat in the first 20 feet of the boiler, where the fire lies, and the last 20 feet, where it is much fainter. The heat of the fire being much stronger, in proportion to the amount of iron used, and the water being carried much lower than at present, was one of the great causes of explosions of former days.

COPPER PIPES FILLED WITH WATER,

USED FOR GRATE BARS.

About thirty-five years since I recollect the steamer *Aurora*, which had copper tubes about 2 inches diameter, used for grate bars. Being young at the time, and not acquainted with the engineers, I did not ascertain what their object was in using them, but will give you my opinion. In the first place, in those days the ash pits were only about 8, 10 and 12 inches deep, and fire on top and below made the bars red hot; the ash pit being paved in with brick, I have no doubt they burnt out grate bars very fast, and suppose this might be one object for using the copper tubes. Another reason might be to assist in generating more steam by using up the heat that would be in the red hot grate bars. I remember that every tube had on the end an oblong cap, with two bolts, for the purpose of taking off to clean them out. I forget how they were attached at the back end, but suppose it might be to a cross boiler. This boat, I believe, had 4 boilers; the next time I saw her they were taken out and grate bars used in their place. I suppose the reasons for taking them out were, there would be danger when throwing heavy wood on top of them; and also, in stirring the fires, unless very careful, they would spring a leak; they would also be liable to leak more or less at each end where the joints are made; and the copper pipes being about 2 inches in diameter and filled with water, would be black and exclude the air, so as to prevent the fire from burning freely.

The engine, which was puppet valve, worked with four short levers—they stood square across the cylinders. The cross shafts were worked with bevel gearing.

MATERIALS USED FOR MAKING BOILERS.

Copper, iron and steel are used for making boilers. Copper was used in early days; on ocean, bay and salt river steamers, it was preferred to iron, on account of not being liable to corrode, as iron was, from the effects of the salt water. The copper boilers cost from six to seven times as much as the iron, and they are not as strong.

I saw one of these large, low pressure copper boilers perform on the Chesapeake Bay, on my way to the gold mines, to get some information about engines and machinery, as we had a number to build for Dr. Hussey, Avery & Co., of Pittsburgh, for California. Whilst traveling on this boat on the bay, I saw there was great danger of the boat taking fire, as the boiler was down in the hold, and all around it was filled up with dry pine wood, which contained more or less turpentine. I thought then, and do still think, it very dangerous to crowd the wood too close around the furnace, for a spark might set it almost instantly in a blaze. In such boats I would advise to have more room in front of the boilers, for the storage of wood, so as to keep it out of the reach of sparks and danger from the heat of the furnace.

IRON BOILERS.

Wrought iron boilers are almost universally used, it being the cheapest and best material known for this purpose. In early days, the boiler and flue iron was heated in an oven red hot, and bent over cast iron plates made to suit the different diameters. This was a good plan in some respects, and very bad in others; it was good on account of softening the iron, it was more pliable, easier calked, and less liable to break and crack at the holes in drifting. But it was bad on account of opening the pores of the iron; the heating raised a heavy scale on each side of the sheet, making it lighter than before; the boiler was not so smooth, stiff, or strong, and it required a great deal more time to heat it than to bend it in the rolls.

CAST IRON BOILERS.

Cast iron boilers have sometimes been used. I saw one that was employed to run a small engine. There is another kind of boiler built at Angelica, New York, that has the inner sides made of cast iron, with copper tubes, and the outer shell wrought iron. This is a costly and complicated boiler, hard to clean out, and almost impossible to repair at any reasonable cost when out of order. Such boilers are hardly worth putting up, unless room become such an object that no other kind could be put in the place.

GLASS BOILERS.

Glass boilers have been used for small models, and also for running small engines for public exhibition. In these boilers you can see the water boiling up, and foaming under a full pressure of steam, which becomes white when it comes out from the cylinder, or is blown off from the boiler at the safety valve; but when confined, it is invisible. You can see through the boiler, with a full head of steam up, just as transparent as though it was entirely empty. I have seen four of these boilers in operation in Pittsburgh, three of them on exhibition driving glass engines, two of them driving the low pressure steam engine Monitor. You could see the piston head moving up and down in the cylinder, also the force and air pump, valves, &c. in motion when the engine was running. The cylinder and heads, piston rod and head, valve rod and valve, steam chest and walking beam, pitman and pillar blocks, water wheels and boilers, &c., were made of variegated colors of fine glass. It was the most splendid piece of workmanship ever exhibited in Pittsburgh. There was one here some years before this, but not so complete. Oliver Evans also used a glass boiler to experiment on the fusible metal for his safety guard for steam boats.

DIRECTIONS FOR BUILDING BOILER WALLS, STACKS, &c.

If you are building in the city, the first thing is to get the grade from the City Regulator. This may be the means of saving you thousands of dollars in after years, as by building at random many have had to pull down their buildings and make them to suit the grade. The foundation for good substantial buildings should always be below the frost, which is generally from three to four feet deep, but some extra cold seasons it has been from five to six feet deep. Stone is always better than brick for a good foundation, and should be built two or three courses above the ground. Stone will resist the frost and the wet better than brick. Brick foundations, especially in a damp place, will always be more or less wet, and cause the wall, the plaster and the paper to be damp several feet above ground; and unless the bricks are very hard, they will waste away and the plaster fall off the walls.

Another cause of buildings cracking is, when the building is on the side of a hill, one part of the foundation is several feet above ground, whilst the other is as much below, and the sun beaming on one side more than the other, the foundation on that side may be frozen hard when the other is several feet below its reach, and the frost expands the walls and causes them to break in settling, &c. The mortar becomes decomposed, and loses its strength and falls off, and the building, in consequence of being damp, is rendered unhealthy and unpleasant.

In commencing to build the foundation, see that the ground is equally firm and solid upon which you are to build, by examining it with a battering ram or sledge; and if there should be soft and spongy places here and there, which is often the case from a variety of causes, let them be hammered down and filled up until perfectly solid. If the ground is marshy and soft, as is sometimes the case and will not allow of this, then piles should be driven in endwise and plank or heavy timbers laid on top, as the case may require. The neglect of this care about the foundation is the cause why so many buildings after having been put up have in a short time been cracked, causing the shutters and window frames to be thrown out of square, so that the one would neither shut nor the other hoist. In commencing to lay the foundation, the largest stones should be in the bottom, and laid on the softest parts of the ground. If there is any danger of water soaking in, water cement ought to be used; and if the building should be put up in very warm weather, the stones and bricks should be wet, and every tier of the stone and brick work slushed or grouted with thin mortar, so that every crevice in the wall may be filled up and the bricks and stones take a firm bond.

HEIGHT OF STACKS.

No certain rules can be laid down for the height of stacks for several reasons. Much depends on the position. It is difficult to get a draft in a place surrounded by high hills, as the current of air passing over, often by a whirling motion blows down into the stack. In cities this is seen to be the case when there is a high wall on one side and a low one on the other. In such positions the higher the stack is raised the better. To a certain extent, the rule, "long stacks for long boilers," is good; still I have known high stacks to draw badly, and low stacks to draw well. Care should be taken that the opening of the stack be sufficiently wide, if it be too small the draft cannot be good.

Stacks should always be high enough to carry away the smoke and sparks from the top of the building. It is possible to have too much draft; when this is the case the heat is carried away from the boiler without having time to act on it. A safe rule is, to have the opening in the stack fully as large as the opening in the flues of the boiler or boilers, or better, one-fifth larger.

Care should be taken not to have the stacks any narrower inside on the top than at the bottom, as it would be calculated to retard or destroy the draft, but have it all of a size. If there is any difference, it would be better to be a shade larger at the top. Three or four courses of the top bricks on the stack should be laid in water cement, as it is more durable than the common lime mortar, which very soon decomposes on the top courses, and the joints open and the bricks spread, and in a few years come tumbling down whenever a heavy blast of wind occurs, and endangers the lives of those below. Stone coping on the top would be still better, but a little more costly; and some have thin cast iron plates, cast in one or two pieces, and bolted together, owing to the size of the stack, with a small flange projecting down 1 inch or more to fit the outside brick of the stack and to keep it from spreading, and the plate ought to be wide enough to project from 2 to 4 or 6 inches, owing to the size of the stack, on the outside, to throw off the water.

LOCATION AND HEIGHT OF STACKS, &c., TO GUARD AGAINST FIRES.

In the erection and construction of buildings for mills, factories, &c., all things should be taken into consideration before you commence to build, so that every thing may be so arranged as not to need changes after the work is begun. You should have your stack located on the side of the mill toward which the wind generally blows, so that the smoke and sparks may be carried away from the mill, and also some distance from the surrounding houses. This can easily be done, especially in the country. I know the wind varies and changes, but I mean, to get the advantage as much as possible of the general current. The stacks should be built some distance above the highest part of the building; it gives a better draft, and carries the smoke and sparks away from the roof and also from the surrounding buildings. The sparks are more likely to die before alighting. Some persons may say they seldom use wood, but all use it more or less for kindling, &c.

I will mention some fires that originated in this way; two of them I was at when they were burning, and in the other case I was called upon to examine the engine, &c., after the mill and neighboring dwelling houses were consumed. The first I mention, was Michael Stackhouse's engine shop, in Pittsburgh. It caught fire about twelve o'clock midday, by sparks coming out of the boiler stack, and alighting on the roof. They usually used coal for their boiler, but at this time they were burning the shavings from the pattern shop, and the stack being entirely too low, the sparks fell on the roof and burnt up the shop, engine and patterns in a few minutes, notwithstanding the fire engines were promptly on the ground. Had the stack been high, the sparks would most likely have been blown away or died out before they fell.

I was an eye-witness to the burning of a large steam engine shop in Wheeling, formerly used by Smith, Wallace & Co., but latterly occupied as a glass warehouse, and at the time stored with considerable amount of ware. It took fire about day-break, by a spark or sparks coming out of the glasshouse stack alongside of the building, and owned by the same person, Thomas Sweney. I would remark here, that this stack was also very low, and the fire engines here were promptly at work, but notwithstanding this, both buildings were burnt to ashes in a few minutes. The third I will mention was Mr. Wilson's grist mill, a few miles from the city of Pittsburgh. The mill took fire in the night, said to be from sparks out of the stack, and the wind being high, set fire to the dwelling houses across the road, and some distance from the mill, and being in the night, and no help at hand, the mill and houses were burnt to ashes immediately. Had the dwelling houses been at the other end of the mill, I have no doubt they would have been perfectly safe, as the wind was in the other direction; so I believe it was in the other two cases. In the first one the stack was at the wrong end of the building, and in the second the engine shop was on the wrong side of the glasshouse stack, and the same with the buildings last mentioned. I was called on to examine the engines, &c., of this mill after the fire.

The fourth case was one of the most splendid, new and largest grist mills in its day in Westmoreland county, belonging to Major Weaver, of Greensburg. It took fire one morning while they were at breakfast; was supposed to have caught from the stove pipe of the office in the second story. If the pipe came out at the side of the building, as is too often customary in such cases, it probably did not come through far enough to keep the heat and blaze off the building. In case of a large fire in the stove, and especially if the wind was blowing against it, it would blow the heat, sparks and blaze, if any, against the building and set it on fire. This is one of the ways it might have caught; and another is, that the stove pipe may not have been properly secured between the outside of the pipes and the wood work of the building; the hole for the pipe may have been too small to keep the wood work cool; it may also not have had a lining of iron, stone, brick, or crock, as it should have had, and from negligence and want of forethought in this way, it no doubt was the cause of burning up in a few minutes.

One more instance and the last that I will mention. We were putting up an engine in a large saw mill, on the Allegheny Mountains; they had a temporary stove and pipe erected to keep the hands warm whilst at work, until the mill was finished. I told the foreman that he ought to have his stove pipe fixed better than it was. I reasoned with him, and told him it was very dangerous, &c.; he said it was only a temporary concern, to warm the hands for a few days until the mill was finished. The pipe went straight up through the roof, and one side of the pipe was leaning against it on the wood; the mill was high and the pipe very long, and I suppose on this account they thought there was less danger than would be with a short one. The morning was desperately cold; I put on a large fire in the stove, and before I knew what I was about, either I or my little boy discovered the mill to be on fire. It was early in the morning, and I think there was not more than one hand besides myself and boy; there was not a single bucket to be had, and the storehouse belonging to the mill was some distance off. There was an overhead cistern, which was frozen; I broke the ice, carrying it in my hands, and was immediately on the roof in time, and laid it on the high side of the roof along side of the stove pipe, and the flame and heat melting the ice and I rubbing it over the burning parts, was instrumental in putting out the fire. This fire no doubt was put out owing to the fact that we discovered it at the very beginning. Had it gone on five minutes longer the building would have soon been in ashes. I do not suppose we could have raised half a dozen of men in the neighborhood to help, it being on the mountain.

I mention these five establishments that were burnt, so that in the erection of mills, factories, &c., you may see the necessity of building your stacks high, and in that part of the mill that the wind will most generally carry away the smoke and sparks from the building. There is also danger from large flakes of burning soot alighting on the roof from the stack. I would also state that you cannot be too careful with stove pipes and chimneys. See to it that the opening is cut out large enough, and made secure, so that if the stove pipe were red-hot there would be no danger of it setting fire to the building. Let me prescribe how this should be done. Say your stove pipe is 6 inches in diameter; cut out the hole in the floor and lathing below at least 12 inches, or more, if the space between the joists will admit; then get three sheet iron rings, one 8, one 10 and one 12 inches in diameter, with a flange on each ring riveted on to a sheet iron plate large enough to cover the hole above, with 1 inch or more lap all around on the floor; then set the stove pipe in the centre, and have three or four lugs riveted on the above plate to keep it in its place, leaving 1 inch between the pipe and the first ring for air to pass through. It would be advisable to let the ring next the pipe stand down two or three inches or more below the lath, and then plaster the outside crevice close to the outer ring. Stove pipe coming sideways out of frame buildings, should run out, if possible, at least 2 feet, and then be carried up to the top of the building, so as to keep the smoke from blacking the glass and house, and also to make it more secure from fire. I believe thousands of buildings have been burnt from stove pipes in this and various other ways. It is just what might be expected where a stove pipe is put out at the side of a frame house, reaching say 6 or 8 inches through the side of the building, the blaze sometimes coming out, and the wind blowing it back on the building.

There is also danger from chimneys used for steam boilers if not properly secured. Where you do not find it convenient to use sheet iron casing, you may use cast iron, or stone or crock, &c., but there should be fully as much care to make the stacks, pipes, &c. fire-proof as in putting up the building. You talk of steam being dangerous, and so it is, unless properly cared for, and laws are made to inspect boilers and engines, &c.; why not do the same with the use of fire? It is equally as dangerous as steam, and destroys millions of dollars' worth of property yearly, as well as many lives, by burning ships, steamers, houses, &c.; and you say these things cannot be helped, they were accidents. So I say the explosions were accidents also; but the one could have been helped just as much as the other, if it is carelessness, which I acknowledge it most generally is, but not always; for there have been some explosions mysterious and difficult to account for, as well as some fires that have originated no one knows how, perhaps from spontaneous combustion, or some other unknown cause.

HOW TO SET BOILERS AND CLOSE IN THE BRICK WORK.

In setting stationary boilers, the end where the blow-off is should be about 1 inch low to every 20 feet, so that when you clean and wash out your boilers the water will run out, instead of having to be bailed and swept out, as is often the case. The boilers should never be put up close to the brick stack, because then the expansion of the boiler, which is about $\frac{1}{16}$ of an inch to the foot, will all be one way, and press the fire front out and cause it to lean over so that the doors will not stay shut unless braced; besides, they will be in danger of falling down, and may wound or kill those within their reach. After building the stone foundation a few inches above ground, then build the brick work about 2 feet high, and let the wall dry a few days before putting the boilers in. Build your bridge wall at the end of the grate bars, and also a foundation for the boiler stand to rest on. Then put timbers across the walls, and roll in your boilers and block them up; then set your fire front, making it to lean inward at $\frac{1}{8}$ or $\frac{3}{16}$ of an inch to the foot, so as to brace against the boiler expansion, and to keep the furnace doors shut. The space between the boilers on the outside and the wall, for small boilers, ought to be 3 inches, and for large boilers 36 inches and upward, 4 inches is plenty; and the boilers should be constructed so as to have the same distance between them, then you can use brick for closing in, as tile is expensive and cannot always be had. Leave a recess in each side of the furnace walls at the front end, one or two bricks below the tops of the grate bars, and 6 or 7 feet back, to receive a single lining of fire brick up to the low water gauge. The boilers should always be closed in at the low water cock, never above, and if the courses of brick do not come exactly right, it would be safer and better to close 1 or 2 inches below. The flues in the boiler should be constructed so that the lower gauge will be 5 or 6 inches or more above the centre, so as to give the boilers a chance to hold the bricks up from tumbling down, as they are sure to do when put in at the centre; and if you should close in above the centre for the purpose of holding up the bricks, as is frequently done, you will be sure to spring your boiler and cause it to leak and crack at the rivet holes. This is the reason why so many boilers have to be repaired, hence the necessity of having the lower gauge 5 or 6 inches above the centre of the boiler. The walls should be 18 inches thick for a first-rate job, 13 might do for some temporary concerns. If built in warm weather the brick should be wet, and the walls either grouted or slushed, so as to cause the mortar to take a bond. If the furnace should be too deep or too shallow, this can be remedied in part by raising or lowering the back grate bar bearer a few inches. The bridge wall should come up within from 4 to 6 inches of the boiler; it is sometimes close at the end of the grate bars, and sometimes a little farther back, especially about saw mills where long wood is used for fuel. Sometimes the boiler walls are bound together by six or eight cast iron plates, three or four on each side, with a plate the whole length of the walls, even with the top and outside of the walls. This prevents the wall from spreading and opening with the heat of the furnace, and also the expansion of the boilers. Those who are not willing to go to this expense use wood, and the majority do without. But there is no job complete without being iron bound, because the walls are sure to crack and spread; this destroys the draft, lets the heat escape, fills the place with smoke, and may be the means of firing the building by sparks, &c. See to it that this part of the work is properly done. It is customary to leave a temporary door in the side, and sometimes one in the back of the flue, to get in and clean out the ashes. Cast iron doors and frames are the best, but if these cannot be had, build your brick on top of a few bars of iron, and close in single thickness with brick, which will have to be taken down and built up every time you go in and out. Sometimes the fire fronts are fastened by bolts running the whole length of the wall, and sometimes half length, and some do without. Sometimes we build two or three pieces of 1 inch gas pipe in the wall, to see how far the flame reaches under the boiler, and how it operates. If you have no pipe, leave your bricks ½ inch apart for that purpose, and have a stopper for the same. Some build a damper in the stack, some on top of the stack, and others have it to slide up and down at the end of the boiler where the flue enters the stack. As the damper when closed will cause the smoke and blaze to come out at the furnace doors, I prefer the ash pit door, as this shuts the air out from below and stops the fire from burning, and at the same time leaves the flue in the stack clear for the smoke to pass off.

Lastly, there is a part of vital importance, seldom done right, either for want of knowing how, or to avoid labor and expense; this is the closing in of the space between the end of the boilers and the brick stack. This has reference only to cylinder boilers. To do this right it is necessary to build the brick work at the end of the boiler or boilers even with the top of the boilers at the back end, and have a straight smooth surface all the way across, then have an offset in the stack 4½ or 9 inches wide, or more, and then you can build fire brick or tile solid to the offset in the stack, so as to allow the boiler to come and go under the brick or tile covering as it expands or contracts. This is very easily done. You can commence the offset in the stack and build it to the exact height after the boiler is set; and if your stack should be built without an offset, it is a very easy matter to build a temporary 9 inch wall alongside of the stack for this purpose. The covering over the space between the boiler and stack may be built fast to the boiler, in case the recess on the stack is not wide

OVERSIZED FOLDOUT

2 COLOR ILLUSTRATIONS

was removed after page(s) 70
for in-house scanning

On 8.18 2000

enough; but I prefer it on the stack, which should be wide enough if made 9 inches. The boiler need never be more than 1 or 2 inches clear of the stack, as the boiler only expands $\frac{1}{40}$ of an inch to the foot. Cast iron plates could also be used here, if they were not considered too expensive. This is the only way to make a complete job of this part of the work. (For particulars, see plate A, with side view of boiler.)

STEEL BOILERS.

"Some very practical, thorough and interesting experiments have been made in Prussia with steel steam boilers, an account of which has been published in *Dingler's Polytechnic Journal.* A steel boiler of the egg-end shape, 4 feet in diameter and 30 feet in length, without flues, was tried. It had a steam drum 2 feet in diameter and 2 feet in height, and the plates were $\frac{1}{4}$ of an inch in thickness. Beside it there was placed another boiler, similar in every respect, excepting that the plates were of iron 0.414 of an inch in thickness. The steel boiler was tested by hydraulic pressure up to 195 pounds on the inch, without showing leakage, and both the iron and steel boilers were worked under a pressure of 65 pounds on the inch for about one year and a half. During this period, the steel boiler generated 25 per cent. more steam than the iron one, and when they were thoroughly examined after eighteen months practical working, there was less scale in the steel than in the iron boiler. The former evaporates 11-66 cubic feet of water per hour; the iron boiler 9-37 cubic feet.

The quantity of coal consumed was on an average 2,706 pounds for the steel one in twelve hours, and 2,972 pounds for the iron boiler. The plates of the steel boiler over the fire were found to be uninjnred, while those of the iron one were about worn out. In Prussia several worn-out plates of iron boilers have lately been replaced with steel, which, it is stated, lasts four times as long. As steel is twice as strong as iron, thinner plates of the former may be employed for boilers, and more perfect riveting can be secured. A greater quantity of steam can also be generated in the steel boiler on account of its thin plates, and thus much fuel may be economized. Such steam boilers should engage the attention of all who make and use steam boilers for engineering and manufacturing purposes."

The above is from the *Scientific American.* I refer to it to show that there is evidently an error in the statement of the relative durability of the two kinds of boilers. It is well known that an iron boiler will, with ordinary care, last from ten to twenty years. In the case mentioned where the boiler was worn out in eighteen months, there must have been some other cause than the material of which it was made. I have no doubt that the thickness of the boiler more than 4-10 inch was the main cause; and I am persuaded that if the case had been reversed, with the iron ¼ inch and the steel 4-10 inch thick, then the result would have been the very opposite—the steel boiler would have given way first. The outside of the boiler at the laps, being so far from the water, is kept constantly at a high degree of heat, and consequently soon burns and cracks.

STRENGTH OF STEAM BOILERS.

"I do not intend here entering into the causes of the large number of boiler explosions that take place, but having lately read in the daily press accounts of the bursting of several locomotive boilers, it struck me that some simple and general rule by which to ascertain their strength would be useful to all who either make or use them; and especially because, although the general principle herein conveyed is well known, still I have found few, especially amongst practical men, who have any idea of the actual pressure it would be safe to test boilers to. I therefore subjoin a table I have worked out, which shows one-third of the pressure per square inch a boiler 1 inch in diameter will bear without bursting, and no material should be loaded with a greater strain. For boilers of any size it is only necessary to divide the number of pounds in the table, opposite the thickness of plate used, by the diameter in inches; the result will be the greatest load that ought to be put on a safety valve in pounds, per square inch. The iron used is understood to be of the best quality, with a tensile strength equal to 70,000 pounds per square inch. Although all boilers should be tested to the extent given by the table, they should not be regularly worked up to that pressure, on account of their depreciation by wear and tear, by oxidation and otherwise, which, according to the time they have been in use, will of course proportionately lessen their efficiency.

1-8th-inch plate,.................................... 2,500 pounds.
3-16th-inch plate,.................................. 3,750 pounds.

1-4th-inch plate,	5,000 pounds.
5-16th-inch plate,	6,250 pounds.
3-8th-inch plate,	7,500 pounds.
7-16th-inch plate,	8,750 pounds.
½-inch plate,	10,000 pounds.
9-16th-inch plate,	11,250 pounds.
5-8th-inch plate,	12,500 pounds.
3-4th-inch plate,	15,000 pounds.

"Suppose, for instance, we have a locomotive boiler made of 5-16th-inch plate (their usual thickness) and 45 inches diameter, the table would give 6,250 45= 139 lbs., the greatest amount to which the safety valve should be loaded; whereas another boiler, 35 inches diameter, and the same thickness of plate, would, by the same rule (6,250 35.) bear 178 pounds per square inch, without any extra strain on the iron. If, however, we make the 35-inch boiler of 1-4th-inch iron, we find opposite 1-4th-inch, 5,000, which, divided by 35, gives 143 pounds, showing that 1-4th-inch plate in a 35-inch boiler, will bear more pressure than 5-16th-inch plate in a 45-inch boiler. This also shows conclusively that by making two boilers of different diameters, that have to work at the same pressure, of the same thickness of plate, that either one is too weak, or there is a waste of material in the other."—*Wm. Tosbach, in Scientific American.*

INSPECT YOUR STEAM BOILERS.

"Boiler explosions are becoming remarkably prevalent. Scarcely a day passes but what, from some part of the country, remote or near, we receive intelligence of a great disaster. It is perhaps inevitable that some boilers should explode, out of the vast number in daily use on land and sea, in the factory and on the rail; it would be strange indeed, if that curse of humanity—carelessness, was not felt in its magnitude; for, reason and theorize as we may, it is a well-settled fact in the minds of scientific and practical men, here and abroad, that to this cause most of the accidents with steam may be traced. It is carelessness that makes boilers on bad plans, of poor workmanship and material; it is carelessness which omits the thorough inspection which boilers should have every thirty days; it is carelessness which permits crownsheets and flues to be burnt from scarcity of water, and water-bottoms, legs, and fire boxes to be bent, burnt and distorted from deposits of mud, scale, or refuse that is suffered to accumulate; it is carelessness which allows safety valves to be jammed or overloaded, feed pumps to look after themselves, braces to be slack where they should be taut, and the pins in the braces not turned, or bent over, so that they cannot slip out; such cases have been known. It is more than carelessness which allows imperfectly welded wrought-iron sleeves for the socket-bolts to be used to cover the same, for the water has free access through the open seams, and destroys the bolt as quickly as if there was no 'protection.' Cast-iron sleeves are now used in the best shops, and besides being a perfect protection to the socket-bolts, they are more durable and much cheaper. From the first hour of its practical operation until the day of its final condemnation, a boiler is constantly growing weaker, and it should be so cared for that the work it is obliged to do is proportionate to its strength each year. To ascertain what the strength is, we must test it, and this can be done in a simple, cheap, and expeditious manner by water and heat. If a boiler be filled *full* of water up to the very safety valves, and all apertures closed, when a fire is built in the furnace, the water will be expanded, and raise the valve, if the boiler is strong enough to withstand the strain, but if it is not, the weakest part will be shown and sometimes sheets are torn out by this method. Steam is not generated from the water during this test, and if a rupture does take place in the boiler no one will be injured by it. The safety valve must be loaded to the utmost limit of strain that it is supposed the boiler will bear; and if the test is favorable, only three-fourths of the load on the safety valve must be employed for the working pressure.

"It has never been proved beyond question that a steam boiler exploded from any of the theories put forth in each disaster. Some persons have a passion for 'explaining' matters that they do not understand by something else they are ignorant of; and we have had hydrogen gas brought forward as an agent in causing explosions; water suddenly flashed into steam as another; electricity for another; and so on, through the category. These are simply excuses on the part of some one at fault for the disaster. *After* a boiler has exploded, it seems almost supererogatory to go and look at it, and say what caused the disaster. We have heaps of smoking ruins, iron bent and blackened, and in most cases each part is a fac-simile of every other explosion; the torn sheets are gravely examined and the conclusion arrived at is that 'somebody was to blame.'

"We have no desire to treat the matter with levity, but is it not time that we had more careful superintendence of steam boilers and fewer inquests? In some cases, the cause of the accident may be pointed out after the explosion, but in such it might have been done equally well before. As we have before remarked, it is to be expected that some boilers will explode in spite of all inspection, just as cannon do with the most careful gunners; but it is a part, and a most important part of an engineer's duty, to be thoroughly convinced of the soundness and strength of his boiler. When we see how seldom accidents of this kind occur to marine boilers, we have positive proof of the value of thorough oversight and watchfulness; and we feel that we cannot speak too strongly or too often upon the necessity which exists for prompt, thorough, and frequent inspection of steam boilers."—*Scientific American.*

CONCERNING STEAM BOILERS.

"We have in previous numbers of the *Scientific American* frequently called the attention of engineers and manufacturers to the condition of their steam boilers; for we have felt, and still feel, that in too many cases they are neglected and overlooked. If there is any department where false economy is out of place it is certainly about a steam boiler; and by this we mean a disposition to let repairs go until a more convenient season, or as a person once said in our hearing, 'till it gets so that it is worth mending;' this is false economy. The tailor's proverb about 'the stitch in time' is eminently true of steam and the apparatus driven by, or the vessels containing it. All the leaky rivets (if any) should be driven tight, slack braces set up to their duty, seams calked where they require it, ashes kept away from water-drip when it falls on the sheets, clinkers prevented from forming on grate bars (where anything like decent coal is provided, no excuse should be received by manufacturers for this neglect), safety valves overhauled and put in working condition (too many of them are mere percussion caps, so to speak), flues swept at least once a week, ashes and soot kept out of the smoke box; every ounce of it is a non-conductor that robs the boiler of its rightful heat. In short, every detail and appurtenance of a steam boiler requires conscientious, thorough, and continual supervision; then there will be fewer lives lost, less property destroyed, and a better class of engineers and manufacturers generally. That is the true way to raise the wages of engineers and make business pay; elevate the standard of the services rendered, and, our word for it, manufacturers will accede to all reasonable requests.

"The terrible effects of carelessness are too apparent when steam boilers explode, and blow to the four winds of heaven all that a man has been able to accumulate in a lifetime of hard labor. See to it, then, you manufacturers, and you, engineers! that there are no half-way measures adopted; that no 'penny wise and pound foolish' policy prevails; keep the boilers in the best possible repair and condition; buy none but the best fuel; hire only capable, conscientious, and *sober* men to oversee them; and the rate of insurance will be lower, higher profits will accrue, and steam power be rendered what in fact it is—an energetic, easily-managed, and economical servant."—*Scientific American.*

INCRUSTATION OF BOILERS.

"We have frequently referred to this subject and the different remedies for it. One of the most reliable is the 'Anti-incrustation Powder' of Mr. H. N. Winans of New York, to which we drew especial attention in our issue of June 21, 1862. Since then we have seen a number of additional testimonials of its operation, and from all we can learn, it is perfectly reliable. Messrs. Bement & Dougherty, Philadelphia, after two years successful use, pronounce it uninjurious, and George Shield, Chief Engineer of Cincinnati Water Works, after five years use, says it not only has no injurious effects, but prevents the iron from oxidizing. These valuable recommendations, with many others, induce us to give it our approval and to recommend it to all using steam. With the high price of fuel and the immense loss in generating steam, occasioned by the formation of scale in boilers and the conseqnent injury to the iron by overheating, we consider almost any expenditure an economy which will effect a remedy, and this we believe Mr. Winans' material will do without injury to the boiler. We therefore advise our readers to make a trial and save fuel, repairs, &c."—*Scientific American.*

THE WAY BOILER SCALE IS DEPOSITED.

"Carbonate of lime is scarcely soluble at all in pure hot water, is a little soluble in pure cold water, and quite soluble in water containing carbonic acid. Cold water, exposed for a long time to the atmosphere, always absorbs its own bulk of carbonic acid; and if, while thus mixed, it comes in contact with carbonate of lime, a portion of the stone will be dissolved. Hence the hard water of our springs and wells. If this water is placed in a boiler and heated, the first action of the heat is to drive off the carbonic acid; and this action, with the raising of the temperature, deprives the water of its power of holding the carbonate of lime in solution. The salt is consequently precipitated, and deposited as a hard scale in the boiler."—*Scientific American.*

RUPTURING BOILERS.

Boilers are ruptured from different causes, and one very common reason is, on account of the brick work on the outside and between the boilers being closed in several inches above the low water line. This is sometimes done designedly for the purpose of super-heating the steam by getting more fire surface, but most generally it is done carelessly, or for want of thought. Bricklayers are not posted up as they should be on this subject, and they do not always receive particular charge and instructions how to do this part of the work as it should be done, and this is the cause of boilers so often rupturing and giving way about the low water line. The fire operates on the boiler several inches above the low water line; and when the water gets below the regular gauge, which it often does, the iron above is heated a great deal hotter than the balance of the boiler, sometimes almost red hot, and the water rising and falling the iron is exposed to frequent and sudden heating and cooling, and crystallizes, which makes it brittle and causes it to crack from one rivet to another, sometimes the length of several sheets at a time. I saw one boiler that gave way on the side, blew the brick work down, and scalded the engineer so that he died shortly after. Boilers have given out on the river the same way and from the same cause.

There is another cause which seldom happens. I saw a boiler that gave way on the bottom over the fire, which the foreman told me was caused by local heat on the bottom of the boiler, and the heat being thus confined to one spot, became so intense as to burn the boiler and cause it to bag, &c. It was caused by burning slack and not stirring it up as often as it should have been to let the air in and make the blaze run along in the bottom of the boiler; thus the heat became very intense on the one spot of the boiler, and caused it to burn notwithstanding it might have plenty of water. Another cause, is leaving blankets, brooms, &c., in the boiler when cleaning out; and another for want of being properly cleaned out.

Boilers often rupture owing to corrosion. Supply and stand pipes underneath the boilers, and also the steam pipes on top, being suffered to leak, oxydize and waste away the iron very fast. These pipes should be kept perfectly tight and dry, in order to keep them from speedy decay. Another cause: unless the boiler or boilers are kept under a tight roof, they may in this way become so badly rusted in parts as to cause them to be so weak as to yield to a heavy pressure.

After all, boilers have exploded where the cause has not been satisfactorily ascertained. We submit whether the sudden decomposition of water thrown into a boiler red hot, and its conversion into its constituent gases, might not cause a boiler to explode. The gas being highly inflammable, would take fire, and its effects would be the same as the ignition of gunpowder. It is ascertained that the increase of heat, unless water be added, will not increase the power of steam, but it will decompose it into its constituent gases. And perhaps electricity, of the nature of which so little is known, may be a cause of explosion.

TO PREVENT BOILERS EXPLODING AND FLUES COLLAPSING.

It was customary, in early days, to put a lead rivet on the top of each flue at the back end of the boilers, so that if the water should get below the top, the lead would melt, and the steam whistling through the rivet hole would give the alarm before the flues had time to become red hot. It is also a good plan to put one lead rivet on each side of each boiler hull, cylinder or flued, in the second sheet above the fire at the low water line, for the same purpose. The object of putting them in both sides of the boiler, is, in case the fire might be hotter on one side than the other, it would be sure to melt without danger of being overheated. There is no doubt that the lead rivet in the boiler hulls over the fire would melt out first, as the heat here is much greater than at the back end of the flues. Lead rivets in the course of time might waste away, and would have to be renewed.

"Of the intense heat that steam sometimes attains, even without causing explosion, the following instance may be cited: the packing of the piston of a steamboat, working with steam of a tension no greater than an atmosphere and a half, burst into flame on opening the cylinder, at least half an hour after the fire had been extinguished. Here it is evident, that any mixture of heated water with this steam might have caused explosion."

In France, every steam boiler is required by law to be furnished with a safety plug of fusible metal. It is composed of tin, three parts; lead, two parts; bismuth, four parts.

"Another method which promises to be effectual in many cases, is to form a part of the boiler of a plate of metal fusible at a comparatively low temperature. Such is an alloy of bismuth, lead, and tin, by varying the proportions of which a considerable difference in fusibility may be attained. They ought to be of such a mixture as not to melt, until heated beyond the temperature assumed as the limit of the heat to which it is ever desired to raise the steam, but fusible at one considerably below that at which the boiler becomes red hot. From 20° to 40° above the maximum heat the steam is meant to attain, will be well suited to the purpose, for they will then melt before any part of the boiler can become red hot. These plates must be adapted to the upper part of the boiler, and be of course in contact with the steam; they are inserted at the end of tubes fitted steam-tight to the boiler. As they are apt to soften long before they melt, they ought to be covered by a diaphragm of wire gauze. When thus protected, they have been found not to give way until they actually melt. As different parts of the boiler may acquire different temperatures, two such plates will be needed upon its outer surface, at the two ends; they ought to be as near to the body of the boiler as possible. When flues pass through the boiler we conceive that it would be a proper precaution to furnish them also with plates, of this description, but in this case, the metal might be less fusible, and lead unalloyed would suffice."

I am not in favor of using the fusible plates unless they are very small, because if large it would be very dangerous to be near them when giving way. The fusible plugs are greatly to be preferred, both because they can do no harm if properly arranged, and they cost but a trifle compared with that of the patent alarm detectors. Many of our first class engineers say that these detectors are not reliable after remaining in the boiler for some time, as the plug of fusible metal becomes coated with lime, and hardened by constant heating, and its fusibility is destroyed. For this reason the fusible rivet would be far superior, for when overheated it will be sure to melt and tell the tale. If the water should be very strongly impregnated with lime, it would be well when cleaning out the boilers to see that the lead rivet heads are clear of having scale, lest after the lead had melted the scale might form so thick as to prevent the steam from blowing through, but I do not think this is at all probable; but by examining it occasionally you have a sure thing, and if soft water is used there is no necessity for examination. Keep your boilers clean, and after cleaning them out be sure to leave no blankets, brooms, or any thing else behind, as boilers in this way have often been bagged and burnt. There is very little difference between the simple fusible rivet and the patented safety alarm whistles. They both alike melt and give the alarm when the water is too low. The patent one, after having given the alarm can be stopped immediately by shutting off the steam; with the other you must get the steam down so as to allow you to put in another plug. Many prefer the latter, rather than pay the high price for the former.

EXPLOSION OF STEAM BOILERS.

An arrangement which has been brought out for preventing explosions in steam boilers is thus described: The apparatus consists of an elbow-pipe, connecting the furnace with the side flue; it is fixed just below the water level in the boiler, but may be fixed at any elevation, or in any position requisite, and can be applied to any kind of boiler, as an opening into a side or centre flue is all that is required. The pipe is perforated with a number of holes, half an inch in diameter, so placed as to be subject to the immediate action of the furnace fire; in these holes are metal plugs, more or less fusible, according to the working pressure of the boiler. The moment that the boiler, from neglect or otherwise, is heated below the level, and leaves this pipe bare, the heat from the furnace acts upon the plugs, which melt, and the steam oozing through the holes, immediately relieves the pressure in the boiler and extinguishes the fire, making explosion impossible.

EXPLOSION OF A BOILER AND ITS CAUSE.

"A steam boiler exploded at the factory of I. M. Singer & Co., Delancey street, New York, by which three men who were employed on the premises lost their lives. A coroner's inquest has been held on the bodies of the victims, and a decision rendered to the effect that the deceased came to their deaths by injuries received by the explosion, and that 'the jury believe that the engineer and the fireman of the factory are censurable for the explosion; the fireman for starting the fires after he had been informed of the state of the boiler, and the engineer for not making a thorough examination of the boiler and its connections after being notified of the trouble.'

"To understand the nature of this decision and the charge against the engineer, William Ford, and the fireman, Michael Reagan, it is necessary to give the substance of some of the evidence before the jury: The private watchman of the establishment stated that he had examined the four boilers in the factory on the evening before, and found that no water would flow out of some of the gauge cocks, although there was a high pressure of steam on. He then went for a boiler maker named M'Given, with whom he was acquainted, and both of them tried to raise one safety valve with their hands and were unable to do so. It pressed against the rafters so firmly that they could only slightly raise it with a piece of timber placed under the ball. He informed the fireman of this next morning, and also the engineer. The fires were started before sufficient water had been let into the boilers, and the pumps did not seem to operate well.

"William M. Storm, a mechanical engineer for the Police Department, stated that three of the four boilers in the establishment were uninjured, and upon examining their safety valves he could lift three easily, but the safety valve of the one which exploded was fast; the lower gauge cock was also immovable. The four boilers were in a gang—all alike and set side by side. Their connections were such that they could work all together or in pairs. They have return flues 14 inches in diameter, and both flues of the one that exploded were collapsed from end to end and torn away at their junction with the ends of the boiler. Joseph E. Coffee, engineer and boiler inspector for the Metropolitan district, stated that he had examined the exploded boiler, and that the safety valve had been shut at the time of the explosion. All the four boilers had their feed water pipes open, but two of them had their steam pipes, which led to the engine, closed, and only one of these exploded—the one which had its safety valve fast. There had been fire under all the four boilers. The steam which was generated in the two boilers that were disconnected with the engine, forced the water out of them, as the pressure increased, into the other two boilers, thus nearly emptying the two former boilers. 'The flues of these then became overheated, and one gave way with an ordinary pressure of steam.' This was the cause of the explosion, in the opinion of Mr. Coffee, and it is very evident that it is a clear explanation of it. Mr. Coffee also stated that had the boiler been full of water and the safety valve in proper order the explosion would not have taken place. It was the duty of the engineer to see that the connections were in proper order. Mr. B. G. Lord, sergeant of the sanitary police, stated that the engineer who had charge of these boilers, had no certificate from the Police Department.

"Nine-tenths of all the explosions which take place are the results of similar causes."—*Scientific American.*

I would add, that it is a bad plan to put fire under the boilers before the water rises to the lower gauge, as there is danger of overheating the boiler iron, and burning it below the low water gauge, on account of the lack of the regular supply of water; and it is running a considerable risk, where you are using a force pump, that is known not to be reliable, and which sometimes works and at other times refuses. There are many pumps of this description now in use.

It is customary to put a lead rivet in the centre of the crown sheet of locomotive boilers, for the purpose of giving the alarm in case the water from any cause should be suffered to get too low; this is done by the heat melting the rivet, and letting the steam escape, which gives the alarm, by blowing through the rivet hole and whistling.

PANTING OF BOILER HEADS AND HULLS.

There is no doubt that one of the causes of boiler heads blowing out is produced by the panting of the boiler head. I recollect a first rate engineer telling me that when he was on the river, he applied a straight edge to the back boiler heads, and every time the engine would take steam the boiler heads would spring in, and then out, from $\frac{1}{8}$ to $\frac{1}{4}$ inch. This is calculated, in the course of time, to weaken the flange on the boiler heads, causing it to crack and give way. Wherever this is the case, you may depend on it that the heads are not as stiff nor as well braced as they should be; they should be made so strong as not to spring, nor pant in the least.

John Warden told me that he had seen large low pressure boilers, on the lake, panting on the sides. Every time the steam was let into the cylinder the sides of the boiler would shrink in, and when the valve was shut they would swell out constantly whilst the engine was running—just the same as a man's chest heaving out and in every time he breathes, inhaling and exhaling the atmosphere.

SUGGESTIONS TO CAPTAINS OF STEAMERS.

It is the duty of every captain having charge of a steamboat, before putting out of port, and also when landing, to give the engineers special orders to have the water in the upper gauge cocks, or as much higher as it can be carried, so as not to hinder the running of the engine by drawing water into the cylinder. The object of this is to guard against the many accidents that are continually occurring by boats being listed, when putting out and landing, and also occasionally when rounding to in putting out, and in taking in passengers. When such accidents occur you often hear the cause assigned, that the boat was listed very much to one side, which may be occasioned in different ways. One very common way is, that when putting out or landing, the passengers generally rush to the shore side; and also the rush from the shore to get on board is on the same side, so that instead of causing surprise or furnishing any apology for any accident to the boiler or flues, it is just what might in such a case be expected; and hence the necessity of precautionary measures to prevent this, by always having in the boilers a surplus of water, and being careful, when going out and coming into port, not to have the steam at its highest, nor the fires at their hottest, until you are fairly under full headway. There are other causes for boats listing, as when caught in a heavy storm. This might be called unavoidable; but as you generally have indications of storms before they come, it would be well to be prepared for them in the same way. Boats when turning in strong water are listed with the current.

Great care should also be taken, in running in low stages of water, to keep the passengers as much as possible from the steam pipes and boilers, as there is great danger in case the boat should rub hard or strike a rock. I saw four deck passengers who were killed in this way on board the steamer *Nimrod*. As she came over the bar in low water, she struck, and the jar sprung a leak in the copper steam pipe leading from the boiler into the cylinder; it was a short pipe, about a quarter circle. When she landed at Cincinnati, I heard of it and went aboard. There were a man and his wife lying side by side, and two other passengers, who were scalded to death in this way on the upper deck above the boilers. To avoid accidents of this kind, some have a long crook sideways in the steam pipe leading from the boilers to the cylinders, say 2 feet or more offset, with 18 inches between; this will allow the pipe to spring a great deal before giving way, and if there had been on the *Nimrod* such a pipe as this, I do not think anything would have occurred.

By way of caution to passengers who know little or nothing of the dangers they are exposed to when traveling on board of steamers on low water, I would advise them to choose as the safest part of the boat, the berths farthest from the steam pipes and boilers, which would be at the stern in side wheel boats; and in daylight, when passing over shoal places, keep as far out of the reach of the boilers and pipes as possible. I went on board the new steamer *Vermilion* at Louisville, when putting out to go over the Falls of the Ohio; the boat was drawing 3 or 4 inches more water than there was on the falls. The canal, I think, was not in operation at this time, as it was about thirty years ago. She was bound to go over if possible, as she was intended for the lower trade. Before leaving Louisville they prepared for the worst, by having the boilers as full of water as they would bear, so as not to hinder the engine from working; and when we were getting into the strong water and nearing the falls, we took hold of the railing, as in case of getting a little to one side or other of the channel she would be thrown over to one side, and might possibly throw those who were not on their watch into the river, but we kept straight in the channel, and went over flying.

Pilots should also, as a general thing, keep in the channel as much as possible, because when out of the channel they cannot tell what they may come in contact with. I was once coming up on a steamer on the Ohio, when she ran foul of a snag which was invisible, as it was under water. A number of others and myself were seated around the stove, and we were nearly pitched into the fire. The boat was so badly snagged that all hands were called to work, some to pumping, some to bailing with tubs and buckets, and others to stopping the leak in the bow, which was done by building a temporary bulkhead and stuffing blankets into the hole. It was with difficulty we kept her from going down. Another caution to pilots: they cannot be too careful to land boats easy; if they come in hard they jar the boat, and are liable to break the pipes or spring leaks.

To give an idea of the danger of a boat when listed, with the flues bare on one side, I refer to a draft, on page 92. The boat is supposed to be in the act of rounding to in strong water, and is listed, and whilst in this condition has collapsed one of her flues, in consequence of becoming red hot for want of water. You see the flue A in the plate rent on the right side; the upper deck is represented as having been blown off, and the movables scattered in various directions, attended with loss of life, &c.

OVERSIZED FOLDOUT

COLOR ILLUSTRATION

was removed after page(s) 92
for in-house scanning

On 8·18 2000

TO FIND THE WEIGHT OF STEAM IN THE BOILER.

In the first place, it will be necessary to show how the notches in the safety valve lever should be laid off. Care should be taken, to have the spaces between the notches cut equal to the space between the fulcrum and valve stem, so that by counting the notches, you may tell exactly how much weight is carried. And let it be always remembered, that the first notch from the valve stem counts two, because the distance between it and the fulcrum is twice the distance between the notches. To make this plainer, suppose twelve weights were put on the top of the valve, they would be just equal to one weight in the twelfth notch of the lever.

The next thing will be to ascertain the net amount of weight there is on the safety valve seat from the weight of the lever, valve stem, valve, &c. This is done by a pair of steel-yards or spring scales, hooked to a string fastened to the lever at the centre of the safety valve stem.

(See draft in which the safety valve calculations are made.)

The last thing, is to get from the position of the pea on the lever, the amount of pressure on the safety valve. Multiply the weight of the pea by the number of notches in the lever, always bearing in mind to count the first notch two. Then divide this amount by the number of square inches in the safety valve seat, which is found by multiplying the square of the diameter by .7854, (see example below,) and the result will be the amount of pressure of steam you are carrying in the boiler, with the weight of the pea, and to this you add the additional weight caused by the lever, valve stem, valve, &c., and those two products, added together, will be the exact weight of steam carried in the boiler.

Example.—The opening in the safety valve seat is 3 inches in diameter, the pea is 50 pounds, and there are 8 notches in the lever, counting the first notch 2; what is the weight of steam per square inch?

```
      3
      3
      —
      9
  .7854  a decimal.
 ———————
 7.0686  Product of the multiplication of 7
         square inches in the safety valve seat.
```

Multiply a 50 pound pea by 8 notches and divide by 7 the number of square inches in the safety valve seat, and the product will be the weight of steam in the boilers produced by the weight of the pea on the end of the lèver; to this you add the additional weight caused by the lever, valve, valve stem, &c.

```
                         50  lbs. weight of pea.
                          8  notches on the lever.
                        ———
Divide by 7 square  } 7)400  lbs.
inches in valve seat, }   ———
                        57¼  lbs. per square inch.
                         3
                        ———
                        60¼  lbs. of steam per square
                                 inch.
```

Suppose the lever and rigging to weigh at the centre

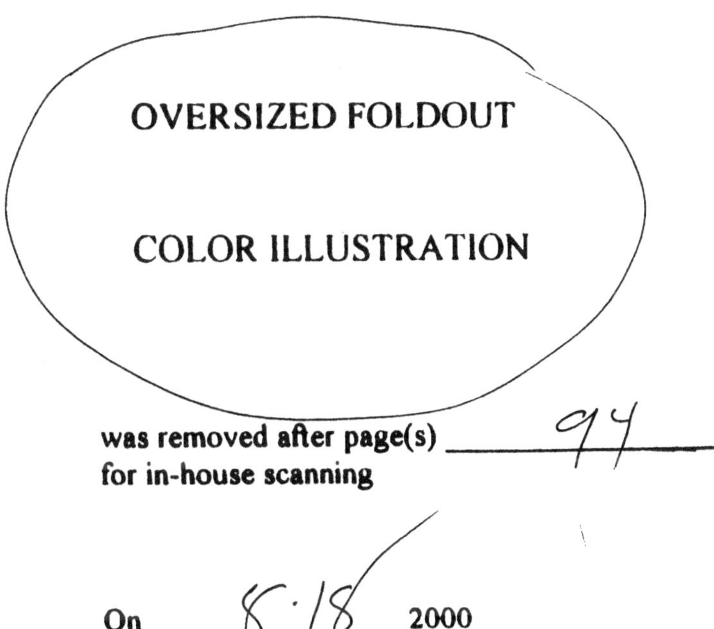

OVERSIZED FOLDOUT

COLOR ILLUSTRATION

was removed after page(s) 94
for in-house scanning

On 8·18 2000

of the valve stem 21 pounds, which, divided by the number of square inches in valve seat, which is

7)21 lbs.

3 lbs. to the square inch to be added for the lever, valve and valve stem.

ANOTHER RULE.

"The apertures for safety valves require no nice calculations. It is only necessary to have the aperture sufficient to let the steam off from the boiler as fast as it is generated, when the engine is not at work.

The safety valve is loaded sometimes by putting a heavy weight upon it, and sometimes by means of a lever with a weight to move along to suit the required pressure.

When the whole weight is put on the valve, to find the pressure to each square inch:—

Multiply the square of the diameter of the valve by .7854, and this product will give the area, or number of square inches in the valve.

And if the whole weight upon the valve, in pounds, be divided by the number of square inches in the valves, the quotient will give the number of pounds pressure to each square inch in the valve.

Ex.—If a weight of 40 lbs. be placed upon a valve, the diameter of which is 3 inches, what will be the pressure to each square inch?

$3^2 \times .7854 = 7$ square inches; then, $40 \div 7 = 5\frac{5}{7}$ lbs. per square inch."—*Norris' Hand Book.*

JOHN WALLACE'S VERTICAL STEAM BOILER.

This boiler having for a long time engaged the attention of the inventor, is now before the public. It has been thoroughly tested, and we think proved to be superior to all other upright boilers now in use, being less liable to explosion. It is so constructed that with a full head of steam, and while the engine is in motion, the sediment can be dislodged, and then discharged through the mud valve, thus relieving it from the danger of choking up with mud and sediment, to which small flued and tubular boilers are so liable. It is cylindrical, and easily transported. It requires no fire front, no boiler stands, and no furnace of brick or mason work, (the furnace being entirely inside of the boiler,) and not over one-third the grate bars requisite for ordinary boilers. The furnace in this boiler being entirely surrounded with water, there is but little danger from fire, and insurance companies have insured factories where these boilers have been used, for 25 to 40 per cent. less than they would do when the common boilers were used. The vertical boiler occupies about one-tenth only of the ground space required for a horizontal boiler, and when we consider this fact, the economy of space becomes a matter of great importance, and particularly so in large towns and cities.

All orders promptly attended to.

W. W. WALLACE,
319 *Liberty street, Pittsburgh.*

OVERSIZED FOLDOUT

was removed after page(s) 96
for in-house scanning

On 8/18 2000

VARIOUS KINDS OF FUEL.

STONE COAL AND SLACK.

More work can be done with less boiler, with a superior article of coal; and the difference between the amount of labor performed by the different kinds of fuel will be equal to the difference in the quality. I have had experience in this matter, and have been able with good lump coal to keep steam up and blowing off with ease, whilst with the same boiler and engine, in using slack or inferior coal, every thing would drag and we could not get along to advantage. Where you intend to use slack, or an inferior article of coal, make your calculations accordingly, getting an extra amount of boiler to make up for the defect in the quality of the fuel, or otherwise you will come short of realizing a sufficiency of steam. If slack is used, the spaces between the bars should be from $\frac{3}{8}$ to $\frac{1}{2}$ inch wide.

DRY AND GREEN WOOD.

Wood can be used to better advantage on flued boilers than any other kind of fuel. It is also much cleaner, and easier on the boilers, being less liable to injure them by excessive heat. It keeps up a more constant flame than any other kind of fuel, with the exception of pine knots. It blazes until almost entirely consumed, and the flues in the boiler remain clean for a much greater length of time, and consequently require less sweeping out, than when using bituminous coal.

Green wood makes a slow but very hot fire; and where it is intended to be used, as it generally is about saw-mills, you should calculate on having from 75 to

100 per cent. more boiler than if dry wood were to be used. Where green wood is used about saw-mills it is sometimes customary to have a double tier of grate bars, 6 and 8 feet long, for burning slabs, &c.

WOOD AND COAL MIXED.

Wood and coal mixed is said to make the hottest fire for raising steam that can be used. This is owing to the wood being scattered through the coal, keeping it more open and porous, and allowing the air to circulate more freely, thereby causing it to burn much better and brighter than either would separately.

SAW DUST AND SLACK.

It is customary, especially about city saw-mills, where fuel is high, to use up the sawdust. In order to do this to advantage, it is necessary to mix in a small quantity of slack, which makes it burn better. Where this kind of fuel is used, it is now becoming common to have the furnaces 20 or 24 inches deep between the bottom of the boilers and the top of the grate bars. It is also coming into use to have two tier of 3 feet grate bars, making the fire-bed 6 feet long. The spaces between the bars require to be so close as to prevent the sawdust from falling through. It is economy to use this kind of fuel, as it costs little or nothing; but wherever it is used it is necessary to have from 75 to 100 per cent. more boiler than would be requisite with the best of fuel.

TAN BARK.

It is a common thing for the tanners about Pittsburgh, Cincinnati and elsewhere, to use the tan bark in the boiler furnace. These furnaces are of a peculiar construction. The boiler is down in a pit. It is customary to have a division in the furnace even for one boiler; the furnace is about 2 feet deep and 4 feet long; it is made low so that the bark can be emptied into the vault from the wheel-barrow by lifting off the cap. The object of the division in the furnace is to fill the divisions time about. As the bark is put in wet, it will not do to fill them both up at the same time, as it would smother the fires; but the idea is, always to have one burning bright whilst you are filling up the other. In all such cases you must calculate on double the amount of boiler that would be necessary with good fuel. In using this waste bark for fuel, several good purposes are answered. It saves cost in purchasing fuel, it saves the expense of hauling it away, and gives more room for storage, and when burnt the ashes are sold to the farmers for manure.

ANTHRACITE COAL.

Anthracite coal is generally used in the cities of Philadelphia, New York, &c. It is found in the east at a great depth, some of the mines are hundreds of feet deep. It is hard and flinty, clean, and makes no smoke. It takes a great while to kindle, and when kindled will burn almost half a day before requiring to fill the furnace again. These fires do not require the shaking and stirring that bituminous coal does. Where this kind of fuel is used they require about 50 per cent. more boiler than with bituminous coal. It requires to be kindled with wood, bituminous coal or charcoal.

PINE KNOTS.

Pine knots are got in the South. They are full of turpentine, and do very well to mix in with wood or coal. They make a very hot fire, but using them altogether is not so good; the flues would soon fill up with soot, and if used alone they would make all blaze and little or no red fire. I used some of them on a steamer at Florence, Alabama, when I was engineering on the Tennessee river.

HOW TO PUT ON COALS IN BOILER FURNACES.

Great skill is required in firing under the boilers, in order to produce the greatest amount of steam with the least amount of fuel, and also to prevent waste and save labor. The best mode of putting on coals is to scatter them thinly over a clear red fire, and let it burn until it forms a regular crust, then open it up with the poker, to let the air circulate freely through it, and as soon as the fire becomes clear and red hot fill up in the same manner as above. Avoid all unnecessary shaking of the fires, as it wastes the fuel, and makes a great many more clinkers than would otherwise be made. In burning saw dust or tan bark, the less slack used the better. You require enough barely to cover the grate bars, to prevent the sawdust or tan bark from falling through, and more than this would choke the fires so as to exclude the air from passing through, and prevent the fires from burning.

BOILER TUBES.

"According to the experiments made by Prof. Fairbairn, the law of resistance for cylindrical tubes is *this:*

a tube having the same strength of material, and being of the same diameter, will resist double the pressure of one having double the length; or, the collapsing pressure, other things being the same, varies inversely as the length and inversely as the diameter. Experiments made with elliptical tubes showed that in every construction where tubes have to sustain a uniform external pressure, the cylindrical is the only form to be relied upon, and that any departure from the true circle is attended with danger. The experiments also tended to confirm the conclusions heretofore arrived at, namely, that the strengths of riveted joints of malleable iron plates are nearly as the numbers 100 for the plate, 70 for double riveted joints, 50 for single-riveted joints."

I endorse the above statement, that the cylindrical tube is the only form to be relied on, and that it is less dangerous than other kinds. I will give an example. Some years ago, a steamship was fitted out here by a New York company. The boilers were flued, the flues having the shape of a triangle with three equal circular sides. The object in making them so, was to get more fire surface. (For particulars, see draft of an end view of boiler and flues, on page 93.) I understood that on her first trial trip, she collapsed one or more of her flues. They were taken out and cylindrical ones put in their place.

I have seen in a patent boiler, a large elliptical flue, the object of which was to gain fire surface. The flue was supported inside here and there with water pipes, as you see in the draft of an end view of boiler, on page 000. Neither of these kinds of flues are worth putting in, as their strength is greatly diminished on account of their shape. You might, with the same propriety, introduce an elliptic boiler, for the sake of gaining fire surface. The one is equal to the other. Boilers and flues of this description would be dear to put in use, if you could get them for nothing; and, not only this, but it would cost more to make them than the cylindrical boiler and flues.

EXPERIMENT TRIED ON A NEW BOILER.

An experiment was tried here on a double-flued 40-inch boiler, 12 feet long, with two 16-inch flues. The iron was heavy, ¼-inch; the best charcoal Juniata; the heads ⅝ of an inch thick. It was made on purpose to try it with the test pump, to see what amount of pressure it would stand. It was tested by the United States Boiler Inspector. It began to leak at the seams on the side at 230 lbs. pressure, and gave way at 290 lbs., at the back head around the flange of the flue, which cracked and opened a space of 10 inches. The head sprung out 1⅝ inches before the flue flange gave way. I suppose the yielding of the head was what caused the rupture. The boiler head had no braces in. There is no doubt in my mind but the boiler would have stood more pressure had the heads been well braced, as the rupture in the flue flange was evidently caused by the head springing out 1⅝ inches.

DEPOSIT OF LIME ON BOILERS.

To persons having the care of steam engines, the following from the *Laurenceburg Register* may be valuable: "Mr. Ira Hill has informed us, that he has accidentally made a valuable discovery, by which the deposition of lime upon steam boilers may be obviated. Two or three shovels of saw-dust are thrown into the boiler; after which process, he states, he never had any difficulty from lime, although using water strongly impregnated with it. He has always found the inside of his boilers as smooth as if just oiled. Whether the lime attaches itself to the floating particles of saw-dust, instead of the boiler, or whether the tannic acid in the oak saw-dust forms a salt with the lime which will not attach itself to the iron, remains to be explained. The saw-dust was placed in the boiler for the purpose of stopping a leak. The experiment is cheap and easily tried."

WEIGHT OF STEAMBOAT BOILERS, &c.

The following tables of the weight of steamboat boilers, including fire bed, breeching, chimneys, guy rods, fire fronts, grate bars, bearers, liners, check, blow-off and safety-valve chambers, including all the wrought and cast iron required for the same, are given for the benefit of those who are about to negotiate for the building of steamers, mills, factories, &c., in order that they may ascertain the cost by knowing the weight, and be better prepared to make their calculations understandingly. It is said, that the cost of boilers, when rigged out complete, is about one-half the whole cost of the boilers and engine. I believe, in many instances, this is correct, and in others, the cost may be more and sometimes less. This depends altogether on circumstances. I merely throw out the hint, so that when you have the price of the boilers and all belonging to the same complete, the cost of the engine will not vary much either way from that of the boilers and rigging. Another advantage to steamboat men is, they can better ascertain the amount of water the boat will draw, by previously knowing the weight of the machinery; and, by having the weight of the boilers and engine, they will know better where to place them on the boat, so as to make an equal draft as much as possible fore and aft.

Weight of Steam Boat Boilers, Single and Double Steam Drums, Mud Receivers, Boiler Stand Pipe, Man and Hand Hole Plates, Bolts and Gaskets, all complete.

No. of Boilers.	Diameter of Boilers.	Length.	Thickness.	Light.	Heavy.	Boiler Head Thickness.	Number of Flues.	Diameter.	Thickness of Flues.	Number of Flues.	Dameter.	Thickness.	Light.	Heavy.	Weight of Boilers, Man and Hand Hole Plates, Arches, Bolts, Gaskets and all, complete.	Weight of Double Steam Drum and Boiler Stand Pipe, all complete.	Weight of Double Steam Drum and Boiler Stand Pipe, all complete.	Weight of Steam Dr'm, Mud Receiver and Boiler Stand Pipe, all complete.	Weight of Boilers, Man and Hand Hole, Plates, Bolts and Gaskets, Steam Drum, Mud Receiver and Stand Pipe, all complete.
															lbs.	lbs.	lbs.	lbs.	lbs.
1	30	12	3/16	...	...	7/16	2	10	3/16	...	...	...	...	...	2,690	350	......	......	3,040
2	30	20	3/16	...	...	7/16	2	10	3/16	...	...	...	...	...	5,528	500	......	......	6,028
2	32	16	...	1/4	...	7/16	2	11	...	...	...	...	...	1/4	6,450	551	......	......	7,001
2	36	20	...	...	1/4	5/8	2	13½	...	...	...	...	...	1/4	13,560	......	1,720	......	15,281
3	36	18	...	...	1/4	1/2	2	14	...	...	...	...	...	1/4	17,165	1,638	......	......	18,803
3	38	22	...	1/4	...	1/2	2	14½	1/4	...	...	...	...	...	16,009	1,290	......	......	17,299
3	38	22	...	...	1/4	1/2	2	14	...	...	...	...	...	1/4	17,165	1,638	......	......	18,803
2	38	26	...	1/4	...	1/2	2	14½	...	...	...	...	1/4	...	14,000	675	......	......	14,675
3	40	24	...	...	1/4	1/2	2	12	1/4	2	8	...	...	3/16	24,000	......	......	2,306	26,306
3	40	26	...	...	1/4	5/8	2	15	...	...	...	...	...	1/4	20,475	2,107	......	......	22,582
4	40	38	...	...	1/2	5/8	2	12	1/4	2	8	...	...	3/16	35,300	......	......	3,600	38,900
2	38	18	1/4	...	1/4	1/2	2	14	1/4	...	...	...	...	...	8,840	1,200	......	......	10,040
2	36	12	...	...	...	1/2	2	13	...	...	...	...	1/4	...	5,476	1,175	......	......	6,651
2	36	16	1/4	...	...	1/2	2	12	1/4	...	...	...	...	...	5,852	1,190	......	......	7,042
2	40	22	1/4	...	...	1/2	2	15	1/4	...	...	...	...	...	10,698	1,400	......	......	12,098

Weight of Boilers, Single and Double Steam Drum, Mud Receiver, Boiler Hand Pipe, Man and Hand Hole Plates, Bolts and Gaskets; including Fire Fronts, Grate Bars, Check, Blow-off and Safety Valve Chambers, and all other Castings belonging to the same.

Number of Different Sizes.	Number of Boilers.	Diameter.	Feet.	Weight of Boilers, Man, and Hand Hole Plates, Arches, Bolts and Gaskets, all complete.	Wt. of Fire Bed, Breeching, Chimney, and all wrought iron work for the same, all put up on boat.	Wt. of Fire Fr'ts, Grate Bars, and Bearers, Check, Blow-off, and Safety Valve, Chambers, including all castings belonging to the boilers, fire bed and chimney.	Weight of Steam Drum, Mud Receiver, Boiler Stand Pipe, Fire Bed, Chimneys, Fire Front, Grate Bars, Check, Blow-off, and Safety Valve Chambers, including all castings and wrought iron work belonging to the same.
				lbs.	lbs.	lbs.	lbs.
1	1	30	12	3,040	480	1,100	4,620
2	2	30	20	6,028	2,400	2,890	11,318
3	2	32	16	7,001	2,989	3,100	13,090
4	2	36	20	15,280	10,399	3,850	29,529
5	2	36	18	18,803	7,252	5,800	31,855
6	3	38	22	17,299	8,157	5,000	30,456
7	3	38	22	18,803	8,509	5,900	33,212
8	2	38	26	14,675	12,269	4,250	31,194
9	3	40	24	26,306	8,900	6,450	41,656
10	3	40	26	22,582	9,159	6,600	38,341
11	3	40	30	38,900	21,384	7,500	67,784
12	2	38	18	10,040	10,150	5,250	25,448
13	2	36	12	6,561	8,500	5,100	20,251
14	2	36	16	7,042	9,900	5,200	22,142
15	2	40	22	12,098	8,000	4,300	22,998

Weight of Flued Boilers, Diameter, Length and Thickness, including Man Plates, Arches and Gaskets.

Diameter of Boilers.	Length.	Thickness.	Light.	Heavy.	Head.	Number of Flues.	Diameter of Flues.	Thickness of Flues.	Light.	Heavy.	No. 2.	No. 3.	No. 4.	Weight of Boilers.
In.	Ft.	In.	In.	In.	In.		In.	In.	In.	In.				lbs.
28	8	1/8	...	...	1/4	1	8	1/8	...	...	...	...	...	486
24	10	3/16	...	...	1/4	2	7	3/16	...	...	...	...	...	1221
26	12	3/16	...	...	3/8	1	11	3/16	...	...	...	...	...	1186
28	10	3/16	...	...	3/8	1	10	3/16	...	...	...	...	...	1282
28	12	3/16	...	...	3/8	1	10	3/16	...	...	...	...	...	1384
30	10	3/16	...	...	3/8	2	10	3/16	...	...	...	...	...	1517
30	12	3/16	...	...	3/8	2	10	3/16	...	...	...	...	...	1850
30	16	3/16	...	...	3/8	1	16	3/16	...	...	...	...	...	2055
30	18	3/16	...	...	3/8	2	10	3/16	...	...	...	...	...	2600
30	20	3/16	...	...	7/16	2	10	3/16	...	...	...	...	...	2764
32	12	3/16	...	...	...	2	10	3/16	...	...	...	...	...	1900
32	14	3/16	...	...	7/16	2	10	3/16	...	...	...	...	...	2050
32	16	1/4	...	...	7/16	2	10	1/4	...	...	...	...	...	3225
32	18	3/16	...	...	7/16	1	16	1/4	...	...	...	...	...	2275
32	18	1/4	...	...	7/16	1	16	1/4	...	...	...	...	...	3640
32	20	3/16	...	...	7/16	2	10	3/16	...	...	...	...	...	2820
32	24	3/16	...	...	1/2	2	11	3/16	...	...	...	...	...	3773
34	18	3/16	...	...	3/8	2	12	3/16	...	...	...	...	...	3038
34	20	1/4	...	...	7/16	2	11	1/4	...	...	...	...	...	3421
36	12	1/4	...	...	7/16	2	13	1/4	...	...	...	...	...	3038
36	14	3/16	...	...	...	1	14	1/4	...	...	...	...	...	3505
36	16	3/16	...	...	7/16	1	17	1/4	...	...	...	...	...	2585
36	18	1/4	...	...	7/16	2	12	3/16	...	...	...	...	...	4013
36	20	1/4	...	...	...	2	13	1/4	...	...	...	...	...	4692
36	22	1/4	...	...	7/16	2	13	1/4	...	...	...	...	...	4400

Weight of Flued Boilers, Diameter, Length and Thickness, including Man Plates, Arches, Bolts and Gaskets.

Diameter of Boilers.	Length.	Thickness.	Light.	Heavy.	Head.	Number of Flues.	Diameter of Flues.	Thickness.	Light.	Heavy.	No. 2.	No. 3.	No. 4.	Weight of Boilers, Man and H'd. Hole Plates Bolts, Gaskets, &c.
In.	Ft.	In.	In.	In.	In.		In.	In.		In.				lbs.
36	24	$\frac{3}{16}$	...	...	..	1	16	$\frac{1}{4}$	...	...	...	...	...	3640
36	20	$\frac{1}{4}$	...	...	...	2	13	$\frac{1}{4}$	...	...	...	...	...	4273
38	14	$\frac{3}{16}$	...	...	...	2	13	$\frac{3}{16}$	...	...	...	...	...	3070
38	14	$\frac{1}{4}$	...	...	...	2	14	$\frac{1}{4}$	...	...	...	...	...	3120
38	16	$\frac{1}{4}$	...	...	...	2	13	$\frac{1}{4}$	...	...	...	...	...	3540
38	16	$\frac{1}{4}$	...	...	...	2	14	$\frac{1}{4}$	...	...	...	...	...	3740
38	18	$\frac{3}{16}$	...	...	...	2	13	$\frac{3}{16}$	...	...	...	...	...	3496
38	18	$\frac{1}{4}$	...	...	...	2	14	$\frac{1}{4}$	...	...	...	...	...	4420
38	20	$\frac{1}{4}$	...	...	...	2	13	$\frac{1}{4}$	...	...	...	...	...	4765
38	20	$\frac{1}{4}$	...	...	...	2	14	$\frac{1}{4}$	...	...	...	...	...	4935
38	22	$\frac{1}{4}$	...	...	...	2	14	$\frac{1}{4}$	...	...	...	...	...	5257
38	24	$\frac{1}{4}$	...	...	...	2	$14\frac{1}{4}$	$\frac{1}{4}$	...	...	...	...	...	5820
38	26	$\frac{1}{4}$	...	...	...	2	14	$\frac{1}{4}$	...	...	...	...	...	6200
40	16	$\frac{3}{16}$	...	...	$\frac{7}{16}$	2	12	$\frac{3}{16}$	...	...	...	...	...	2830
40	16	$\frac{3}{16}$	...	...	$\frac{7}{16}$	2	14	$\frac{3}{16}$	...	. .	...	...	...	3012
40	18	$\frac{3}{16}$	...	...	...	2	15	$\frac{1}{4}$	...	...	...	...	...	4260
40	20	$\frac{3}{16}$	...	...	...	2	14	$\frac{3}{16}$	...	...	...	...	...	4330
40	20	$\frac{1}{4}$	..	...	...	2	15	$\frac{1}{4}$	...	...	...	...	...	4718
40	20	$\frac{3}{16}$	...	...	...	2	15	$\frac{1}{4}$	..	...	...	...	...	4650
40	22	$\frac{1}{4}$	...	...	...	2	15	$\frac{1}{4}$	...	...	...	...	...	5643
40	24	$\frac{1}{4}$	...	...	...	2	15	$\frac{1}{4}$	...	...	...	...	...	6020
40	26	$\frac{1}{4}$	...	...	...	2	15	$\frac{1}{4}$	...	...	...	...	...	6510
40	28	$\frac{1}{4}$	...	...	...	2	15	$\frac{1}{4}$	...	...	...	...	...	7210
42	16	...	$\frac{1}{4}$	...	...	2	16	....	$\frac{1}{4}$	...	...	...	...	4210
42	18	$\frac{1}{4}$	...	...	...	2	15	...	...	$\frac{1}{4}$	...	....	...	4640
42	18	$\frac{1}{4}$	...	...	...	2	16	....	...	$\frac{1}{4}$	...	...	...	5165

Weight of Flued Boilers, Diameter, Length and Thickness, including Man and Hand Hole Plates, Arches, Bolts and Gaskets.

Diameter of Boilers.	Length.	Thickness.	Light.	Heavy.	No. 2.	No. 3.	No. 4.	Number of Flues.	Diameter of Flues.	Thickness.	Light.	Heavy.	No. 2. Heavy ¼.	No. 3. Light ¼.	No. 3. Is 7-32.	Weight of Boilers.
In.	Ft.	In.	In.	In.					In.	In.	In.	In.				lbs.
42	20	3/16	...	...	....	...	...	2	14	3/16	...	...	....	...	...	4330
42	20	...	¼	...	....	...	...	2	15	..	¼	...	...	...	...	4718
42	20	¼	...	...	....	....	...	2	14	¼	...	...	...	...	...	5050
40	22	¼	...	...	...	....	...	2	15	¼	...	...	...	...	...	5643
42	22	¼	...	...	...	...	...	2	16	¼	...	...	...	...	...	5960
42	24	¼	...	...	...	...	...	2	16	¼	...	...	...	...	...	6330
42	24	¼	...	...	...	...	...	2	16	¼	...	...	...	...	...	6100
42	26	....	...	...	...	...	...	2	16	¼	...	...	6	...	...	6675
42	26	....	¼	...	...	3	...	2	16	...	¼	...	...	3	...	6840
42	28	¼	...	...	...	...	...	2	16	¼	...	...	...	...	...	7830
44	18	3/16	...	...	...	...	...	2	16	3/16	...	...	...	...	...	4500
44	18	¼	...	...	...	...	...	2	16	¼	...	...	...	...	...	5385
44	20	¼	...	...	...	...	...	2	16	¼	...	...	...	...	...	5690
44	22	¼	...	...	...	...	...	2	16	¼	...	...	...	...	...	5590
44	24	¼	...	...	...	...	...	2	17	¼	...	...	...	...	...	6775
44	26	¼	...	...	...	...	...	2	17	¼	...	...	...	...	...	7340
44	28	¼	...	...	...	...	...	2	17	¼	...	...	...	...	...	8050
44	30	...	..	¼	2	...	...	2	17	...	...	¼	2	....	...	8825
44	26	¼	...	...	...	..	...	2	17	¼	...	...	...	....	...	7755
44	24	...	¼	...	...	...	...	2	17½	...	¼	...	...	3	...	7050

Weight of Chimneys and Breeching.

Diameter of Chimney.	Length of Chimney.	Thickness of Iron No.	Weight of Chimney.	Weight of Breeching.	Diameter of Chimney.	Length of Chimney.	Thickness of Iron No.	Weight of Chimney.	Weight of Breeching.
In.	Ft.	In.	lbs.	lbs.	In.	Ft.	In.	lbs.	lbs.
15	20	...	280	120	50	60	14	3,877	361
15	20	16	275	120	46	60	14	3,020	......
16	20	18	254	251	38	48	14	2,014	......
16	20	...	262	251	40	42	14	1,944	......
15	20	...	247	119	36	38	14	1,215	......
18	20	14	389	270	40	46	14	1,866	......
18	20	...	304	142	38	44	14	1,627	......
20	30	18	400	160	26	32	14	660	......
24	36	16	782	180	52	52	14	3,000	......
22	40	16	820	170	38	40	14	2,014	......
30	36	18	740	190	36	38	...	1,379	......
24	40	16	944	395	36	22	...	660	......
30	30	15	863	250	40	40	...	1,759	......
40	46	15	887	......	20	30	18	400	......
38	48	14	4,250	......	...	...	...	....	......

Weight, Sizes and Thickness of Cylinder Boilers, with Wrought Iron Heads, Man Plates, Arches, Bolts and Gaskets, all complete.

Diameter of Boilers.	Length.	Thickness.	Light.	Weight of Cylinder Boilers, with Wrought Iron Heads, with Man Plates, Arches, Bolts, and Gaskets, all complete.
Inches.	Feet.	Inches.	Inches.	Pounds.
30	20	......	¼	2275
30	26	......	¼	2960
24	12	......	......	1035
36	28	¼	......	3505
40	40	¼	......	5530
42	16	¼	......	2975
24	14	......	......	1390
30	20	......	¼	2275
32	40	¼	......	4810
28	10	......	......	1010
30	18	......	......	1810
32	22	......	......	2874
36	26	......	......	3590
36	32	......	......	3791
40	16	......	......	2643

Pressure allowable on Boilers of Various Dimensions.

Adopted for the guidance of Local Inspectors.

DIAMETER OF BOILERS.

Pressure equivalent to the standard pressure of a 42 inch Boiler, ¼ in. iron.

Wire Gauge.	Thick. of Iron	34 Inch. Diam.	36 Inch. Diam.	38 Inch. Diam.	40 Inch. Diam.	42 Inch. Diam.	44 Inch. Diam.	46 Inch. Diam.
		lbs.	lbs.	lbs.	lbs.	lbs.	lbs.	lbs.
1	$\frac{5}{16}$	169.85	160.41	151.97	144.37	137.50	131.25	125.54
2	$\frac{14}{48}$	158.52	149 72	141.84	134.75	128.33	121.50	117.17
3	$\frac{13}{48}$	147.20	139.03	131.76	125.12	119.16	113.75	108.80
4	¼	135.88	128.33	121.57	115.50	110.00	105.00	100.43
5	$\frac{11}{48}$	124.55	117.63	111.44	105.87	100.83	96.25	92.06
6	$\frac{10}{48}$	113.23	106.94	101.31	96.25	91.66	87.50	83.69
7	$\frac{3}{16}$	101.91	96.24	91.18	86.62	82.50	78.75	75.32

JOINTS.

VARIOUS MATERIALS FOR MAKING JOINTS.

The following are the principal materials used for making joints, viz: lead, copper, iron, brass, sheet lead and tin, gum, gasket paper, canvas, canvas and sheet lead, packing yarn, rope, pine board and leather.

CEMENT JOINTS.

There are various kinds of cement, used for making different kinds of joints, but I will speak of but two kinds that are used for cementing iron. Cement joints, such as are generally used about the steam engine, oil stills, hot blast pipes, &c., are made of cast iron borings or turnings, mixed with water enough to cover them. Then take a piece of sal ammoniac $\frac{3}{8}$ of an inch round, pulverize it, take a quart of the iron borings, and mix and stir them up several times, and if possible let them stand at least half a day or more, to give the sal ammoniac time to dissolve, and also to thoroughly saturate the borings. If too much sal ammoniac is put in, it will weaken the joints by burning them, and if too little, it will not rust sufficiently to cause the borings to cement. A small amount of sulphur used to be put in to help the joint to dry faster. This is now generally dispensed with.

In cold weather joints should be done in a warm place, and not exposed to the frost, nor suflered to freeze before getting perfectly dry. The joints would be all the better for standing three or four days or more, so as to get dry and hard before using them. They have been used in a few hours after making, but it is running somewhat of a risk, and this should be done only in cases of necessity. The new steamer *Jubilee*, a four boiler boat, with steam up, freight and passengers on board, when about ready to put out, blew out one of the connection joints between the boilers. The river at this time was falling, and no water to spare in the channel. The captain was threatened damages to the amount of several thousand dollars. Fearing he should lose his present trip, and be detained until another rise, the boilers were cooled down, and the joint made in haste, and she put out next day. A good deal depends upon the inner gasket being made tight, which will take the strain off the cement joint and give it time to dry. But should the gasket leak on a green joint, it would be very likely to blow out. Care should be taken to have the borings and flanges free from grease, as grease prevents rusting, which is indispensable to a good joint.

LEAD JOINTS.

Lead joints are often used about various parts of the steam engine—for boiler stand pipes, and connections, steam pipes, chests and caps, valve seats, cylinder heads, man and hand hole plates, caps, &c. For boiler connections they answer very well, as long as the water is kept to the guage, but they are likely to melt out when the water is low. Cement would stand the heat better, but neither of them would answer after being heated too hot. The gummets on the heads of the connection bolts inside of the boilers would be sure to burn off, and this itself would slacken the bolts and cause the joints to leak, saying nothing about burning the cement or lead. It might or might not stand; this depends on the amount of heating it would get. I mention this to show that all centre boiler connections ought to be forever abandoned. These connections, blocks or pipes, would get red hot much quicker than the boiler in case of low water, on account of their being away from the water. The boilers should always be connected below by large stand pipes, or on either end of the boiler heads, or on both, if you please. Boilers connected as the above, were connected about the centre, and sometimes 2 or 3 inches below; this kept the water course open longer than it would at the centre. One object of using these boiler connections in early days was partly for the purpose of holding the boilers together at the front end, on account of the rolling and surging of the boat. But if it is considered necessary to have any extras for binding the boilers together more than the fire fronts, steam and stand pipes, it would be better to bind them together at one or both boiler heads fore and aft, by bolting or riveting a flat bar of iron, to hold each pair of boilers firmly together. Lead joints may be used to good advantage about almost every other part of the engine, as long as they will last without corroding and wasting, which will be much longer in places less hot, than where it was more hot. When corrosion commences the joints and gaskets will require to be renewed.

HOW TO RUN A HORIZONTAL LEAD JOINT.

To do this requires judgment and practice. Failures arise from several causes. Sometimes the lead is too cold, and chills; or this may take place if the lead be sufficiently hot, but poured in too slow. Sometimes the space between the bolts and the inner gasket is too small for the lead to pass, and the same may be the case on the outside, the bolt being too near the edge. Sometimes the clay being sandy will not adhere and let the lead run out. Sometimes the joints are too close to receive the lead. The lead should be very hot, and poured in with two or more ladles, according to the size of the joint. When the space between the gasket and the bolts is found to be too small, cut a little out of the gasket back of the bolts; if the difficulty is on the outside, enlarge by setting out the paper. Fire clay is the best; when this cannot be had, get the toughest clay you can. Care should be taken to have the joint well vented, that the air may escape before the lead, otherwise it will blow and be a failure. It is necessary to have some person at hand with clay to apply in case of a leak.

HOW TO RUN PERPENDICULAR JOINTS.

A great many joints of this kind are lost, on account of having the lead too hot, and pouring it in too fast, and in one spot. It melts the inside lead gasket, and the lead runs into whatever you may be pouring into, and in order to get it out, you may have to undo and run over three or four more joints, as the case may be. Some persons, in order to avoid this, lap the gasket with packing yarn. In running these joints the lead ought to be so cool as not to set fire to a dry pine stick when put in to ascertain the right heat before pouring it. The gate for pouring should be as wide as possible on the top, and the lead as cold as it will run without making cold shuts. In this case there is nothing to chill the lead, when running into the joint, until it reaches the bottom. Not so with the horizontal joint; the lead chills almost as soon as poured between the two flat surfaces, whilst running, and frequently chills before being filled. It will not be necessary to have any additional gate for vent on the upright joint, as the gate itself is sufficiently large for this purpose, if the lead is poured slowly, as it should be, so as not to choke the entire opening. In pouring in the lead, you should shift the ladle from side to side, so as to prevent its melting the gasket, by pouring it constantly in one place.

Thus it will be seen that the lead for running a horizontal joint requires to be very hot, and poured very fast, whilst the upright joints require the lead to be just as cold as it will run, and poured as slowly as practicable.

HOW TO PREPARE A JOINT FOR RUNNING.

Take a strip of gasket paper about $\frac{1}{8}$ of an inch thick, and if it is too stiff to bend around the flange, wet it in water until it becomes pliable, then tie it firmly around it, and cut a piece out of the paper to pour in the lead at one side, and leave another opening opposite for a vent; the paper all around should be plastered with fire clay to keep the lead from running out. Where gasket paper cannot be had leather may be and often is used, but this is more expensive, and does not last so long, as the heat burns it and soon makes it hard. Packing yarn is often used, and does very well; or a small rope about $\frac{3}{4}$ or $\frac{1}{2}$ inch tied tight over the joint, pulling it to one side where you pour in the lead. The two last require less time than the former. The only objection to these joints would be where you want a smooth finished outside; they would be rough with the packing yarn or rope. They would also be a little hollow, equal to the size of the rope pressing into the joint; but for durability and strength they cannot be beat.

SHEET LEAD JOINTS.

Sheet lead, such as was taken out of tea boxes, was used in early days for making joints about the steam engine, and they answered a good purpose. In those days I believe there was no other kind to be had in the West.

SHEET LEAD AND CANVAS JOINTS.

In the early days of steamboating, when cast iron steam and supply pipes were used, the joints were generally made with cement. They afterward substituted for it sheet lead the same as above, and canvas, which was better on account of its elasticity, yielding to the springing and settling of the boat. It was also customary to have the pipes to fit in each other with a stuffing box and packing yarn, to accommodate the expansion and contraction of the pipes when heating and cooling. The joints were made by putting a layer of sheet lead and one of canvas alternately, until they were made the desired thickness. Coating them with white lead would be an improvement, if there is time for it to dry before using, otherwise it would run off like grease and daub the machinery. The expansion of pipes is about $\frac{1}{40}$ of an inch to the foot.

ROLLED SHEET LEAD JOINTS.

Rolled sheet lead can be had of various thicknesses, and is often used for making joints about steam engines, and for various other purposes. Where the two joint surfaces are planed or turned, the lead may be very thin. It may or may not be coated with white lead, it will do very well without, but it would be better with it, if it has time to dry and harden. These joints last a long time until the lead corrodes and loses its life, and then it will be necessary to renew them with new material.

RED LEAD JOINTS.

Red lead joints are generally made in the following manner: the two joint surfaces are planed or turned true, and then coated with red lead, and screwed up tight; when dry it is as tight as a bottle, and lasts almost forever. Red lead is said to be superior to white lead for joints, as its being burnt removes the acid which is said to eat or corrode the iron, and when dry it makes a hard cement, and is not so liable to decay as white lead.

WHITE LEAD JOINTS.

There are certain joints about the steam engine that would be better of being coated with white lead, especially if it had time to dry before using, such as paper around the heat, and other parts of the engine; for steam and supply pipes, joints, &c. It is also used about gaskets that have been lapped with packing yarn, such as man plates, cylinder heads, valve caps, and various other lap joints about escape pipes, hot and cold water pipes, pumps, &c. Unless the white lead has time to dry before using it, it will do very little good, as the heat will cause a great portion of it to run off. White lead is frequently used between iron plates and surfaces for the purpose of making tight joints, and answers very well, but it is not so good or desirable as the red lead, and is liable to oxydize and decay sooner.

In taking off man plates for the purpose of cleaning out the boilers, and also cylinder heads for the purpose of tightening up the packing, &c., it is customary with many engineers to coat the face of those gaskets that have been well fitted and bedded with white lead, and then raise steam immediately. In such cases it would have been much better to put on none, for as soon as the engine is heated up, it runs off like so much grease, and daubs every thing it comes in contact with. As a general thing, it is almost useless to put it on, unless it has time to dry before using.

SCREW PATCH JOINTS.

There is a cement made of iron scales, got from the anvil block—the proportions are as follows: to the white of one egg, add one table spoonful of flour, one table spoonful of iron scales, or equal portions of each, mix them together, breaking the scales fine. This makes a good cement, and is frequently used about salt works, for salt pans, steam boilers, &c. The joint is made as follows: take two pieces of boiler iron, dish them a little, say from $\frac{1}{8}$ to $\frac{1}{4}$ inch, according to the size of the patch, and put one or more bolts, as may be needed, through them; fill the patches with cement, and screw them tight, and if you have time to let them dry a day or two before using, all the better; but they have been, and can be used as soon as made, in case of an emergency. I am told that steam boilers and salt pans, that have been cracked six or seven inches long, have been mended in this way, and some also requiring patches as large as 8 inches square. These large patches would require six or eight screw bolts. These are made tight by the cement, and do not require any gummets on the heads of the bolts. I mention this for the benefit of those not acquainted with these facts, so that in case of an emergency they can make a cement of this kind, where the other could not be had without having to send a great distance; and I have no doubt the owners of hundreds of country mills have gone to a great expense in getting boiler makers to come from a distance, or in hauling the boiler to town for repairs, when if they had been acquainted with this fact they could have had the boiler mended at home for one-tenth or one-twentieth of the cost, saying nothing about loss of time, disappointment of customers, &c., and expense of keeping hands unemployed, as well as the capital invested standing still.

COPPER AND SHEET IRON JOINTS.

Copper joints are used in various parts of the steam engine. I have known sheet copper to be used between the bottom of the boiler and the flange on top of the stand pipe, instead of lead or cement, as was formerly used. There was no danger of this either melting or blowing out. In using the sheet copper, it was necessary to have the circular flange on the stand pipe chipped and filed up true and straight, so as to fit the boiler neatly. Before putting the copper in, it should be coated on both sides, and also the boiler and cast iron flange, with red or white lead; then bolt or rivet them together as you please, riveting would be the best, but it is the most expensive. The copper in this case would be about $\frac{1}{4}$ inch thick. Sheet iron is also used frequently instead of copper. The reason of using the sheet copper and iron, is owing to having a cast iron flange on the stand pipe for the purpose of calking the joint between the boiler and the cast iron flange, to make a tight joint. Where wrought iron stand pipes and flanges are used, it is not necessary to put anything in between, but calk the wrought iron flange on the pipe. Copper is preferable to wrought iron, as it is softer, and yields and bends itself easier than the iron. Thin sheet copper is often used between valve seats, caps, cylinder nozzles, steam chests, caps, &c. In such cases, it is necessary to have the faces turned or planed up true, and coated with red or white lead; this will make a better joint than without.

Copper rings are frequently used for gaskets for loose cylinder heads, man hole plates, &c. They are made in the following manner: get a $\frac{5}{8}$ or $\frac{3}{4}$ inch copper pipe made to suit the diameter of the cylinder head, or man plate, bore some holes in it and run it full of soft lead. This makes an excellent gasket, where it is necessary to be taken apart often. Owing to the outer surface being harder than the lead, it lasts much longer, and is not so easily dinted. Square copper gaskets $\frac{5}{16}$ and $\frac{3}{8}$ inch square, may be made use of to good advantage inside of cement joints. They are preferable in some respects to lead, as lead gaskets have been known to be eaten entirely out, leaving the whole pressure of steam on the cement alone. Copper is much more durable, and being of a soft nature may be made steam-tight before driving in the cement. Square iron gaskets have also been used for the same purpose; they are used with and without lapping. If the flange is very narrow, and not much room for cement, the iron had better be lapped to insure a tight joint; if the flange is very wide, and plenty of room, it will do without. The bolts should not be drawn up very hard until the joints are made, and when made try and get a quarter or half turn of the nut more, to make the joint tight as possible.

GROUND JOINTS.

Ground joints are mostly used on locomotive engines, and also on various others. The object of using them is to make a more substantial job, and also to dispense with the use of gaskets. In order to keep them in good repair, it is necessary to oil them occasionally, to prevent them from rusting, which would be very destructive and also eat them in holes. It will be necessary, also, to grind them anew occasionally with oil and emery. These joints are very costly, and when once made should be kept in good order. In screwing them up, great care should be taken to screw them up evenly as possible, for by having one side tighter than the other, it would be liable to leak, and in this case you would require to slack the bolts on the high side, or otherwise by screwing up to make it tight, you would be sure either to spring the cylinder head, cap, or whatever it may be, or break the bolts, if not both, owing to the great leverage of the plate on the gasket, which may be ten to one. This is what is called "foul play."

There is another advantage of ground joints on the loose cylinder head, the clearance is always about the same, whereas with a lead gasket you may have $\frac{3}{4}$ inch thick when new, and only $\frac{1}{4}$ or $\frac{1}{8}$ when worn out. In this case you actually require as much more extra clearance at the beginning, in the packing end of the cylinder, as the gasket will be reduced by wear and waste about $\frac{1}{2}$ inch, otherwise when the gasket becomes thin, the piston head bolts will strike on the cylinder head and break it; especially if there should be any false motion in the pitman box, or the key become slackened. The loss of steam in this way, in the course of a year, would amount to considerable. Say $\frac{1}{2}$ inch less the diameter of the cylinder every revolution, and the engine makes 108 revolutions per minute, there would be 84 inches or 7 feet dead loss of steam per minute, 420 feet per hour, 4200 feet per 10 hours or in a day. In this item alone there would be steam enough lost to run the engine 25 minutes every 10 hours or 1-24th part of the whole amount, supposing the cylinder to cut off at 12 inches of the stroke. 1-24th part of the power and fuel used on locomotives in a year would be a considerable item alone.

UNIVERSAL STEAM PIPE JOINTS.

Universal cast iron steam pipe joints are now being used on locomotives, instead of copper as formerly, for the following reasons: the copper steam pipes used for conveying the steam from the boiler to the cylinder were continually giving out by corroding and wasting away, and they tried to prevent this by lapping the copper with sheet iron and wire, but to little or no purpose.

It is possible the escape steam and ashes might have something to do with this. The copper no doubt was preferable to iron on account of yielding to the motion of the cars without breaking, but these pipes, owing to their peculiar shape and short bends, were hard and expensive to make, and required to be replaced frequently with new ones, hence the necessity of resorting to cast steam pipes with universal joints, made so as to yield to the spring of the cars. There are two joints on each pipe, one on each end; they are turned beveling, similar to a valve and seat, only the one is a little round, and the other a little hollow, so as better to suit a rotary motion. These pipes are said to be much better than the copper, inasmuch as they last much longer and do not eat out like the copper. The ashes and escape steam appear to be as destructive on the copper steam pipes of locomotives as the ashes and sweating are to supply drums of marine and stationary boilers for engines; they too frequently have had to be replaced on account of corrosion. It is necessary that these pipes and drums should be kept clean and dry, in order that they may last longer.

FIRE FRONTS, &c.

FIRE FRONTS AND BACK PLATES.

Heretofore, plain fire fronts were made without any lining whatever, and consequently often became so hot as to scorch the clothes of the firemen. The fronts on which the boilers stood would frequently bend and give way under the excessive heat, and had to be replaced often the same as we have now to replace our grate-bars. They were very dangerous, especially in case of collision.

FIRE FRONTS LINED.

Fire fronts have been made to receive different kinds of linings. Cast iron liners have been frequently made, but were found not to answer the purpose on account of having to be often replaced with new ones. At the present time it is common to line fronts with fire-brick, which is by far the best plan of any yet adopted. Sometimes the liners that are to receive the brick, are cast on the fire fronts, and at other times cast separately, and bolted on to the fire fronts with screw-bolts. The latter is the best plan. These fronts are quite cool and pleasant for the firemen, and seldom need repairing. Another great improvement in fire-fronts would be to let the grate-bar bearer, in front of the liner, extend 5 or 6 inches beyond the liners, having a recess for receiving another course of brick, the narrow way, [see letter B, inside view of boiler, page 126,] (or lengthwise, if you please, 9 inches,) the casting to be, say 4½ inches in the clear. This would keep the furnace doors still more cool, and be easier on the edges of the liners. The fire in this place can do no injury to the fronts or liners, for want of air. Fire-fronts made according to this plan are the most durable that can be made.

BURNING OUT GRATE-BARS.

In order to prevent the burning out of the grate-bars, it is necessary that the ash-pit should be kept well cleaned out. Some ash-pits require cleaning out oftener than others—depending altogether upon the depth. Formerly ash-pits were made so shallow as to require almost constant cleaning, and still they were continually burning out the grate-bars. Now they are much deeper, but still they must be cleaned out occasionally, yet not half so often as the shallow ones of former days. Another cause is, the bars are made entirely too light, with a thickness on top of about ⅜ of an inch, and as soon as the top edge burns off, the bar is done.

BACK PLATES.

Back plates should be firmly fastened to the boilers. They are sometimes laid on top of the brick wall and on the top of the flue, with nothing to hold them fast to the boiler when expanding or contracting, and the result is, that the draft is partially destroyed, the smoke and sometimes sparks escape, making it quite disagreeble. There is also much danger to be apprehended of fire from the sparks. The best plan for fastening them securely to the boiler, is to cast lugs on the back plates, drill holes in the lugs and boiler heads, and tap them, and then fasten the plate to the boiler head with set screws. The holes in lugs should be a little larger than the set screws, and a little oblong, so that in case the boilers or walls should settle, there would be less danger of breaking the lugs off the plates. Care should be taken to have the bolts, when screwed up, to be slack enough to yield on the bolts, without which they would be liable to leak in case the boiler or the walls should settle. Cover the joint over with mortar, and the job will be complete. [See back plate on draft C.]

STEAM AND STAND PIPES.

CAST IRON STEAM PIPES.

In the early days of steamboating, the pipes used on steamers were made of cast iron altogether. The steam pipe, from the boiler to the cylinder, had a stuffing box and a slip joint allowing it to come and go as the spring of the boat might require. The supply pipes, from the force pump to the boiler, were also made of cast iron. These were the kind of pipes used on the Western steamers about the year 1820. They answered very well for slow running boats, but as the speed of steamboats began to increase something of a more malleable nature was required,—something that would yield and accommodate itself to the spring or settling of the boat, and not be liable to break or crack. But a few years elapsed, however, before this deficiency was supplied, and the cast iron were superseded by the copper steam and supply pipes, which proved to be far superior, and are still in general use.

But we wish to call your attention more especially to the cast iron steam pipes, now gradually going out of use. Where they were strong they answered a very good purpose. Frequently, no doubt, steam and stand pipes have been broken by the boat being ladened out of trim, or by its settling. Steam pipes are less liable, however, to be broken by the settling of the boat than stand pipes. Steam pipes have frequently been broken by coming too suddenly in contact with the shore when landing, or striking a bank or bluff, seriously injuring those on board by being scalded with hot steam. Pilots cannot be too careful in landing a boat, and should approach the shore as steadily as possible.

Wrought iron steam and stand pipes, we think, are still better, and will soon come into general use. They will come and go without danger of suddenly breaking. In this they are similar to the copper, but in other respects they are vastly superior to the cast iron pipes; they need no joints, being riveted close to the boiler.

We would recommend to all those who wish to fit out good boats to have wrought iron stand and steam pipes, and copper or wrought iron steam and supply pipes, from boiler to cylinder, and from force pump to boilers. Then there would be less accidents and fewer lives lost.

I recollect some years ago the steamer *Pulaski* came in collision with the steamer *Forest* whilst running on the Allegheny river, which threw the boilers of the steamer *Pulaski* down, breaking the cast iron steam and supply pipes, and there were several persons killed, and eight or nine whom I visited were so badly scalded as to die in a few days afterwards.

The wrought iron pipes are much lighter than the cast iron, and on this account are preferable for marine engines, as it is desirable to have the machinery as light as possible, so as to have a light draught boat and be able also to carry more freight.

CAST IRON STANDS CONNECTED WITH COPPER PIPE.

The plan of cast iron stands with copper connecting pipes was in use at an early day in the history of steam. The boilers rested upon the stands, which were connected, one with the other, by copper pipes, on each end of which were stuffing-boxes, so arranged as to allow them to come and go, so that there would be less danger of their breaking or leaking from the springing and surging of the boat. This, while it answered the intended purpose, was attended with great labor and expense.

WROUGHT IRON STEAM PIPES AND DRUMS.

Wrought iron steam pipes, placed upon the top of the boilers, are considered a great improvement, as there is no danger from breaking or cracking from the setttling or springing of the boat. Another advantage is the steam drum on the top of the boiler, which acts as a small reservoir, and is a preventive to the drawing of water. If any water at all may be drawn by the steam in this drum, it has a chance to go back and return again to the boiler. It is not good policy to have too large a steam drum. We would say that there might be as much capacity in the steam drum as in the two cylinders. If it goes beyond this, the drum will act as an unnecessary condenser. It acts as a condenser at the best; still, it may be a necessary evil to prevent the drawing of water and give dry steam to use in the cylinder.

It is not essential that the drum be very large, so that the openings from the boiler to the steam drum are sufficiently large to prevent the water from rising with the steam, as it is taken from the boiler into the steam drum.

But if you wish to carry water high for the purpose of getting more fire surface in the boiler, then it would be necessary to have a large drum for a steam reservoir. The size of the steam drum would in this case depend on the extra height the water is carried in the boilers. Say you carry the water three inches higher than is usual, and by raising the brick work on the sides of the boiler 3 inches, also, on each boiler 20 feet long, it would give 10 square feet more fire surface on each boiler; this would make a considerable amount of extra steam over what would be lost by condensation and by carrying the water extra high, it would be far safer, especially for flued boilers. By this mode more steam would be made with the same boilers and fuel, from the very fact of increasing the fire surface. This is the great object, to create the most steam with the least amount of fuel and boiler. It would also be less dangerous, especially for flued boilers; in such cases there would be comparatively little or no danger of flues collapsing from the surplus of water carried in the boilers. I would recommend its use on board of steamers where fuel and steam are objects of the utmost importance, and by all means let this plan be adopted on marine engines.

WROUGHT IRON SUPLY-PIPES.

Wrought iron supply pipes are now coming into general use, and we would say that they are superior to any heretofore in use. There is one thing, however, which we wish to impress upon the minds of persons fitting out large steamers, (or even small ones with large boilers.) It is, (and they should see to it,) that the last sheet of iron in the bottom of the boiler, on which the stand pipe is riveted, and upon which one end of the boiler rests, should be ⅜ inch in thickness. It will then take a more general bearing upon the body of the boiler, than the small stand pipe with a narrow flange can do. This we consider essentially necessary to the making of a better and a stiffer job than can be done without it. It is the lack of stiffness in the boilers, at this point, owing to the small bearing of the stand-pipes on ¼ inch iron, which causes them to spring up and down like a basket, or as though they were resting on a spring-board. When they come into rough water, or the waves caused by the passage of another boat, the safety-valve will spring up and down, bound and rebound, and causes the blowing off more or less steam, in proportion to its height in the boiler.

We would say to those who wish the boilers to stand on a good foundation, try the recommendation above noted; you can lose nothing by it, but will be sure to gain what we have mentioned. The boiler will be stiffer and firmer than it was on the former plan.

No donbt this is one cause of the many accidents that have occurred by the breaking of steam and supply pipes, and joints, and scalding many persons to death and injuring others. The flanges on the stand pipes should be large in diameter, so as to take hold on the body of the boiler as much as possible, that it may by this means have a more substantial foundation to rest on.

DIFFERENT PLACES FOR ATTACHING STEAM AND STAND PIPES TO BOILERS.

As a general thing, steam is taken from the boilers at the most convenient place, to the engine. For our part, we do not think it makes much difference from what point it is taken. If we had our choice, and it was convenient to do so, we would prefer supplying at the back end of the boiler always, both river and land engines, and take the steam from the middle of the boiler, or from the end over the fire, where it is hotter and stronger. But on steamers, some take it from the back ring of the boiler, some from the second, some from the third, some from the fourth, and some from the middle, &c. But we do not think that it would make any material difference where it is taken from; we would prefer, however, to take it a little distance from where the water comes into the boiler.

STEAM TAKEN FROM END OF PIPE.

It is known by experience, to all those who have taken steam from two, three, and from six boilers, &c., at the end of the steam pipe, that it always draws the water to the side of the boiler from whence the steam is taken. On the side from which the steam is taken, the water will be found above the upper gauge cock, while in the far boiler it will be below the lower gauge cock. The diagonal line drawn on the six boilers [draft C, page 70,] shows the position of the water in the boilers. By the exercise of a little judgment in this case, the water may be brought very nearly to a level in the boilers; by opening the furnace doors beneath the boilers farthest off from where you take your steam, and firing up hard under the opposite ones. But to do this and keep up steam, would require more boilers than would be otherwise necessary. The steam should be taken from the centre of a double or single steam pipe attached to the boiler, where there are three, four, five, six, or more boilers, as seen on draft, page 71.

BEST MODE OF TAKING STEAM FROM TWO OR MORE BOILERS.

The best place for taking steam from two boilers is the centre of the connecting pipe. It may be taken from the side or top of the pipe; the top would be preferable to the side, as the water is drawn more or less by steam, and would be more likely to settle and fall back into the boiler. But it ought never to be taken out from below, if it can be avoided, because all the water drawn into the steam pipe, as well as the condensed steam, would have to pass off through the cylinder cocks and escapement, which would cause the engine to drag, as well as to be liable to burst or break the cylinder.

Where the steam is taken off three or more boilers, the double steam pipe has been invented, having as many branches as boilers, fitted to the boilers, and on this pipe is another pipe having two openings, one on each side between the centre and each outside branch. This is truly a great improvement, as will be seen by the accompanying drafts. (See page 144, pipe A.)

STEAM TAKEN FROM STEAM DRUM.

On two-boiler boats, many of which navigate our rivers, the steam is taken from each end of a steam drum. This is the safer and more practical mode for boats of that class; but it is said to be better that three and four boiler boats should have but one pipe from the centre of the steam drum, branching off to connect with the two engines. For four, five, six or more boilers, there should be two steam pipes, taken from the back of the steam drum to each engine.

It would be a good plan, on large drums, to have a man-hole plate on each, so that the boilers can be cooled down sooner, when required to be cleaned out in a hurry, as they often have to be, especially about blast furnaces. I will state one instance. We made eight large boilers for a blast furnace, with steam and supply drum; we had in them twenty-four man-hole plates, one in each end of the boilers, and one in each end of the steam and supply drum. This gives more air within, and makes it more pleasant to the men, when cleaning out the boilers.

STOP-COCKS, CYLINDER LUGS, &C.

DANGER OF BRASS STOP-COCKS BETWEEN THE BOILER AND THE FORCE PUMP.

Brass keys in stop-cocks require to be tightly screwed, to prevent them from leaking, and when thus secured, they are likely to corrode, and require the nut to be slacked off below, or the key to be hammered back, before they can be turned; and unless there be a good thread and nut on the bolt below, they are liable to fly out in the act of turning them. Every engineer has witnessed this fact. If you turn the cock after it has been slackened, it will demand some effort to tighten it again. A slight frost will so far destroy brass keys that they cannot be used until repaired. Thus it will be seen, they are more troublesome than profitable.

The only way in which they can be used with safety for stop-cocks, between the boilers and the force pumps, is to screw the keys in with a bridle and a set screw. For this purpose, the stop-valve is used in its place, in which it is superior.

The key blew out once when I was engineering on the Tennessee river. Owing to some defect in the force pump, I had occasion to shut the water off between the force pump and the boilers, until I would make an examination, and put the pump in order; and knowing that the screw in the key was not very good, being almost stripped, I went cautiously to work to turn it, and prepared myself for the worst, fearing it might blow out. I put a long wrench on the top of the key, and then took hold of a stanchion, and told those standing by to keep out of the way. I then turned the wrench with my foot, and out came the key and emptied the boilers, immediately filling the boat with steam and hot water. The steam was low and the fires were burnt down. No one was injured. I saw two other keys partially blown out in a similar way, one at an engine shop in Louisville, when the hands were at work, a little after dinner, another at a machine shop in Pittsburgh, whilst in the act of turning the keys.

BLOW-OFF STOP-COCKS ON BOILER STANDS.

This was the mode of blowing off the water from steamboat boilers in their early history; they are, however, liable to get out of order in the several ways already mentioned. Their place has been superseded by the use of the blow-off valve, which is superior to the old plan, being much safer.

FREEZING OF STOP-COCKS.

This is one of the greatest objections to the use of the brass stop-cock about a steam engine. They are liable to be continually out of order, especially when subject to frost. They are more a matter of expense than profit. When used, great care should be taken to prevent them from freezing, by covering them and keeping them warm; and where this cannot be done, it will be necessary to stop and let out all the water, to prevent damage being done by the frost.

VARIOUS MODES OF CASTING CYLINDERS.

It was customary to cast two nozzles on the one end of the cylinder in the early days of steamboating, and upon this plan were the majority of our engines constructed. Latterly nozzles were cast upon each end of the cylinder. This plan was superior, on account of the side pipes being built on the nozzles, which were all cast on the cylinder. There was no necessity for taking them off when reboring the cylinder, as was done on the former plan. It made a much better and neater job, although it was attended with more risk in casting the cylinder, in case the top parts should be in any way deficient, for want of metal.

FOUR LUGS CAST UPON THE CYLINDER.

In early years, cylinders were made much shorter than those now in use. Four lugs might well do for them, while they would not answer for the long cylinders now in use. Every old engineer has had the trial of them, and finds that the keys could not be kept tight on account of the continual expansion and contraction of the cylinder. If, when hot, it were closely keyed up, there would be danger of the lug breaking when the cylinder contracted by cooling. Who has not experienced this in practical engineering? The only way in which four lugs can be made to operate correctly, is to key fast one on either side, and leave the other without keys. This will do, but it leaves the expansion and contraction confined to one end of the cylinder.

One plan of making the bed plates and keying up the cylinder lugs was to have the bed plate between the two end lugs even with the top of the lugs, and to have an offset at each end of the bed plate, equal to the thickness of the cylinder lugs; then one key was driven in at each of the offsets in the bed plate, on the inside of the lugs, to hold them fast, and there were no jogs nor keys on the outside of the lugs at either end. This was the worst plan that could be invented, because you could not key one lug tight without keying both tight, and to key both tight, when hot, would be apt to cause them to break when cooling. The cylinder I allude to as keyed up in this way, had one lug broken off. I did not understand how it was done, but no doubt this was the cause. A gentleman with whom I was talking on the subject, said he had one broken off in the same way. Doubtless there have been many others broken in a similar manner.

Another late improvement is to cast both the side pipe and four valve-seats together. This is a good plan, as it takes up less room and requires fewer bolts and joints, and is less weighty, and, upon the whole, saves considerable labor; and in this way, there is no danger of blowing out joints around the valve-seats, as formerly, as none are required on this plan.

FOUR NOZZLES CAST ON THE CYLINDER.

It was, for a long time, considered an improvement to cast four nozzles on the steam cylinder, because it looked better and was more pleasing to the eye than the plan previously used. It made an artistic job. And when the cylinder required to be bored out again, it would not be necessary to take off the side pipes and fast cylinder head, as had to be done on the former plan.

SIX LUGS CAST ON THE CYLINDER.

The casting of six lugs on each cylinder has been done for many years, and has been found of great utility. The cylinder is keyed fast by the centre lug, and screwed fast to the cylinder timbers by the four end lugs. This gives the cylinder a fair chance to come and go, from the centre each way, to accommodate itself to the expansion and contraction, without danger of breaking the lugs, as formerly.

SUB-CYLINDER.

In the early history of constructing steam engines, there was much uncertainty connected with the casting of cylinders. For the purpose of avoiding risk and diffiulty, there is no doubt the experiment of casting the sub-cylinder was adopted. The main cylinder was cast without any nozzles, and but two on the sub-cylinder, which is bolted to the main cylinder; and the other two nozzles are cast on the cylinder-head.

The first engine of this construction was placed upon the steamer *Hercules*, and was afterward used on the steamer *Samson*. It was the only one of the kind which came within our knowledge; and facts compel us to say, it worked admirably. It was constructed at Pine Creek, (near Pittsburgh,) Allegheny County, by Mr. Belknap. But as there is less risk in making castings now than formerly, it would not be advisable to adopt this plan, as it requires more metal, labor and joints.

STROKE OF CYLINDER.

In the early days of steam, we used much smaller cylinders with longer stroke than we now do, and worked steam, nearly full stroke on the piston, $\frac{3}{4}$ to $\frac{7}{8}$, &c. Our cylinders in use at the present day are nearly twice the diameter and half the stroke of those formerly used, and the steam generated in the boilers raised to a much higher pressure to the square inch. They cut off more closely in the cylinder—sometimes $\frac{1}{2}$ stroke, $\frac{5}{8}$, and $\frac{3}{4}$, &c., in order to make as much from the expansion of the steam as possible.

The remarks in regard to the long and short boilers, may well be applied to the long and short stroke cylinders. When persons are about changing from one thing to another, and find the change for the better, they are

OVERSIZED FOLDOUT

COLOR ILLUSTRATION

was removed after page(s) 142
for in-house scanning

On 8·18 2000

apt to carry it to the contrary extreme, and overdo their work in their search after improvement. The medium stroke, between the long and the short, as a general thing, is the safer, more economical, more powerful, and of more utility for all practical purposes.

It is customary to make the stroke of stationary engines twice the diameter of the cylinder. There are exceptions, where the stroke is longer or shorter. The advantage of short-stroke engines for stationary purposes, is to get a fast speed, in order to avoid the necessity of using so much gearing, as was customary when using the long-stroke engine.

SLIDES, PITMANS, PILLAR BLOCKS, &C.

BEARING, THICKNESS AND WIDTH OF SLIDES.

SLIDES should be so made as to have a large bearing on the part where the shoving-head jaws are to run, in order that they may bear up under the weight of heavy pitmans, shoving-head, piston rod, &c., otherwise the cylinder cannot long continue in line. Our slides formerly had not more than one-fourth the bearing they should have had, to stand the wear they were subject to, and which the necessities of the boat which they were propelling required.

The slides should be much thicker than they are ordinarily made, so that both the bearing and the balance of the slide will not spring in screwing down. Slides are very often made too narrow, and by reason of this, they do not get sufficient bearing on the timber to keep them from rolling. There is another thing which should, as much as possible, be guarded against; that is, the putting of bolts in a straight line in the centre of the slide, as may be seen in plate F. They should be placed out and in, as may be seen in draft, plate K. This holds them more firm than when on a straight line.

OVERSIZED FOLDOUT

was removed after page(s) 144
for in-house scanning

On 8·18 2000

On the timbers H, may be observed another mode of putting on slides, which was in use in the early stages of steamboat navigation. (See plate H, page 144.) In the middle of the slides there should be a groove, planed within one or two inches of each end, to retain the oil, so as to lubricate the slide to better advantage.

LENGTH OF SLIDES.

The length of the slides, for river engines, should always be from one to one and a half inches shorter than the stroke of the engine and the brass in the shoving-head, so that the jaws will work over the slide at each end in such a manner as to keep a lump from rising on the end of the slide, as would inevitably be the case were the slide longer than the stroke of the engine and shoving-head jaws. If the slides be longer than this, and the jaws screwed close to the slides, to keep them from back-lashing on the slides, which they are likely to do, the lump would be in proportion to the amount of room or space left between the shoving-head jaws and slides. If the jaws are as close to the slides as they should be, and the slides longer than we have mentioned, after having been worn for a season, they will have a rise on each end of the slides, just equal to that which has been worn down; and as the pitman shortens by wear, it forces itself upon the thick part of the slide, and may stress the thread of the bolt, thus causing the engine to labor as it revolves over the centre, especially if it pinches tight on the slides.

If backing be put in, to lengthen the pitman, it will

work the same at the other end of the slides. This is the reason why we think it would be better to have the slides a little short; thus you need have no charge on your mind for the safety and security of the engine. All the intricacies about engines, beyond what is absolutely necessary, should be avoided. They not only tend to confuse and puzzle the engineer, but cause him unnecessary labor. The more simple the engine can be constructed, so that it has all necessary appliances, the better; it will take less labor to manage it, and engineers are well aware that they have little time to lose while running the plainest and best engines.

SHOVING-HEADS BORED OUT.

Shoving-heads should always be bored out in a lathe. The centre of the wrist on the shoving-head should be parallel with the centre on the lathe, while the opposite end is being bored out. This is the only way that the centre of the piston rod can be brought true to the centre of the wrist on the shoving head. In early days, they were bored out with a reamer and lever by hand, and it was a rare thing to get a true hole in this way. If it happened to be in the centre, all was right, and if not, it was thought that it made no particular difference. If the jaws on the shoving-head stood a little above the centre or to the one side, they generally set the slides to suit them. This mode of doing business was not correct; nevertheless, these things I know to be facts.

BOLTS FOR SHOVING-HEAD JAWS.

It is within my recollection of once having witnessed a steamer with four boilers. Were it necessary her name could be given. She had twenty-four inch cylinders, and from five to six feet stroke. We give it not as a certainty, but as recollection warrants. She had but one bolt in each of the shoving head jaws, and we understood from the engineers that it answered the purpose for which it was intended.

We do not approve of shoving-head jaws, large or small, with only one bolt. They are not safe, for this reason: there is nothing to prevent the bolt from working out, if the nut happened to be a little slack. The bolt will instantly drop from its position, because there is nothing to hold it. In order to keep the nut from turning and working, it should be a little tight—that is, the nut on the end of the bolt. The bolt will then drop out while the engine is working, unless a jam nut be used.

It is within the knowledge of many engineers, that this has happened, even with two bolts in the jaws. When this has happened, the nuts were made fast from turning, by a piece of wood being driven between the nuts; the bolts will then sometimes, after all precautions, turn and find their way out.

The object we have in view, in reference to two and three bolts, is that the nuts upon the shoving-head jaws may be locked so that they cannot be turned; this may be done by driving a piece of wood between the nuts. If this should not answer, it is necessary that the bolts should be kept from turning. This may be done in two ways: one is by having square holes in the lower jaws; the other, by making such large heads upon the bolts so that they cannot pass one another. The latter is considered the easiest plan, and will answer all useful purposes. In this way, and by these means, the nuts may be held fast to the bolts.

The reason why two or three bolts should be preferred in a shoving-head jaw, is simply this: when they are secured, as above mentioned, they are safe in the hands of any person, whether he understands his business or not. It would also be safe in the hands either of a fireman or a boy, because the bolts are thus rendered stationary, until they are unlocked by drawing out the wood or iron which may have been put in between the nuts for the purpose of holding them fast. Now, by way of contrast, the author will give his views, while he feels the spirit and interest of the subject strongly upon him. The subject now in review may seem a small matter, but it is truly important. In the beginning of the remarks upon this branch, it will be remembered that strong objections were made against the use of but one bolt in the jaw of a large shoving-head, for the reason that it might possibly work out or break. It might do so, in case of friction produced by working dry slides, or from other causes, which nothing but experience and practice can avoid.

It should be impressed upon the minds of all who read and understand what they read, that that which is perfectly safe within itself, and completely under the control of one man, would be quite dangerous and unmanageable in the hands of another. Now, the author can, and there are many others within his acquaintance who can take the largest steamer that floats on the Ohio, and run her engine with safety with but one bolt in the shoving-head jaw, provided that bolt is as perfect as it ought to be when it comes from the hands of the machinist who forged it. The nuts should not be loose upon the bolts, but should, on the contrary, be so tight as to turn easy with the short wrench, accompanied by the use of a second wrench to hold the head of the bolt below. They must be screwed hard and fast to the papers between the shoving-head jaws, in order both for safety and use. If the slide be constructed on the long order, as heretofore described, as the pitman shortens it will crowd upon the thick part of the slide, and be very likely to strip the thread or break the bolt. Herein lies the difficulty with all but the most experienced engineers; for if the nut be put on slack, or loosely, as it is in many other places, the engine will become unsafe and unmanageable. All having control of steam engines should be careful to understand this, as much harm might readily result from neglect, carelessness or inexperience. Therefore, it is better that two bolts be used, because where the inexperienced may not be able to get along with one bolt, the scientific man might work his engine with a bolt even of smaller dimensions. The one would not know how to keep it in position. A jam nut might answer the purpose, but there are many who have not sufficient constructiveness to think of such an expedient.

But lest the length of the remarks upon this branch should weary the reader, it may be said, in conclusion, that although some persons can work with but one bolt where others could not, on account of the superior skill and judgment which some possess in a greater degree than others, yet it would be the sounder policy that all engines, from the smallest to the largest, which have labor to perform, should be supplied with two bolts to the smaller, and three to the larger, for the reason that if by chance or accident one bolt should break, the other one, or two, as the case may be, will altogether likely hold out until it has been discovered wherein the weakness consists.

It may well be considered a nice matter, where paper is used in a shoving-head, to so adjust it as that in every way it shall fit on the slides, both above and below, as well as upon the outer and inner edges of the slides. There is a great degree of skill required on the part of those who undertake this difficult job, to accomplish it as it should be done; and when it is well done, it is, in many respects, far superior to any set screws which may be used for regulating the brass liners which are movable on the jaws.

There has been much said on this branch of the treatise, and much more might be said, but prudence requires that it should be cut short, as there are other branches that require attention.

LENGTH OF PITMANS.

It used to be a general rule to make pitmans three times the length of the stroke. Some have used them shorter than this, say about two and two and a half lengths of stroke; but these are considered, however, exceptions to the rule. It has been customary for rolling mills to construct their pitmans one foot longer than three lengths of the stroke. We do not vary but slightly from this rule at the present day in the construction of land engines. But for river engines, they should be about four times the length of the stroke, as a general thing. There may, however, be exceptions, and more or less length used in order to accommodate the peculiarities of the engine for which they are intended to be used. There may be forcible objections urged against the use of long pitmans. They not only are more liable to spring in their working than short ones, but add much to the weight which bears upon the top of the slides, and on the crank-wrists to which they are connected. Thus it will readily be observed that the friction must be greatly increased. There is a medium between the long and short pitmans which should always be observed by the builder. Extremes ought, in all cases, to be avoided.

Some pitmans have been made of locust, and others of curly maple, and others of hard wood, but as a general thing they are made of white pine.

WOODEN PITMANS.

The pitmans of our steamers are mostly, if not in fact universally, made of wood (light pine wood), and this has been found to answer the purpose admirably, when carefully watched and kept in perfect working order. Exceeding caution should be observed in the adjusting of the pitman straps, in order that the timbers be not cut too lean next the brass boxes, because this would, when screwed up, throw the jaws too wide apart at the point.

On eastern American rivers, as also on ocean steamers, pitmans are all made of wrought iron. A wooden one would be as great a novelty to them as a wrought iron one would be to those who navigate the western waters.

IRON PITMANS.

Iron pitmans for the most part remain about the same as when first constructed; but wooden ones require continual watching, and more or less screwing up, as the timber from which they are made shrinks; and moreover, there is much danger from their liability to rot. The exposure to which they are subject, in all kinds of weather, is certain, sooner or later, materially to affect them. This fact requires vigilant watching on the part of those in charge of river engines.

PLACING IN WRISTS.

In order that wrists may be kept firmly in their place, it will not answer to give too large a draft, because the larger the draft, the more wedge-like it becomes; hence the easier pulled out. It ought not to taper more than one-fourth of an inch to six inches in length, and give three-eighths draft in the key-hole; when drawn firmly up, split the key or keys, and all will be right.

COLLAR-WRISTS AS FORMERLY USED.

(See plate 4, A.) This was a bad way of putting in wrists, and the only object that could have induced its adoption, must have been to save a little iron on the back of the collar, but its construction costs more in labor than the difference of iron would amount to.

If this wrist should at any time be drawn np to the collar, and should happen to work loose, it could not be ascertained by reason of the collar, without especial attention. If it be found loose, the only remedy is to take it out and bush it. It would be found that the fault consisted in making the wrist too small to allow sufficient bearing to hold itself in form without chawing and working loose.

WRISTS AS NOW USED.

Either of the secured wrists will answer the purpose. (See diagram H, No. 5.) The wrist B was not brought into use until long after the wrist A, which has heretofore been fully alluded to. It was of greater utility, and worked to better advantage, because it had no collar to prevent its being drawn up if slack; nor had it any obstruction to prevent its being bushed, if found necessary.

It was found to be much more convenient, and far more practical, because it worked more easily. It had no collar to look after and fit in or see to, when it became loose; nor had it any play from the motions of the engines. By use of a large wrist, there is greater strength and more bearing, which prevented hard keying and heavy pressure upon the wrist, when performing its labor, and from bedding itself in the eye, as a small wrist will always do.

C is a wrist which is larger on the back end; this was found necessary from the use of wrought-iron cranks, for the purpose of boring out the holes, both of them true from one side, without changing the crank in the lathe; whereas, if it were changed, in order to bore out the other side, it would be almost impossible to get the two holes as true to each other as on the former plan. The outside collar is sometimes separate, and screwed on with a set-screw. The only object of this would be to save iron; it is bad policy, although it has, in many instances, been found to work well. In many more, it might be found the cause of much trouble. The wrist should be in one piece, as may be seen in plate I.

WRISTS WITHOUT KEYS.

This plan has been introduced lately upon the Western waters. It is the putting in of wrists, in the cranks of our steamboats, without keys. They are made with little or no draft, and are forced in by means of a screw, which being properly adjusted, the wrist is riveted in, or hammered a little around the outside edge of the wrist. This plan has been practically tried, and many engineers bear testimony that it has answered the purpose admirably; but in all cases it would be much better that the wrists should be firmly keyed in, so that they could be taken out, and turned anew, after having been used for a while, and worn out of true.

If it becomes necessary that a wrist should be taken out, which has been forced in and burred, it would, beyond doubt, become necessary to take off the crank and carry it to a shop, in order to have the burr cut off, and it will require to be placed under a screw, in order the more conveniently to be taken out.

BOTTOM BRASSES IN PILLAR BLOCKS.

In the early history of our steamers, as a general thing, they made no use of bottom brasses, but instead thereof used side brasses, considering this sufficient, inasmuch as the labor of the engine is principally fore and aft upon the side boxes. Notwithstanding this, there was still found to be considerable wear on the bottom blocks, owing to the weight of the main shaft and fly-wheel; and owing to a little wear of the pillar-blocks (for want of the bottom brasses) the whole block might be lost, which otherwise would last as long as the rim of a fly-wheel that would be as good when the boat is worn out as on the day when it was placed on board.

KEYS IN SIDE BOXES.

Side boxes are frequently keyed up to the journals by means of narrow keys through the caps, with four holes cast in the pillar block, for the purpose as well of securing the keys as they are driven down, as of keeping the side-boxes tight to the journals. Objections to the use of these keys may be urged for many reasons: they weaken the cap as well as the pillar block; they may slip back and leave the boxes loose; and being thus exposed to view, at all times, they may often be driven down when there is no occasion, and thereby heat the shaft, and on this account produce unnecessary friction. Sometimes the keys are drawn up with a screw through the cap, having the thick part of the wedge below. They are also liable to cut the shaft and boxes unnecessarily.

BACKING IN SIDE BOXES.

This mode may be considered much better than any other plan now in use. When the boxes are once keyed up to the place, and the caps on, there is no danger of your backing coming out; and at any time when side-boxes are becoming slack, the cap can be taken off (which should be done immediately on discovery of looseness), and the slack may be taken up by putting in a thin piece of sheet-iron.

SET SCREWS FOR SIDE BOXES.

Set screws are also used for tightening up side boxes, but there is the same danger in using them, as in the keys; there is danger of screwing them up too tight, and thereby heating and cutting the side boxes and journals of the shaft, and causing the engine to labor and drag. And owing to the small size of the set screws, and the heavy pressure on the side boxes, when the engine is running, they are liable to bed the points of the screws into the side of the boxes, and work holes in them, and, at the same time, stave up the points of the set-screws, so as to render it difficult to get them out. They are also more expensive to fit up. When they are used, it would relieve the set-screws to fill in between them with backing.

BORING OUT PILLAR BLOCKS.

To make anything like perfect pillar blocks, it is absolutely necessary that they should be bored out as smooth and as true as a cylinder, and each block faced off on each side perfectly true in the lathe. In early days, they were used as they came out of the foundry, after scraping off the sand and chipping off the lumps; and, on this account, the friction of the engine was much greater, and the shafts wore out much more quickly, than those of the present day.

LARGE COLLARS ON SHAFTS.

Our large steamers should all have large collars on each side of the journals, varying from one to one and a half inches, as the collars on the shaft always bear hard on the pillar blocks, when the boat is on a list. Thus it will be sufficiently plain that a false motion is continually on the increase; this can be remedied by cutting the side-boxes in two pieces and driving a key between the brass and the collar on the pillar blocks.

SMALL COLLARS ON SHAFTS.

In the early years of steamboating, there were four shafts, and they all had small collars. In a very short time, during the running of the boat, these collars would be found to have bedded themselves in the pillar blocks on both sides; and this, in addition to the back lash in the coupling blocks then in use, would make a tremendous noise as the boat would roll from one side to the other, while making short turns, which would be quite as unpleasant to a nervous or sensitive person, as the sound of trip-hammers.

JOINTS.

CONTINUED.

PINE BOARD JOINTS.

JOINTS have frequently been used on our steamers, made of white pine, mostly between the bottom of the heater and side-pipe flange, for the escape of steam. I am also informed that pine has been used for the supply pipe leading from the force pump to the boiler, and that it stood well. If it stood the pressure here, I believe it would stand it for the steam pipes also. There is no doubt about this, if the flange is wide and has plenty of bolts. These, like all other joints, require to be watched and screwed up occasionally, until they are perfectly bedded and solid.

PACKING YARN AND ROPE JOINTS.

Gaskets for man and hand-hole plates, also, cylinder heads, valve caps, &c. have often been used, made of the above materials, and answered very well. I have used them for the man-hole plates, when running as engineer on the Ohio and Tennessee rivers, and never had any trouble. If the place between the man-hole plate and the boiler head is not true, as is often the case, and if the man-plate casting should be warped, something more pliable than lead should be used, as lead is hard to bed up, and there is danger of breaking the plates, lugs, &c. When lead gaskets are used, they should be round or diamond, then they will bed up easily.

CANVAS JOINTS.

Canvas joints are used to good advantage for steam and supply pipe joints. Take three or four layers, owing to the thickness required to make the joints, putting a coat of white lead between each layer. Then screw it up tight, and, if you have time, let it dry a few days before using, to harden the lead. If heat is applied immediately, it melts the white lead out, and it runs away. These joints are equal, if not superior, to gum; and country millers, as well as others, could use old wornout bags and canvas of almost any description, and joints made in this way would not cost more than about one-twentieth part of the price of gum. (N. B. There are two kinds of gum; the one is mixed, and the other is filled in with several layers of canvas, and is preferred for steam-joints on this account. It costs more than the mixed. I believe, if the canvas is tolerably good, not too old, and well saturated with white lead, and has time to dry before using, it will make a more solid and durable joint than gum.)

GASKET PAPER JOINTS.

Gasket paper has been universally used for making certain joints about the steam engine, such as the joints between the heater and the side pipe, and all the water pipes connected with the heater, also the feed pipe from the heater to the force pump. It has also been used in all joints about the steam engine, excepting those connected with the boiler, steam and supply pipes, &c. I mention this for the benefit of employers, as well as engineers, as a great many use gum, where paper would do as well, and costs only about one eighth the price. I have known paper to be used on the outer end of the boiler stand pipes, for the blow-off cock of high pressure engines, about thirty-five years ago. They were almost equal to a ground joint, only they would be required to be made anew every time they had to be taken apart, which was seldom necessary, unless the cock should get out of order by the frost or otherwise.

About the year 1860, I was called on to make some alterations on the steamer *Wm. Dennis*. Her engines were built in Buffalo, N. Y. I had occasion to take off the steam chest and cap, which were both planed up, and had thin gasket paper joints about one inch wide, above and below. I was surprised, never having seen it in use here before. I asked the owners how it stood; they said, first-rate. From this time my attention was called to this fact, and I thought I would try it also, not seeing why it would not do. I have tried it since on the fast-head of a cylinder used at Shoenberger's rolling mill, where steam is carried at about 120 lbs. per square inch.

I have used it also about the check blow-off and safety valve chambers for two double-flued boilers, to drive Bollman & Garrison's new engine. I have also tried it on many other engines, and find it to answer very well.

Since writing the above, I have inquired of one of my old bosses, who was one of the best engineers of his day on the western waters, and who has been engaged for about twenty years in Pittsburgh, building the largest class river and lake steamers, about using gasket paper joints for steam pipes, &c. He told me they were used for the steam pipe joints leading from the boilers to the cylinders, and also for the blow-off cock joint on the outer end of the boiler stand pipe, &c., and he said they answered very well. On the next day, I met John Warden, his old partner in engine-building, and asked him if the paper joints were used in early days. He said they were, and that they answered a first-rate purpose. He told me he believed the paper to be better than gum. The reason he gave for this was, the gum being so very soft would squeeze outside of the flange, while the paper, being hard and solid, would not. In one instance, he said, the gum closed up the opening so much as to prevent the engine from running, and there was considerable time lost and search made before the cause of the difficulty was discovered.

I mention this, because I believe there have been many instances of a similar kind; and although the opening in many cases may not be entirely closed, so as to stop the engine from running, yet it may be closed so much as to cause it to labor very hard by holding the steam back, and causing it to be wire-drawn, by forcing its way through a small opening, and destroying in a great measure the force of the steam on the piston head. I have tried the gasket paper for joints at home, first on our own engine, and then I tried it abroad, and am satisfied that it will hold steam or hot water, as well as gum. (N. B. As the paper is very hard and solid, and will not yield so much as gum, hence it will be necessary that the faces of the castings for the joints be tolerably true, and have a sufficiency of bolts.)

VARIOUS CAUSES FOR JOINTS BLOWING OUT, AND LEAKING.

In the early days of steamboating, it was very common for some one or other of the joints about the engine to blow out or commence to leak badly. I will mention some of the joints that were most likely to give out first, and then tell you the different causes. First, the connection block joints between the boilers, the steam and stand pipes for the same, cylinder heads and valve seat joints, and in fact there is very little dependence to be put in any of the joints the way they were made. Joints, in early days, were mostly made of cement, formed of iron borings and sal ammoniac. The connection blocks between the boilers and the stand pipes below were made of this kind of cement, and they would often leak and blow out. No doubt, one cause was the want of more screw bolts. The joints may have been tight where the screw bolts were, but the space between the thin boiler plate being so great, the iron would swell up between the bolts so as to allow the joint to leak, whereas there should have been another bolt between every two then in use. Another cause for leaking was owing to the cement not having been sufficiently tight driven in all round, leaving the joint open and porous. There is another cause, which perhaps has given more trouble than any other about the steam engine. I allude to the gummets used on the bolt heads for the boiler checks and stands, also on the heads of the bolts inside of the heater, &c. These gummets are mostly made of packing yarn, fitted tight around the heads of the bolts to prevent them leaking; but in a very short time they will require to be watched, and frequently screwed up, in order to keep them tight. If this is neglected, the bolts will commence to leak, and then the joints will cut and blow out. Another great source of annoyance to engineers has been, that the holes in the boilers, and also in the heaters, have generally been made round, and the bolts were also made round to fit the same, whereas the holes should be square, with square necked bolts.

GUM JOINTS.

Gum joints are one of the latter-day inventions, and when first introduced, were looked upon by many with suspicion, and thought to be rather a novel kind of material for making joints. But they soon came into general use, for several reasons: one is, they are easily made, and require less than one-fourth the time to make a lead one, and if the joints when made should leak, the gum will be more easily screwed tight, as it is more pliable than lead, and on this account there is less danger of breaking the flanges by hard screwing, when necessary to make tight joints, as is often the case when the faces of the flanges are uneven for want of planing or turning. I believe gum to be one of the most costly materials that can be used for joints; it lasts but a short time till it burns out, and soon becomes very brittle. If the gum joints require to be taken apart, as they frequently do, they must be replaced with gum, unless it is copper-lined to prevent it from sticking and tearing to pieces, as they generally do, when put on without copper lining. The use of the gum joints I consider one of the most costly items to keep up an engine. I do not allude to the first cost, but they are a continual expense, so that there is no end to the cost; for almost every time you take off a cap, cylinder head, man or hand-hole plate, you will be likely to require some new gaskets.

HAT JOINTS.

For the benefit of the public, and especially country millers, and others living far from cities, I mention that I have tried this experiment. I had to make a new joint under our safety valve pipe, on top of the boiler, and for the purpose used an old hat. It stood first rate, and is still standing. This same material will do for any joints about the engine not exposed to the fire. This information may be very useful to some persons whose engine joints may be burnt or rotted from age, and blown out; and may save them from traveling scores and in some cases even hundreds of miles to purchase joint materials, and in this way the establishment and hands can be kept going, customers accommodated, and much time, expense, labor and disappointment saved. This material will answer as well as gum, and joints made in this way will cost little or nothing comparatively, as they may be made of worn or otherwise almost useless materials.

MUSLIN JOINTS.

Puppet valve seats that have been turned, and the side pipes and cylinder nozzles having been planed up true, joints have been made by putting in a single layer of cotton muslin, coated with red or white lead. When screwed up tight, this makes a first rate joint, and requires a great deal less labor than it would to grind or scrape, and answers every purpose. It will also do for valve caps, steam chests, &c., or any other joint dressed up in similar style, which is not exposed to the action of the fire.

CASSIMERE JOINTS.

Joints for steam and supply pipes have been made out of old cassimere pants, to answer as well as gum, paper or lead. We have an old engineer working with us who has had considerable experience in engineering about salt wells, &c., and has worked many years in Pittsburgh, he says he has made a great many of these joints, and they stand very well. N. B. They can also be made out of an old worn-out overcoat, or cloth of any kind will answer. In this way thousands of dollars might be saved yearly, which are otherwise unnecessarily expended no doubt for want of information on this subject.

HOW TO MAKE AND RUN LEAD GASKETS.

It has been customary with some persons in getting a mouldboard ready to cast elliptic gaskets, to cut them out, in a board, to the shape of the man or hand-hole plate, &c. This is not necessary. Add the long and short diameter together, and one-half of this will be the size to turn your gasket board, and it can be done much neater and better than you can cut it out by hand. I have found out, after many years experience, that it is not a good plan to cast them in this way, as they very often break in shrinking and cooling, unless the lead be extra good and tough. If the lead is second-hand, then it will not pay to cast them in this manner. The better plan is, to bend a piece of ⅝ or ¾ inch round iron, and make a pattern to the size, and cast it in a flask in sand. In this way there will be less danger of breaking, as the sand will yield to the shrinkage. I have seen some break in this may, but not often.

SOFT CEMENT JOINTS.

Soft cement is a composition, made of about ⅓ red lead, ⅔ white lead, and as much clean cast-iron borings as can be worked into it, to make it of the consistency of putty. The borings if not clean should be sifted through a fine sieve. This is said to make a first-rate cement. Such joints, I am informed by a skillful engineer, are used on lake and ocean steamers, and will last several months. He says he has known seams where the boilers have been cracked 4 and 5 feet long, and cracked one-fourth round the boiler; and that boilers 4 and 5 feet diameter have been mended in this way, by taking a piece of boiler plate, 5 or 6 inches wide, and the length of the crack, and making it a little hollow in the middle, so as to receive the cement. The bolts on each side should be as close together as the nuts will turn to clear each other. The plate of boiler iron has a flange turned on each side about ⅛ of an inch, for the purpose of holding in the cement. It is put on in the following manner: Rub the inside of the patch over with a thin coat of white lead, put on the soft cement, about ½ an inch thick, and then screw and hammer it up as hard as the bolts will bear safely. Get a few shavings on a sheet-iron plate, set them on fire, and hold them to the patch a few minutes until it becomes warm, then commence to tighten the nuts again as hard as they will bear with safety, as they will yield considerably after heating. This makes a substantial joint, that will neither sweat nor leak. Then gather and scrape up all the cement you can, outside and inside, roll it up in a ball, and put in a keg of water to keep it moist, and it will be ready for use at all times. This cement is said to be first-rate for bedding down large pillar blocks, bed plates, &c. It is said to be the best and cheapest material that can be used for making stationary joints, and is generally used at sea. I am also told by the same engineer, that at San Francisco, boilers have been made to stand first-rate with this soft cement. It is necessary to have some of this material when out at sea, in case the boilers should give out from rupturing, burning, or any other cause.

SANCUM.

Sancum is made of brimstone dissolved over the fire in a ladle or pan, and filled in with clean cast iron borings, and stirred to mix the borings through and through the same, until it becomes too stiff for stirring, then pour it out into thin cakes, and let it cool, and it will be ready for immediate use. It is used to fill up holes in defective castings; it is also used to fill small holes in cylinders that are too small to get inside to patch. This hard cement is put in in the following manner: take a piece of sancum large enough to fill the hole, and put it on the top of the same, and hold a dark red hot iron on the top till the brimstone begins to melt, and then rub it over it until it fills the hole. This kind of cement is often used, and answers very well.

SLIDE VALVES, CAMS, &C.

SLIDE VALVE, CUT-OFF AND SEAT.

THE slide valve cam and valve are laid out on a different principle from the eccentric or full stroke cam and valve. On page 142 you have a side view of a cylinder and side pipe with a cut-off slide valve and seat. It cuts off at three-fourths of the stroke. I will explain what is meant by cutting off the steam. The cylinder has four feet stroke, and the steam fills the cylinder, whilst the piston travels three feet, and it is immediately shut off by closing the valve whilst running the other fourth. The object of cutting off the steam is to gain additional power by the extra expansion of steam, whilst at the same time the escape steam passes off much easier, and, on this account, the engine will run more freely than those engines working full stroke, especially when cramped in letting out the escape steam, which is said sometimes to produce a reaction on the piston head, and causes the engine to labor and drag heavily. This cam is laid out so that when the piston has traveled three feet the valve closes the opening with equal lap on each side, as you will see in the draft, valve B, whilst the valve at the other end of the seat allows a full opening out into the exhaust until the piston has run nearly the whole length of the stroke, and the valve stands still whilst on the cut-off point, keeping the opening closed until the crank is about coming over the dead centre, and then the valve opens and lets the steam into the other end of the cylinder, and cuts off on each end time about.

This is the most powerful cam that has ever been used, and it is the only one that cuts off the steam at any point you please, and at the same time gives a full exhaust nearly all the time. I recollect an engine that worked a long time using an eccentric cam, and gave entire satisfaction. Another party bought it, and it was guaranteed to drive a certain amount of work, but it would not do it satisfactorily. I then tried a longer valve, to cut off more steam, but it did not answer. Then I put in the regular slide valve cut-off cam, to work in a square cam yoke, and altered the valve to a regular cut-off valve, similar to that in the draft on page 142, slide valve B, and made some few other alterations. It then gave entire satisfaction, and, it was said, took less fuel and less water.

I believe there are a great many medium-sized engines having eccentric cams, that might truly be called steam wasters, working almost full stroke. I believe, in many instances, if they were thrown out and the old slide valve cam used in their place, there would be a saving of about 20 to 25 per cent. of steam and fuel.

The only plan of cutting off steam correctly with an eccentric cam, and at the same time giving a full exhaust all the time, is to use two cams and valves, as formerly used on locomotives, the lower valve being a full stroke valve and the upper valve an independent cut-off. By shifting the cam that works the upper valve, you can cut off at any point you please, and by setting the cam that works the cut-off valve square up, the same as the full stroke cam, the cams being the same throw, they keep time one with the other, and work together, and both cams and valves set in this way work full stroke; and then by turning the outside cam one-fourth round or at right angles with the other cam, you cut off at one-half stroke; putting it only one-eighth round, you cut off at three-fourths; and putting it three-fourths round, you cut off at one-fourth, &c. It is only when the two cams are set together that the valves work full, and the more one cam is set ahead of the other the closer you cut off the steam.

I knew an instance of an engine being repaired which had one of these slide valve cams working in a square yoke. A general repairing had been given it, and a round cam put in the same yoke. After using it a short time, it was found impossible to keep up steam; the round was then taken out and a slide valve cam, similar to the former, put in its place. This answered the purpose much better.

The slide valve cam is made to give two unequal motions; one gives more throw than the other, which accounts for the lean and full side. The first movement of the cam always closes the valve. This rule holds good on all cams, whether for slide, puppet, or any other kind of valves.

The second motion opens the valve and lets the steam into the engine. You will see a ¾ slide valve cam with a lean and full side (it is a ¾ cam), No. 3, on page 172,

OVERSIZED FOLDOUT

COLOR ILLUSTRATION

was removed after page(s) 172
for in-house scanning

On 8·18 2000

marked L on the lean side and F on the full side. This cam is laid out to work the slide valve B, which is laid down in the draft on page 142. The lean side of these cams goes foremost and runs the same way the engine runs. If the engine was one that was intended to run backward, that is, the top of the fly or water wheel running off from the cylinder, then the lean side of the cam would require to be turned round and face the other way. If the full side of the cam is put foremost, the valve, instead of standing still, as it should, on the cut-off point, as soon as the steam is let into the cylinder, for the purpose of retaining the same for expansion, until the piston travels the other fourth, it opens the port, and suffers the steam that should be retained for expansion to escape before its time, and the other end of the cylinder will be closed as much too soon, producing a strong reaction on the piston head and causing the engine to labor. By so doing you lose the expansion of steam as soon as it is cut off, whereas, if the lean side were foremost, the valve would stop as soon as over the opening, and by so doing it would still retain the steam in the cylinder until the piston had run the whole length, and then you would have the benefit of the expansion. When the sides of the puppet valve cams are equal from the centre, it makes no difference which side of them goes foremost, provided the bolt holes are not cast in, and if they are, you will have to set them to suit the holes. And the same with the exhaust or full stroke cams in general, with but one exception, as you will see in plate on page 172, cam 10, which has a sharp point for backing quick, whilst the same cam has the other corner rounded off to run more smoothly, as this side is seldom used. It would be better on all cams to have all the corners made round. The advantage of the sharp over the round is so little that it is of no real benefit, whilst the round corner cam works much smoother than the sharp.

DIFFERENT KINDS OF CAMS.

Cut-off puppet valve cams have four points, giving a double motion, the second motion to raise the levers, and the first to let them fall.

The full stroke puppet valve cam has but one motion, but it is not a continual go-ahead motion, as an eccentric cam. It gives the full movement gradually, and then the lever stands still until the nose of the cam has passed the outer circle, which holds the lever up with a full opening for a considerable distance of the stroke.

The slide valve cam has four points with a double motion and unequal sides, which is required for the reason that the first movement of the cam is equal to the width of one of the letting-on openings and the lap of the valve on the outside of the opening, after the valve has had a full opening, and the steam let into the cylinder. The first motion of the cam closes the opening, with an equal lap of the valve on each side, and the valve stands still on this point until the crank is about ready to come over the centre. Then the second throw of the cam is equal to the distance from the end of the valve to the inner edge of the letting on opening, always making the difference equal to the difference from the inside of each letting-on opening in the side pipe, and each end of the valve B, as it now stands on the seat, which is the width of the opening, with the outside lap less for the end of the valve marked B than the other end marked O.

There is another six-pointed slide valve cam which gives a treble motion, and was used in the early days of steamboating. There were two different steamers using them. I was employed to make new patterns for each, with four points, when at our shop in Louisville, Kentucky. They did not like the ones they had.

ECCENTRIC CAMS.

The eccentric cam is always a full stroke cam, which gives a constant motion to the cam yoke. It is never at rest, as other cams are, for the reason that, although the cam itself is a true circle, yet it has no true circle from the centre of the shaft, neither on the nose, heel or sides of the cams, as the puppet valve cut-off cam, and also slide valve cams have. The puppet exhaust has on the nose and heel only, but not on the sides.

The eccentric cam being round never opens as quickly as those cams which work in a square cam frame, and, on this account, in letting on and off the steam to the cylinder, it is more or less wire drawn.

It is a universal custom in the east to use the eccentric cam on marine and stationary engines. The mode of cutting off the steam with these full stroke cams is by having crooked lifters, one arm drooping down from the other at an angle, say of 45 degrees more or less, owing to the amount of steam you wish to cut off.

ROLLING MILL CUT-OFF AND FULL STROKE CAMS.

The rolling mill cam that I allude to is the one that goes on the cross shafts under the levers, and which is worked by bevel gearing two to one, putting the large bevel wheel on the main shaft. In this case, the cutting off is done by making a narrow nose on the point of the cam, all taken off the lower side.

These full stroke cams are parallel and have flat sides, the nose of the cam is a true circle from the centre to the circumference, excepting the outside points, which are rounded slightly, to enable them to work more smoothly than they would on the sharp corners.

WRIST OR CRANK MOTION.

Wrist or crank motion is the same thing, and gives the same motion as the eccentric cam. It works full stroke, and if there is any steam required to be cut off it must be done by giving an extra length to the valve covering the openings, owing to the quantity of steam to be cut off.

LENGTH OF FULL STROKE AND CUT-OFF SLIDE VALVES.

The length of the slide valve for a long stroke engine and slow motion is generally made as follows: suppose the letting-on openings to be 1¾ inches wide, the bearing on the end of the valve should be at least 2 or 2¼ inches wide, lapping ⅛ or ¼ inch over the openings inside and outside. And when the valve is standing on this point the exhaust opening under the valve should be about one-sixteenth of an inch open, so that when the valve opens to receive the steam the exhaust will be open equal to the lap of the valve, whether ⅛ or ¼ in addition to the extra one-sixteenth, in advance of the receiving opening to let on steam; so that there may be no reaction on the piston head on account of having to force the steam out of the cylinder, as is often the case, especially if the openings are very small.

SLIDE VALVE CAMS WITH EQUAL SIDES.

Some slide valve engines have been worked with full stroke valves. Such valves would require the cams to have equal sides, and the result would be, the moment you cut off the steam you close the exhaust opening, as the valve has say ¼ lap on each side of the opening, and the moment you close the letting-on opening by cutting off, you also close the other opening and the exhaust before the time, and this chokes the escapement and causes the engine to labor very hard on account of the reaction of the remaining escape steam, &c.

The valve and seat should be made the same as the one in the side view draft of the cylinder and side pipe, on page 142, which, after closing the opening, stands still with equal lap on each side of the opening, until the crank is about to come over the centre, leaving all the while a full exhaust opening, as you will see in the draft, valve B. I have frequently made the valves so as to allow but half an opening in the exhaust when the valve is standing still on the cut-off point, but I consider the full exhaust better when the valve is on the cut-off point, as it gives a freer exhaust by letting out the escape steam a shade sooner than the valve with the half opening in the exhaust when the valve B is standing on the cut-off point, as you will see in the draft on page 142. A regular full stroke valve, when over the openings, has seldom more than ⅛ inch lap, and sometimes only one-sixteenth of an inch, and as soon as the valve commences to open the exhaust port ought to be open about ¼ of an inch for the purpose of letting the escape steam pass off more freely than it would otherwise do, if longer detained.

For slow running engines the steam ought not to be let on until the crank has come over the centre and the shoving head about to commence moving on the slides. If let on any sooner, it is calculated to rack the engine fore and aft and destroy the machinery; for all the steam you can give an engine on the dead centre will not bring it over. N. B. I have seen engines brought off the dead centre by giving them steam, but this was owing to a lop or heavy sided fly wheel.

For fast running engines, such as locomotives used for drawing freight trains, the valve has about one-sixteenth of an inch lead when the engine is on the centre, and the exhaust about three-sixteenths of an inch; and for fast running passenger trains the valve has from three-sixteenths to ¼ inch lead, and the exhaust would require from ⅜ to ½ inch lead. The reason for giving the fast running engines more lead than the slow running ones, or giving

OVERSIZED FOLDOUT

COLOR ILLUSTRATION

was removed after page(s) 178
for in-house scanning

On 8/18 2000

them the steam before coming over the centre, is for the purpose of cushioning the engine, or to fill what is sometimes called the dunnage space, which means the clearance between the piston head and the two cylinder heads, and also at the sâme time filling the opening in the side pipe between the end of the slide valve and the end of the cylinder, so that the steam will act immediately on the piston head as soon as it begins to move on the slides, and by thus giving the steam before coming over the centre it prevents the back lashing that would otherwise be caused by slackness in the pitman boxes, &c. And it answers better on this account. If the fast running engines were not to receive their steam sooner than the large slow running engines, the piston head would have moved a considerable distance before the steam would act on it.

When engines have lead in the valve letting on the steam a little before the engine comes over the centre, it always suits better for locomotives or any other double engines than it would for single engines, for this reason: the one engine helps the other over the centre, whereas if the single engine was at the end of the slide, and the steam let on before coming over, the reaction of the steam when the engine was standing would require some hard pulling to bring it over the centre, unless the steam was shut off; but when the engine is running at its full speed, it barely fills the vacant room without having any time for reaction.

Doctor engines running very slow require to work a full stroke valve. They ought to receive the steam as soon as the shoving head begins to move on the slides; the valve, when the engine is on the dead centre, ought to cover all the openings not having more than one-sixteenth or one-thirty-second of an inch lap over each opening and ⅛ of an inch lead in the exhaust.

Just in proportion to the amount of steam you cut off from the engine, you require a heavier fly wheel to bring the engine over the dead centre. And the same with the speed of an engine. In proportion as you run it slow, you will require to enlarge the diameter and weight of the fly wheel rim.

HOW TO LAY OUT A SLIDE VALVE CAM.

(See side view of cylinder on page 142.) First lay out the eye of the cam; next allow a sufficiency of width outside of this, to bolt on to the cam flange, and at the same time allow enough to keep the cam yoke clear of the cam flange on the shaft. Then get the distance from the end of the valve B to the back of the opening, as it stands on the draft, which will always be equal to the width of the opening, including the lap of the valve on the outside of the same, which is sometimes ⅛ or ¼ of an inch, according to the size of the valve. Then draw another circle outside of the heel of the cam for the first movement, equal to the width of the opening and one outside lap included. See valve B, in the draft, page 142.

To get the second movement, take the distance from the other end of the valve to the back of the other letting-on opening, as laid down in the draft, page 142. The valve laid down in the draft at the end B requires three-sixteenths of an inch for the first movement and five-sixteenths for the second. After getting these two

OVERSIZED FOLDOUT

COLOR ILLUSTRATION

was removed after page(s) 180
for in-house scanning

On 8.18 2000

circles on the outer circle, lay off the width of the nose to any size you please. If you wish to cut off at one-half stroke, the cam will be nearly sharp on the point; if you wish to cut off at $\frac{5}{8}$, it will be about three or four inches wide on the nose. After the cam has been laid out, draw a line across the centre and step it off, as you see in draft of cams on pages 172 and 182, and if you find it cuts off too slow or too fast, you can increase or diminish the width of the nose of the cam, until you get it as you want it.

EXPANDING CAMS.

The expanding cam is made in four pieces; each piece is about one and a half inches thick, making the thickness of the cam three inches. It parts up and down in the middle on one side, and at right angles on the opposite, for the purpose of widening and contracting them on the nose, as far as the oblong holes will admit, as you will see in the draft of expanding cams on page 186. C, H and I are cams contracted, whilst J, K, L are expanded. You will also see an edge view of three cams in the same plate, marked A, B, C, D, E and F. If ever there was a time in which we would be justifiable in using these cams, it was in the early days of steamboating, when wood was universally used for fuel, and sometimes you would get it dry as powder, and at other times almost as green as grass, so that the amount of steam made would differ in proportion to the quality of the fuel. These cams never came into general use, and there is less call for them now than formerly, as coal is almost universally used, and if of a good quality, always produces nearly about the same amount of steam.

When using the expanding cam the two inside pieces were made stationary on the shaft, and when the cams were to be made wider or narrower, it was done by shifting the outside pieces of the cam.

SETTING THE FULL STROKE CAM.

These cams are made in two pieces, pivoting up and down straight through the centre; thus when the engine is on the after dead centre the cam stands straight up, and square up from the top of the pillar block when the block stands level with the boat fore and aft, or in other words, stands parallel with the shear plank.

The pillar blocks now in use differ materially from those formerly used. They are not put down parallel with the shear plank, but are laid on an inclined plane in a line with the cylinder and the slides. This is owing to our cylinder timbers being quite differently made from those of former years.

Our cylinder timbers now are skeleton timbers, and they run the whole length on an incline. Those in use many years ago, were filled up of different pieces of timbers, solid, while the cylinder timbers generally in this case run on an incline up to the pillar block, and then this part of the timber was level or parallel with the shear plank, and the pillar block would be parallel with the same. In this case, as we have already described, the centre of the cam would then stand plumb up, or square up from the face of the pillar block, and

OVERSIZED FOLDOUT

was removed after page(s) 182,
for in-house scanning

On 8.18 2000

the centre passing through each half of the cam stands upright and parallel with one or both faces of the cam frame, as may be seen in the full stroke cam and plate, page 184, which has a cut-off cam mostly within the same.

In setting the full stroke cam on our engines at the present day, where the cylinder timber is on the incline, and straight on the top the whole length of the timbers, the centre of the cam is still, as above described, parallel with one or both faces of the cam frame, and of course the centre of the cam is square up from the face of the pillar blocks, the same as the one first mentioned, where the pillar blocks were level or parallel with the shear plank. There is, however, this difference. On the plan which prevailed in early years, the pillar blocks being parallel with the shear plank, in this case, the faces of each cam would also be plumb, or in other words, both faces of the cam frame and the centre of the cam would be square up from the centre of the pillar block; but the faces of the latter, being on an equal inclination with that of the cylinder timbers (as they are now used), the centre line through the exhaust cam hangs as much over the plumb as the face of the pillar block in the same length of cam is below the level.

It should be remarked, that neither the plumb nor the level is used on water crafts, but the author has made use of them, in this treatise, in order that he may be the more easily understood, If the top of the pillar block is level when the boat is in trim, the centre of the cam would be found perfectly plumb. To repeat the substance of what has been already said in regard to the setting the exhaust or full stroke cams, when the engine is on the after dead centre the nose of the cam is up, and the centre line through the middle of the cam is always found to be square up from the middle of the face of the pillar block, and of course the centre line through the cam will be parallel to one or both faces of the cam frame; and the easiest manner in which these cams can be set is to make the centre line through the cam frame parallel, or at equal distances from the face of the cam frame; thus that frame will be equidistant from the centre of the main shaft. This rule will always be found right. It makes no difference if the pillar blocks are on a level with the shear planks, or on an incline. The principle remains one and the same, for horizontal or incline engines.

After the full stroke cam has been set, it is advisable to make a mark both upon the cam and upon the cam flange (opposite the first one), upon the shaft; so that if this cam should slip either way whilst in the act of setting the cut-off cam, there will be nothing to do but bring mark to mark; and when the cut-off cam is properly adjusted it would be well to mark it also, so that in case it should at any time slip by reason of the bolts becoming slack, or from any other cause, it will be much more easily discovered and adjusted, by comparing the marks made on the cam with those made upon the cam flange, or upon the main shaft.

It should be well noted, that double arms upon the rock shaft which is worked with a full stroke cam for backing, and sometimes for going forward, should be taken to the boat by the proper persons, and placed on the cross shaft, and then the cam-rod made to ship on both the upper and lower pin. The arm and rock shaft

OVERSIZED FOLDOUT

COLOR ILLUSTRATION

was removed after page(s) 184,
for in-house scanning

On 8·18 2000

should be marked with a centre punch and the hole drilled; this is the most correct plan of performing this part of the work. These arms are sometimes put on and drilled before coming to the boat; others put them on as before stated.

To those who put these arms on the rock shaft in the shop instead of placing them on in the boat on both pins while the engine is on the dead centre, it will be well to say, that they will sometimes require a little raising or lowering of the bearer of the cam-rod above or below a straight line, as it may require to make the cam-rod ship on both pins in the arm. It is to avoid this, and also to keep the cam-rod bearers in a straight line, that mention has been made of the propriety of not making this arm fast in the shop where the engine is constructed; but rather having it taken to the boat and there set, so that the cam-rod will readily ship on both pins. After which the arm should be marked, taken to the shop, and drilled and made fast. This may be considered the safest and best plan for executing this part of the work.

No. 2 is a draft of an equalizing arm, the object of which is to cut off the steam equally at both ends of the slides, inasmuch as the common cam has failed to do this; the latter cuts off the steam at the lower centre, passing out slower than it comes in at the upper centre. The reason of this will be discovered by examining the shoving-head, when its centre is in the centre of the slide. For instance, suppose the crank to be three feet from centre to centre, when the shoving-head is in the centre of the slide coming over the dead centre the wrist will be about six inches over the centre of the shaft, with a plumb, while on the other centre going out it will be found six inches behind the time. This is why the nose of one cam requires to be considerably wider than that of the other; the deficiency must be made up in this way. The cam is partially double and has an off-set in the cam frame so adjusted as to accommodate the difference of the points as the cam passes over, as may be seen in plate No. 2, page 184.

SETTING THE CUT-OFF CAM.

Where the engine is on the after dead centre, the nose of the cam is uppermost; let the cam then be turned until the consecutive circle comes hard up on the face of the cam frame and ready to move it the moment the wheel begins to move over the centre. The face of both the cam frames, full stroke and cut-off, will be equidistant from the centre of the main shaft.

It is well in this place to make especial note that on upright or walking-beam engines, the noses of the cams stand in an entirely different position to the crank upon the main shaft, from what those used on horizontal engines do.

The reason why the centre line through the nose of the cut-off cam does not stand perpendicular with the nose of the full stroke cam, is because it is a cut-off cam, and narrower on the nose, and on this account the centre line forms an acute angle, as may be seen described on draft, cam No. 4¾ and No. 5, page 184.

The sharper the nose of the cam the greater the angle, and the wider the nose of the cut-off cam the less will be the angle. (See drafts of different cams.)

PUPPET VALVE CAMS.

The names of the various cams used for the puppet valve engine are: Full stroke or D cam, cut-off cam, eccentric cam, equalizing cam, and expanding cam.

To give some idea of the latter cam, it would be well to remark that it was in use on board the large steamer called the *William French.* It was built at Jeffersonville, about the year 1820. This cam is of double thickness, and the object of expanding or widening out the nose, was to enable the engine to work off more steam than it otherwise could, while in the use of good wood or other fuel. When, as is sometimes the case, the wood was quite green and of inferior quality, and would in consequence generate less steam, they would be compelled to draw the cam together at the nose. It was made in four pieces, and when expanded from its ordinary shape, some parts of the working on the frame would only be the one-half thickness of the cam. The two inside half thickness of the cam would remain stationary and close, while the two outside ones opened at the nose; and just as far as the latter passed beyond the former, just so much must be taken off the heel of each inside cam. This is very difficult to be understood from verbal or written description; it must be seen to be properly comprehended, either in practical operation or by model, and then dissecting and laying it down in its different parts, as you will see in draft on page 186.

This cam will be, no doubt, a novelty to most readers, but it was only our purpose in this work to give it a passing allusion, to gratify curiosity and stimulate a desire for more knowledge on this complicated machinery. It may lead to important truths in the use of steam never before known.

This cam when contracted and brought to its narrowest working point at the nose, required the two heels of the inside cams to be cut off as much as the two points of the noses of the outside cam extended over the inner ones. Say, for the sake of illustration, the whole cam was three inches in thickness; then some parts of it, while working in the cam frame, would be three inches in thickness whilst other parts would be but 1½ inches thick—one half the thickness of the cam when closed together.

SLIDE VALVE CAMS.

The names of the various cams used on slide valve engines are: Full stroke cam; eccentric cam; cut-off cam with four points, with one lean and one full side opposite; cut-off cam with six points, with one lean and one full side.

HOW TO LAY OUT CAMS.

I believe there are but few engine builders who know how to lay out a slide valve cut-off cam and valve. Cams were first made for the western waters, about 44 years ago, by Stackpole & Whiting,. a Boston company then carrying on engine building in Pittsburgh. The motion given to the valves, before the introduction of cams, was produced by an arm from the shoving-head, or piston rod, when the piston was near the end of the stroke—somewhat similar in principle to the small pumping engines now in general use. The backing was done by hand. I have had charge of a shop in Pittsburgh for upward of twenty years, and we generally use the lean-sided slide valve cam and valves; and there never has been, in our shop, from the time I took charge of it to the present, one of these cams laid out except by myself; nor have I ever shown but to one person how to lay out such cams. For the benefit of the public, and in order that the idea may not be lost, I now publish the mode of laying them out.

Some have used the full stroke valve to work with a cam having equal sides, similar to those used on puppet valve engines for cutting off; this is all wrong, because almost as soon as you cut off the steam at the one end of the cylinder you close the letting on opening at the other end, and compress the remaining steam in the cylinder that should be allowed to escape, and thus cause the engine to labor unnecessarily, by producing a reaction on the piston head.

The rule for ascertaining how much steam the cams cut off, is, first, to draw two lines on the face of the cam, one straight up through the centre of the nose of the cam, and another square across through the centre of the eye. Take, for example, the half stroke puppet valve cut-off cam (No. 10, on plate B, page 190); there you see the half circle stepped off into eight equal parts; and where the half circle is intersected by the two circles leading down from the point or points on the nose of the cam, marked A and B, the space between A and

B shows the amount of steam let on, and the steam is cut off from the centre line C up to A and B. Or thus: the half circle is stepped off into eight parts, and there are four parts from B and A down to the centre line, or where the valve covers the opening, by moving the valve, which is four-eighths, equal to one-half. The same rule answers for the lean side slide valve cam.

You will see on page 190, plate B, cams Nos. 7, 10 and 11, another rule used by some for finding the amount of steam cut by the cams. Cams Nos. 7, 10 and 11 are three cams laid out on this rule, and No. 11 is laid out on both rules. For example, see cam 10: At the point of intersection you draw the line marked A; from this point through the centre of the eye of the cam; and at the opposite point of intersection marked B, you draw a line square to the line A, which in this cam comes to the centre of the eye, owing to its being half stroke. (In the three-fourth cam below No. 11, below the line B, which is also square out from the line A, and is considerably out from the centre, this rule will not hold good, because the point of intersection is thrown farther round, which is owing to this cam having a wider nose than the other.) Then draw a straight line up through the centre of the nose of the cam, and step it off into any number of equal parts you please, 8, 16 or 32, and take the same distance on the short square line out to the point of intersection, (see plate B, cam No. 10, page 190.) This rule holds good in both cases—the stepping on the half circle and also on the square line A and B. In the half circle there are eight spaces, and from A and B to the centre line there are four spaces cut off, which is equal to four-eighths or one half.

OVERSIZED FOLDOUT

COLOR ILLUSTRATION

was removed after page(s) 190
for in-house scanning

On 8/18 2000

There is one other case where this rule does not apply —see cam No. 11. There are eight spaces in the upright line, and about two and a half in the short line B. Say we put this into $\frac{1}{16}$ on account of the fractional part two and a half, which marks $\frac{5}{16}$ off, leaving $\frac{11}{16}$ on, making it an $\frac{11}{16}$ cam by the lines, whereas by the half circle it would be a $\frac{12}{16}$ or $\frac{3}{4}$ cam.

I have mentioned these two rules to satisfy the curiosity of those who are anxious to know all about the different modes of laying out cams, &c., as well as for the benefit of young beginners, who wish to understand laying out and experimenting on the same, and for want of sufficient practice and training have not yet full confidence in their own abilities. I would recommend the plan of laying out and making small cams, and also frames of thick gasket paper, or thin pine boards, and work the cam in the yoke, and in this way you can experiment until you understand the principle of laying out and working the cams completely.

I hinted in my former book that it was possible I might say something more on this subject, which I could have done then as well as now, but did not see proper to do so: I have now said more than I intended to and could say more, but will let this suffice for the present. What I have said will throw more light on the subject of cams than the former book, and I believe will more than come up to the expectations of many who may peruse the work. It is possible that I may say something more on this subject at a future period.

There is almost an endless variety of ways for making and shaping cams.

No. 1, plate A, is a view of a cut-off cam, for a slide

valve engine, with sharp corners and sharp nose, cutting off at ½ stroke. This cam differs from the puppet valve cam, having its sides unequal, so as to give the motion to the valve that is requisite. A is the lean side of this cam; this side goes foremost, to work the cam frame. B is the full side of the cam. Some engineers, in setting these cams, have put the full side foremost, and said they worked very well, stating that they did not see that it made any difference which side of the cam went foremost. Such engineers have yet to learn how to set a slide valve cam.

N. B.—In setting the full side of the cam foremost, B, you lose the expansion of the steam; for with the full side B foremost, you begin to exhaust the moment you cut off.

No. 2, plate 3, is another slide valve cut-off cam, with sharp corners, having a wider nose than No. 1, and of course, lets on more steam. While this cam travels from A to B, the receiving opening to the cylinder is closed, the steam is cut off and the valve is stationary; because the distance is equal from centre to circumference. Just the same with the nose of the cam; the valve remains stationary from C to D; the distance also is equal from E to F, and from H to G.

No. 3 is another slide valve cam with sharp corners, having a wider nose than No. 2, and of course letting on more steam than No. 2.

No. 4 is a slide valve cam, having round corners. These corners are cut off, and from the same centres that these corners are laid off by, you draw the curves for the balance of the cam, and by this means the cam is made to fill the cam frame all round.

No. 5 is a slide valve cam, similar to No. 4, only having a narrower nose, and of course, cuts the steam off quicker than No. 4.

No. 6 is another slide valve cam, having round corners, and narrower on the nose than No. 5, and cuts off steam quicker.

No. 7 is a full stroke D cam, and such as is generally used on puppet valve engines for backing. This cam has two sharp corners, and the frame stands still while the cam travels from H to I, and holds the lever up more than one half the time with a full opening from the time the lever commences to rise until it is closed. (The levers are down and the valves are closed on our horizontal engines when the cam is in the position you now see it.) The cam in this position gives a motion from the centre A, each way equal, because the distance from A to E is equal to the distance of the centre curve C, between G and E, and the motion is stationary until the cam has passed from I to the point H, and then the curve begins to fall back to the heel of the cam J, at the point nearly opposite I, where the distance is again equal from the centre to the circumference till it reaches the point K.

No. 8 is another full stroke D cam, with round corners, and such as is often used on puppet valve engines on steamers, for backing.

No. 9 is a puppet valve cut-off cam, having both its sides equal. This cam has sharp corners, and while it travels from A to B the steam is cut off, and when traveling from B to C it receives a full opening and remains full while traveling from C to D, because from C to D the distance is equal from centre to circumference.

No. 10 is a full stroke puppet valve cam, used on some of our steamers for backing. This cam has but one sharp corner, and this sharp corner is used for backing. The object of having this corner on is for backing quick, and the object of having the other corner off, is that the cam works more smooth and easy on a round point than it does on a sharp one. By request we had one of these cams made for the *Gen. Brown*, a Louisville boat, about the year 1839, which generally run from Louisville to New Orleans, and which was said to answer the purpose very well. This same boat exploded her boiler about one year after this and killed about 40 persons. She was a four boiler boat, and was again refitted and put in good running order at Louisville.

No. 11 is a puppet valve cut-off cam with round points, and also with sharp corners—the one drawn on the top of the other for the express purpose of showing that there is little or no difference between their motion in the raising of the valves. A great many ignorant engineers, who know very little more about the laying out of cams than the cams know about them, are continually calling for the sharp corners, saying, "we want something to open quick," &c. Now, we say, the corner has nothing to do with the commencement of the opening in any cam whatever, whether slide or puppet valve. Take the cut-off cam No. 11, for example, if you please, and you will see the first motion of the cam from the heel T to C; the cam frame then remains stationary while the cam travels from point C to E, because the distance is equal from centre to circumference. Now, at point C you see the cam with the corner on, and also with the corner off; or you may take a view of the other

OVERSIZED FOLDOUT

COLOR ILLUSTRATION

was removed after page(s) 194,
for in-house scanning

On 8-18 2000

point, G, if you please, at the nose of the cam, where the principle is the very same, and you will at once see that there is but little difference in either the shape or motion of the cam, but there is a material difference in the working of them. The cam with the round corners works more smooth and easy than the cam with sharp corners. The sharp cornered cam can only be used on board of steamboats or some large engine used for other purposes, where the motion is slow; and even then they make a great noise, like beating with a large trip hammer. The reason why sharp cornered cams cannot be used on small engines or locomotives running very fast, is because you cannot make anything that has a sharp corner work well; the nearer round the more smooth and easy it will work.

We are not now to be understood as upholding eccentric cams as the best that could be used for our steamers, although on the eastern steamers they are generally used, where the steamers are much larger than ours and draw from 15 to 22 feet of water, with a full load. Now, for example, suppose the cam No. 11 to give 4 inches throw, and suppose this 4 inches throw to raise the lever one inch at the valve, now in rounding the corner of this cam you take a quarter of an inch off the points G and K at each corner of the nose; now this quarter of an inch of corner taken off, is but $\frac{1}{16}$ of 4 inches, or of the throw of the cam and the raising of the lever. Again, suppose the lever to raise one inch at the valve stem, this is but one-fourth of the throw of the cam, and makes it but $\frac{1}{64}$ part of an inch difference in the raise of the lever, and this is not at the point where the engine takes the steam, as a great many suppose who speak without thinking. Whatever is done or said, should be done understandingly and knowingly, and not at random. But now to the point again.

The cam No. 11, with one-fourth of an inch of the corner off for making it round, reduces the raise of the valve but $\frac{1}{64}$ part of an inch, and that not as the engine takes the steam, but at the point G, when the valve is about its highest point. Now let us look at this again; it is only a point, G, which is gradually cut off from F to G, and then runs out from G to H. Now this point G is no sooner reached than passed, and in our estimation is a mere matter of moonshine; and what we have been trying to impress on your minds is, that our cut-off and exhaust cams would work much better and smoother with the corners off. We agree with John Currey, engine builder, Louisville, Ky. (having been his foreman for some time), in this respect, and we would say for the information of those interested, that almost any one knowing anything about cams, may lay out a cam with sharp corners, but it is not every one that can lay out a cam with the corners off; this requires more skill and is more difficult to do than the one with sharp corners, as will be seen laid down in the puppet valve cut-off cam, No. 11; the sharp cornered cam is first laid out and then the four centres are got, and the four corners O, K, G and C are cut off, and from these four small centres you strike a smaller circle on the outside of the other lines, already struck from the sharp corners, which accounts for the double lines; or in other words, you have a sharp cornered cam and a round cornered cam, one drawn on the top of the other, and you will observe that they are as near alike as possible, and not that difference that would appear to those who have not examined the matter. But still we wish you to remember that the round cornered cam is the smoothest and best working cam.

When I was foreman for Benton & Walker, New Albany, Ind., we had on hands building a large number of engines for steamers, for running on the lower trade, and it was quite a common thing in those days for captains to show off, while at the same time they fancied they would get a better job by having their engineer dictate how such and such parts of the work should be done. These men were often employed some months before the boat was ready for running, at $100 per month, merely for the purpose of walking round and occasionally seeing to matters. While fitting out the engine for one of these boats—a five boiler boat—we proposed to the engineer to make his cam with round corners, to which he would not listen, but said hastily, "O no, O no; I want something to open quick! Give me something to open quick!" as if the round corner cam would not answer at all. We made mention of the circumstance to Mr. Dally, formerly engineer of the old *Red Rover*, an eight boiler boat built at Pittsburgh some eighteen years ago, and who at this time was getting another larger boat at New Albany, Ind., called the *John Randolph*, the engine having been built at Louisville, Ky., by John Currey; and knowing Mr. Currey's opinion on this subject, we stated to Mr. Dally that we wanted the engineer to have his corners off, but that he would not listen to us, believing the cam with the sharp corners to be the best. But when Mr. Dally mentioned the matter, and reasoned with him, and fairly hooted at the idea, he consented at once to have them made with round corners. This same engineer was considered one of the very best of his day, and we believe that he could run an engine as well as any man, and yet he had to come to us while living at Louisville, to show him how to weigh steam, at the time so many explosions of our boats occurred, among them the *Moselle* and others. This was about the period when the inspection of boilers commenced, and he wished to know how to weigh steam, that he might be a match for the inspectors, who were about to examine his boilers, and also to know the amount of steam he was carrying.

No. 12 is a puppet valve cut-off cam, having sharp corners, with a wider nose than No. 11, and of course lets on more steam. See page 195.

OVERSIZED FOLDOUT

COLOR ILLUSTRATION

was removed after page(s) 198
for in-house scanning

On 8·18 2000

PUMPS.

HORIZONTAL FORCE PUMPS.

THE principle of force pumps is the same, whether horizontal or upright. The valves and the chambers are substantially the same thing, the only difference being that one has a horizontal barrel for the plunger to work in, while the other works in an upright barrel. This may be assigned as the reason why one is called horizontal and the other upright. The main object to be attained in using the horizontal force pumps, is the saving of labor and material to the builder of engines. It often, however, increases the labor of the engineer to keep them in order. The horizontal pump dispenses with the use of the pump stands and caps, the pendulum and pendulum shaft, the connecting link between the shoving-head and the pendulum, and the connecting rod from the arm to the plunger. This is no doubt the object of using them in general. In some places there may not be room for an upright force pump, in which case it becomes indispensably necessary to use the horizontal pump in its stead. The latter suits better for short stroke engines than they do for long ones, because they are more easily kept in line. When the brass in the shoving-jaws wears and settles down, it throws the end of the plunger hard upon the barrel of the force pump, and the end of the plunger begins to leak badly, by reason of this uneven wear; and the longer the plunger the worse it is in this respect. Three different times has the author known a horizontal plunger to be turned down on this account, when a larger one had afterward to be put in its place. More engines than one have had their plunger worn flat upon the point on account of the shoving-head sinking down on the slides by wearing. It is worthy to remark in this place, that when these pumps are put in line their centres should not be parallel at both ends with the centres of the cylinder. The centre of the line should be in the centre of the stuffing box, and on the other end the plunger ought barely to clear the bottom of the pump barrel, giving all the clearance on the top of the plunger. Then, when the jaws settle down on the slides by wearing, the end of the plunger will be found to run twice as long as it would otherwise do, before it rubs the top off the pump barrel, owing to the clearance all being on the top at the far end of the pump.

UPRIGHT FORCE PUMP.

Upright force pumps, in a general way, are easier to keep in order than horizontal ones; and usually, if put up true at first, and if on a good foundation, they will need no more lining while the engine lasts. Not so with the horizontal, it is continually getting out of line. The pump itself is stationary, but it is the plunger to which we allude, owing to the shoving-head sinking on the slide, caused by the wear of the brasses in the shoving-head jaws, without taking up the slack. If the brasses in the shoving-head were kept up by set screws this need not be the case, but this is seldom done.

UPRIGHT FORCE PUMPS WITH BORED CHAMBERS.

This pump was considerably used in the earlier years of steam. It is the same in principle with the upright pump last treated of, only differing in this, that instead of using a plunger, they use a piston head packed with hemp; and the two valves, one on each side of the pump barrel, are at the foot of the pump—and on this account are sometimes called foot valves.

RULES HOW TO FIND THE STROKE OF A PLUNGER BY FIGURES.

To find the stroke of a plunger by figures, it is necessary to multiply the stroke of the engine by the length of the pump-arm, and divide by the length of the pendulum from centre to centre, and the product will be the stroke of the plunger.

EXAMPLE.—You want to find the number of inches throw of a plunger. The engine is 5 feet stroke, the pendulum is 72 inches long, and the pump-arm is 16 inches from centre to centre. What number of inches stroke will the plunger have?

```
                 60 inches stroke of engine.
                 16 inches length of pump-arm.
                ----
                360
                60
                ----
Pendulum 72 inches)960(13⅓ inches stroke of plunger.
                72
                ----
                240
                216
                ----
               | 24 | 1
             24--------
               | 72 | 3
```

Persons not being acquainted with the above rule, generally took a strip the length of the pendulum, and the pump arms nailed across each other, and moved the long strip the length of the stroke of the engine, and in this way got the stroke of the plunger.

THE TRUE PRINCIPLE TO MAKE A FORCE PUMP.

Force pumps, having shallow valve chambers, as you will see in the force pump C, will work with low steam, when they will not work if the steam is high. The object of using the bridle D, is to prevent the valve from tipping over, but when the steam is high it reacts on the side of the valve, and also on the top of the valve stem, and the pressure sideways on the valve produces such an amount of friction on the bridle and guide below, that it holds the valve fast, prevents it from falling, and hinders the pump from receiving its regular supply of water. Instead of using the bridle it would be better to bore the pump chambers out, and turn the valve caps, so that they will fit in the chambers easy, and have a large pin cast on the caps, as you will see on the draft of a perfect force pump E; in this pin there is a hole drilled out, say one quarter of an inch larger than the top valve stem, allowing the valve to raise up one-fourth of the diameter. This plan is much better than the bridle, as the back reaction from the boiler comes on the pin on the valve chamber cap, and not on the valve stem, thus leaving the valve at perfect liberty to fall free and easy.

COLD WATER PUMPS.

There is an endless variety of ways for raising water, but there is no plan which can be invented to do it which will require less power than the weight of the water to be raised, adding the additional friction of the pump to that weight.

For raising water there have been invented the screw, working in an outside barrel; a variety of patents; rotary pumps of various kinds; Mixwell's patent double chamber pump with an air vessel; Warner's patent forcing and suction pump, &c. The kind of pumps we generally use are the single and double, and the common well or lift pump, with two boxes, the upper and the lower box. This pump can raise water from 26 to 28 feet high. (See draft of a pump marked I.)

It is said that the pressure of the atmosphere will

sustain a perpendicular column of water 32 to 34 feet in height.

FORCE PUMPS.

The barrel of this pump is generally made of cast iron, bored out true, in which a piston head works with hemp packing, screwed up with a follower, by one nut that screws it down, being attached to the pump rod. This pump has one valve on the inside of the pump chamber, which is the receiving and discharging valve, and sits on a cast iron pipe on one side of the pump, and is screwed together; the valve chamber has another branch pipe upon it for the purpose of carrying off the water as it may be discharged from the pump.

This pump works as well as any one can, when in working order; but in case anything should be the matter with the valve on the inside, the engine would be required to stop for the purpose of taking out the plunger before access can be had to the valve, to ascertain what the matter is. (See the draft of pump marked H.)

SUPERIOR FORCE PUMPS.

The barrel of this pump is similar to the last one about which we have been speaking, but the valves are both on the outside of the chamber, just as they were on the cold water force pumps. The fact of the valves being thus placed on the outside is what gives it superiority over any other pump that can be used, because access to the valves can be had at any time without stopping the engine, and you can get through your examination in less than one-fourth the time it could be done on former pumps. (See pump on draft marked R.)

SUPERIOR FORCE PUMP WITH AIR VESSELS.

This pump is the same in all respects as the above, only with the addition of an air vessel, which is of great benefit toward relieving the pump from surging, where the water has to be thrown to a considerable height above the pump, as it gives elasticity to the non-elastic fluid, thereby enabling the pump to work more easily and smoothly, while at the same time throwing a more regular and uniform stream of water. (See plate S.)

The air vessel B on the left side of the cold water pump C, is a late improvement. On locomotive engines they frequently use two air vessels close to each valve chamber. One object of using them here is, it prevents the valves from beating hard on the caps, and also causes them to bed easier into their seat, &c. Sometimes the valve chamber caps are converted into air vessels; when this is the case it will be necessary to have a bridle in the same to hold the valve to its place. The air vessel B should not be far from the receiving valve; if the pipe should be very long, it might be from 3 to 5 feet off, similar to what you see in the draft B, on page 206. I have been informed that there was an experiment of this kind tried with a pump that had been in use some time before, and did not work very well, but after putting in an another air vessel B, it gave entire satisfaction by throwing nearly double the amount of water that it did before. The flow of water up into the pipe was more easy, regular and uniform, owing to the partial vacuum in the air vessel. As soon as the plunger was up and about to descend, the water would cease flowing into the pump, and run up into the air vessel until the pressure within and without was equal, and the moment the plunger would commence to ascend it would first draw the water out of the air vessel and then up through the pipe.

The object of using the two air vessels A and B, is to dispense with the surging both in receiving and discharging the water. In the air vessel B the air is partially exhausted, which causes a more constant flow into the pipe; and in the air vessel A the air is compressed, and produces a more regular discharge than would be without, and it is easier on the pump and valves in the same proportion that the stream is more regular and uniform.

CAUSE OF FORCE PUMPS AND CHECK VALVES SURGING, &c.

One general cause of force pumps and check valve chambers surging, and very often breaking pendulum shafts, pendulums, pump arms, and bursting the supply pipes that lead from the force pump to the boiler, is that the valve chambers are made entirely too small to allow room for a valve seat large enough in the opening to let water pass through freely. The water being a non-elastic fluid, the opening should not be cramped.

OVERSIZED FOLDOUT

was removed after page(s) 206
for in-house scanning

On 8·18 2000

When foreman at New Albany, I was called upon to make a new pendulum shaft for the large double flued seven boiler steamer *Mississippi*. This boat when coming round a certain bend in the river, could be heard barking at a distance of ten miles. She had frequently broken her pump shaft. I was asked the cause of its surging. I could not say much about it, as I had never been on the boat; we talked the matter over about using an air vessel, &c., and dropped the subject by making a new shaft. We did nothing to remedy the cause of the surging.

The plunger was about 6 inches diameter, and the shaft 5 inches. I was asked the cause of breaking so many shafts, &c., and after talking awhile about using air vessels to relieve the same, put in a heavier shaft. When a boat is lying at the wharf, the water frequently gets low in the boilers on account of blowing off steam, and sometimes the engine is run very fast, for the express purpose of pumping up water into the boilers; sometimes they give the pump a full head of water, and the openings in the valve seats are entirely too small. All these are the causes of so much breaking. Besides in those days the engines were mostly single, and the boats had two water wheels and two main shafts, so as to ship and unship, and as there were no doctors in use then, they would frequently have steam at its highest, and when forcing the water, a non-elastic fluid, into the boiler against a head of high steam, and the engine running very fast, there is a strong reaction, more especially when it is retarded by short elbows in the pipes. This will account for surging, breaking, beating out the valves, &c.

Any one knows where there is surging in the pump, and kicking in the pipes, that something is not right; you are doing violence to the machinery. The general fault is, the openings in the valve seats are seldom more than one half large enough. This is the reason why the valves and seats wear and cut out so fast. The top stem beds against the valve cap, and thus bed and hammer the valves into the seats until the bearing on the valve seat is twice as large as it should be.

To sum up: the various causes for surging are as follows: Too fast or quick motion—high steam—small openings—short elbows, and unnecessarily large plungers. A pump working slow is not likely to surge if every thing is right.

At Shoenberger's rolling mill they had five large double flued boilers, 24 inch cylinder, 6 feet stroke, working a plunger 8 inches diameter, and the engine was run very fast. I had seen the same pump years before, but never made any particular remarks or inquiries about it. As I was walking around one day, I saw they had been cleaning out the boilers, and remarked to the engineer that they had a very large plunger; he said they had, and observed that they had it reduced down to 7 inches diameter, as it kept constantly surging and bursting the copper supply pipe leading from the force pump to the boilers. The present copper pipe was 4 inches in diameter. He told me they ascribed the bursting of the pipe to the copper not being good. I told him almost at the first glance, that the check valve chamber was too small, being only 4 inches clear in the valve seat, and about one-third of the opening was closed up with the bridle; he said one of the coppersmiths told him the same thing, that it was too small. There were 50 square inches in the 8 inch plunger, and $12\frac{1}{2}$ square inches in the opening of the seat, now fully one-third of this must be taken out for the bridle in the seat, and there are only 8 square inches left in the seat, and more than six times this in the plunger working very fast, with high steam.

INOPERATIVE FEED PUMPS.

"Having from time to time seen correspondence upon engineering and mechanical subjects in the *Scientific American*, I take the liberty to forward you my experience with a feed pump to a steam boiler, hoping that it (the experience, not the boiler) might prove serviceable to your readers. In March last the water in one of our cylinder boilers kept getting lower and lower until they ceased to be safe to work. The difficulty was an imperfect operation of the feed pump: the plunger was well packed and the valves apparently in good order; the water was clean and there seemed to be no reason why the pump should not work. Several times the engine was started, but to no purpose, as the pump still refused duty. After much delay, I found on examining the spindle of the feed valve (the seat of this valve had a bridge across it on the bottom, in which a stem on the valve worked to guide it up and down) that it was bright on the end, as if worn. On looking in the valve chamber the source of the difficulty was plainly traced, as the stem rested on the bottom of the chamber and kept the valve off its seat. The valve seat must have worked down, I think, in some way, as the pump had always operated well before. Of course, when I filed "clearance" on the stem there was no further trouble. Hoping that this may be of service to your readers, I send it for your journal." J. H. R.

I would add to the above (from the *Scientific American*) that if the valve seat had been well put in at the first, and firmly bedded on the bottom of the valve chamber, the valve seat could never have worked down as it was said to have done, but I have frequently heard and known of pumps giving out from the same cause. This is owing to the valve stem below being left too long, and not having sufficient clearance left for the wear, it beds and sets down the valve in the seat, and also owing to the small openings in the valve seat, which bring the valve down on the seat hard as though it had beeu struck with a sledge hammer, and thus the valve settles down in the seat, and not the seat in the chamber. I have often seen worn out valves and seats where the fillet, or boss, underneath the valve and around the valve stem, had come in contact with the bridle, owing to the wear of both the seat and the valve, and this prevented the pump from working, in the same proportion that they were brass bound. The other force pump that we have alluded to was inoperative also from another cause: a lead ball was found in the bend of the pipe as they were taking it off to put in a new pump, when they found out the difficulty. It was said this pump was bewitched, owing to the trouble they had with it before making the discovery.

Other pumps have refused to work, on account of the valve stem fitting too tight in the bridle of the valve seat, and to the expansion of the valve stem, with the heat; so that I knew in one instance where it required hard pulling with a pair of tongs to get the valve out of the seat to file the stem smaller. Others have been bound with sand coming in with the water, and others I believe have given out owing to the packing yarn having been drawn into the pump either from the cylinder or from the packing around the stuffing box of the plunger, which being too small to fill the collar in the force pump cuts out the packing. More could be said, but let this suffice for the present.

COLD WATER PUMPS.

Cold water pumps have sometimes been a great annoyance and expense on account of leaks in the pipes, which have frequently been very hard to find out. I recollect of a pump that gave out once, and after they did all they could with it to get it to work, they gave it up and sent for me. I discovered underneath the pipe in the elbow, leading from the pump over the wall down into the well, a leak, which was caused by the shaking of the pump moving the pipe on the sharp corner of the wall, and which wore the pipe through, which was the cause of its giving out.

I know another instance where they had from one to two hundred feet of pipe leading down to the river; the pump gave out, they dug up part of the pipe and put in new pipe, and it cost them between one and two hundred dollars, including the lost time, and after all their labor and expense was in vain, for when they found out the leak, it was in the elbow of the pipe underneath where it was fastened to the pump.

It has been customary in using lead pipe, to widen the lead out, and turn a flange on it with a round nose hammer. The flange is very thin, and liable to be galled in turning it over, and cause it to give out, especially if the pipe should vibrate on the working. The better plan is to have a brass flange cast with a small pipe 2 or 3 inches long, and slip it on the outside of the pipe and solder it on. This makes a good substantial job. A copper pipe and flange would answer the same purpose.

TREACHEROUS FORCE PUMP.

On board the steamer *Comet*, which ran in the Mobile trade, they were occasionally annoyed with their force pump, and it frequently gave out all at once, when they would take off the caps and remove the valves, but finding nothing wrong, the caps and valves would be again returned to their places, and the engine started. The pump would work a day or two very well, and at other times not more than a couple of hours, and then give out, often when most needed. The engineer left the boat, and another took his place, with whom I was well acquainted, and he had the same trouble with the pump as the former engineer. They had ordered another to be made in Mobile, and got along with the old one as well as they could until a new one was made. In the meantime it gave out again, and the captain became so enraged on account of the loss of time, dangers, &c., that he was exposed to, that he determined to never run the boat again with that pump; he said he would burn

OVERSIZED FOLDOUT

COLOR ILLUSTRATION

was removed after page(s) 212
for in-house scanning

On 8·18 2000

the boat up first. They frequently said the pump was bewitched.

When finished, the new pump was brought on board; and as soon as they took off the pipes, to take out the old pump, there rolled out of the elbow of the receiving pipe on to the deck, a round lead ball 1¼ inches in diameter. The copper pipe was 2½ inches inside. After this they never had any more trouble. The engineer said the ball from some cause or other was occasionally drawn up, and got fast between the bridle and valve seat, or between the point of the stem and the inside of the same, and held the valve up so as to prevent it from working, but always when they took off the cap to examine what was wrong, the ball would disappear by settling down in the elbow, and thus they were for a long while puzzled to find out what was the matter, till they were taking off the pipes.

Copper pipes have sometimes been choked on account of the rosin not being entirely melted out. It would be a good plan to try the copper pipes if they are clear, by pouring water through them before putting them on. Sometimes the openings are almost shut up by the gum.

CONSTRUCTION OF A FORCE PUMP.

We have laid down another draft of a force pump with a valve seat and chambers, as they should be made. The valve chambers should be deep enough to allow of a good depth of valve seat and a thick valve. The top of the valve, when up at a full opening, should never be allowed to come above the bottom of the opening in the pipe, but should always be a little lower on the top of the valve than the opening in the pipe, say from ¼ inch to an inch lower, according to the difference in the sizes of pumps. The reaction of water from the boilers upon valves thus below the openings, will assist them to fall or close; as the reaction or pressure of the water from the boiler comes more directly upon the top of the valve, and hastens its fall. The valve F, in the pump E, is a model of a perfect pump. The top of the valve is below the opening in the pipe G, whilst the valve itself is up at a full opening. In this case, the reaction of water from the boiler passes over on the top of the valve (instead of striking on the side of the valve, as may be seen in the valve B in the force pump A,) and helps it to fall into its bed in the valve seat.

How high a valve should rise to make the opening around the circumference equal to the opening in the diameter of the valve.—This rule is very simple, and also very important that engineers should know it. It is equally useful to the builder of engines, to know how high his puppet valves should rise to give the same number of inches around the circumference of the valve seat itself. It is useful also to know how high the force pump, check valves, &c., should rise in order to give as much opening in the valve seat. The rule is this:

The valve should rise one-fourth the diameter of opening in valve seat, measuring it at the smallest place, just at the bottom of the bevel.

Example.—How high should a three inch valve rise, to give as much opening in the circumference as there is in the diameter?

OVERSIZED FOLDOUT

COLOR ILLUSTRATION

was removed after page(s) 214
for in-house scanning

On 8·18 2000

Divide by 4) 3 inches ($\frac{3}{4}$ inches rise.

$$\begin{array}{r} \\ \hline 0 \end{array}$$

And for a 4 inch valve—

Divide by 4) 4 (1 inch rise.

$$\begin{array}{r} 1 \\ \hline 1 \end{array}$$

Table of inches of valves to give the same opening in the circumference that there is in the diameter of the valve:

Diameter of Valves.			Inches rise.	
Divide	by 4)	3	$\frac{3}{4}$	inch.
"	"	$3\frac{1}{4}$	$\frac{13}{16}$	"
"	"	$3\frac{1}{2}$	$\frac{7}{8}$	"
"	"	$3\frac{3}{4}$	$\frac{15}{16}$	"
"	"	4	1	"
"	"	$4\frac{1}{4}$	$1\frac{1}{16}$	"
"	"	$4\frac{1}{2}$	$1\frac{1}{8}$	"
"	"	$4\frac{3}{4}$	$1\frac{3}{16}$	"
"	"	5	$1\frac{1}{4}$	"
"	"	$5\frac{1}{2}$	$1\frac{3}{8}$	"
"	"	6	$1\frac{1}{2}$	"
"	"	$6\frac{1}{2}$	$1\frac{5}{8}$	"
"	"	7	$1\frac{3}{4}$	"
"	"	8	2	"

DEFECT IN FORCE PUMPS MADE IN EARLY YEARS.

Very many of the valve seat chambers in force pumps, used in the early days of steam, were made entirely too shallow. We have seen the top of the valve seats in force pumps, and check valve chambers, about level with the opening in the bottom of the pipe leading from the valve chamber to the force pump, on the one side of it, and on the other side of the pump from the valve chamber to the discharge pipe, to which the pipe is attached that feeds the boilers with water. In some instances the tops of the valve seats were higher than this, in which case the valve stood the thickness of itself above the top of the valve seat. It is no wonder that force pumps thus constructed, could not be depended upon at all times to throw a regular supply of water into the boilers.

In the first place, the valve when bedded in its seat stands above the opening in the pipe; and when raised by the plunger, for the purpose of letting the water pass through into the boilers, the valve being above the opening, it is thrown over on its side by the pressure or reaction back from the boilers, and sometimes remains in this position without falling; and of course, while in this situation, it will throw no water. By frequent tapping with a hammer, the valve may be caused to fall into its seat; it may then work a while; but, after a short time, when the steam becomes a little higher, the pressure on the side of the valve will be greater, and the friction so strong that the valve will not fall, when of course the pump cannot work.

We believe the reason why many force pumps refuse to do their part is because they were not properly designed by their constructors. We have seen and heard of engineers frequently throwing cold water on their force pumps when the engines were running, in order to start them to work when they had quit throwing;

and they would beat the cap of the force pump very frequently with a hammer, for the same purpose. Now we ask what sense there would be in beating upon the cap of a force pump with a hammer, if it were not to bed the valve in its seat, which they must suppose to be up? If it be up, let them ask themselves the cause, and they will find it to be just exactly as we have described it above, viz. that the valve chambers were made too shallow to allow the valve seat to sink a proper depth below the opening of the pipe in the valve chamber.

We do not believe the cause to be what many engineers have stated: "that the water was too hot, and that the force pump was working steam," &c.; but one thing is certain, the pumps frequently refuse to work, and of course, some of our engineers often are put to their wits' end to find out what is the matter. If a bystander were to ask them the trouble, they would feel very strange if they could not answer him. And they (no doubt not knowing the real cause) would think it was occasioned by the water in the force pumps being too hot when received from the heater; but the true reason of the pump becoming too hot, was owing to the valve being up on the discharge side of the force pump next to the boilers. Suppose there was but a little leak on the opposite valve, between the valve and the seat, or between the valve seat and the valve chamber, owing to the lead having partially oxydized or wasted away; in this case the hot water would come back from the boiler through the pump into the heater; this would make the pump as hot as steam could make it.

We have laid down a draft of force pumps with shallow valve chambers, showing how the action of the water operates on the valve, by pressing it over to the one side, as may be seen in the valve B, in the draft of the force pump marked A, page 214.

But perhaps some may suggest the idea of putting a bridle on top of the valve stem, in order to keep it in its place, and from tipping over on one side. They can see the top bridle D in the force pump marked C; but this bridle will not answer the purpose. The reactive pressure being on one side of the valve, the friction becomes so great as to prevent the valve from falling. Engines running very slow might give the valve time to settle and fall, while others would not, on account of the increased speed of their engine. There should be no friction of any kind whatever, to retard these valves from falling in the bridles or guards. Valve stems should fit easy.

HOW TO CUT THE LEATHER FOR A PUMP BOX.

To cut a leather out to fit a pump box, it must be cut circular; aud in order to get the small diameter, it is necessary to continue the flare of the pump box until it meets in the centre, and this will give the distance for the inside circle; and the outside circle will then be as much larger as it is intended the depth of the leather of the pump box should be. A box and leather may be seen laid down in draft: A is the shape of the leather; B is the pump box, and C is the centre. It is upon this principle that strips for laying out boiler iron are made, owing to rings being smaller at one end than they are at the other. The difference of the diameter of boiler

OVERSIZED FOLDOUT

COLOR ILLUSTRATION

was removed after page(s) 218
for in-house scanning

On 8-18 2000

rings at each end, is equal to the difference of the boiler iron; and the strips for laying out the boilers must be laid out accordingly.

BEST KIND OF VALVE SEATS FOR FORCE PUMPS.

The best kind of valve seats that can be used for force pumps, check valves, &c., are made of brass. Brass valve seats stand the water better than any thing else that has been tried; iron seats soon rust out, and wear away much faster than brass.

We have seen another species of valve seats used as a substitute for brass; it was made of cast iron, and in the inside of this valve seat there was a recess turned out about $\frac{3}{8}$ of an inch square, to receive a brass ring which was neatly turned to fit in this recess, which recess in the casting was a little larger at the bottom than at the top, so as to rivet the ring in so tight as to prevent it from coming out, as may be seen in the draft of the valve seat A. The brass ring B, after it was riveted tight into the valve, with a round faced chisel and hammer, was then put into the lathe and turned off. We have tried this plan, and find that it does not answer a good purpose on account of the brass ring becoming loose in the valve seat after using it a short time. We would therefore recommend brass valves and seats as the very best that can be made use of for force pumps, check valves, &c.

VARIOUS MODES OF GEARING PUMPS.

Some are worked upright with a pendulum and shaft, with the motion taken from the shoving head or end of the pitman by a wrist and link, others are worked in the same way horizontally, others are worked by cams, others by cranks and levers, others by belts. It is a good idea to gear pumps so as to run them slower than the engine. One great advantage of gearing hot and cold water pumps to run with belts is, that in case they should be frozen up in winter, as pumps frequently are, there would be no danger of them breaking when starting the engine; in case the ice was not thoroughly thawed the belt would slip and discover the difficulty. Some persons would not have their pumps to work in any other way for this reason, and it is a first rate idea on this account. There is a possibility of breaking a pump gearing when working with a belt, if the belt should be unnecessarily large; care should be taken that this should not be the case.

DANGEROUS CHECK VALVE CHAMBERS.

It was customary in early days to have on valve chambers of force pumps, and also on those attached to the boilers or boiler stand pipes, round caps and flanges, to fit the same, so as to take in at least four bolts; and a less number than this I do not consider very safe, especially for ocean and war steamers. There should be six bolts, made of Juniata iron, in each cap, so that if one or two bolts should break in tightening the cap, there would be no risk in running with the rest. Force pumps, valve chambers and check valves attached to the boilers or boiler stand pipes, are very dangerous; for instance, suppose the check valve chamber attached to a number of boilers, and it has but two lugs, and you have a round lead or gum gasket under the cap. In case it should spring a leak, as they often do, and you commence to screw it up hard, and you should break a lug off the valve chamber or the cap, owing to the leverage the bolt in the lug has outside of the lead gasket, the boilers would be immediately emptied, and under certain circumstances numbers might be scalded to death, and there is no knowing what damage might be done to the boat; especially if coming over rapids, it might prove the loss of the boat; if engaged in a battle, it might be the cause of a defeat; and if caught in a storm, it might prove to be the loss of the vessel and all on board. If valve chamber caps with only two ears and but two bolts are used, I prefer lead gaskets made the full size, of oblong cap, so that there will be less risk and danger of breaking the ears of the valve chambers or caps. I would add, that once when I had charge of an engine on a boat, we had steam up and about putting out, a friend of mine, an engineer on board, seeing the valve chamber cap of the force pump leak a little, took the liberty to tighten it without leave from me, and broke one of the lugs off the pump. I made some shift and soon got it in working order. My object for commenting so much on this subject is to show, first, that all such valve chambers, having but two ears and bolts are actually very dangerous. Always when I am tightening up such caps with a head of steam on, I go very cautiously about it, hammering lightly on the cap, and screwing gently on the bolts, knowing very well what the result would be in case of a break. It has now become the custom here as well as almost every where else to stint the work and shave every thing about an engine as much as it will bear, and sometimes more, so that where the engine builder makes one dollar in this way, the purchaser very often loses one hundred by detention of the boat, including repairs, expenses of the hands, &c.

ACCIDENTS.

A SAWYER named Willson, employed in a mill at East Williamsport, on the Monongahela river, some time ago attempted, in the absence of the engineer, to "tramp the balance wheel over the centre." Having a full head of steam on at the time, the wheel made a rapid revolution, and one of the arms striking him on the head, broke his neck, from the effects of which he died the next morning. I would add that it is dangerous for engineers to get on the fly wheel, to turn it over the dead centre with the steam on, or with a throttle valve which leaks, although it may be closed, for although the engineer knows what he is doing, yet he is very likely to slip when straining to lift the fly wheel over the centre, every thing around being perfectly saturated with grease. And if it is dangerous for the engineer, how much more so for one who understands little or nothing about an engine, and especially in the absence of any person who might otherwise be able to render assistance in case of an accident.

I recollect in the early days of steamboating, of hearing of a man who went to work on the water wheel, and whilst at work the engine was started, and the coupling by some means happened to be on the water wheel shaft at the time, and it split his head. I would suppose from the nature of the accident that he was standing at the side of the wheel shifting the buckets.

Some time after this on board the steamer *Lagrange*, there was a carpenter at work on the water wheel, and the engine was started, and he was killed instantly. Boats in these days had two main and two water wheel shafts, and the couplings were very greasy and loose, and if the boat should happen to be listed considerably, there would be great danger of them sliding on from their own weight.

All such steamers should have at least one strong stirrup attached to an eye bolt made fast in the heavy timber, to slip on the water wheel arm to hold it secure when any one is on the wheel at work. This stirrup is indispensably necessary on another account, in case of a strong current and running drift, as in time of high water. I have been working on the water wheels many a time at the arms, braces, &c., when drift would run against the wheel and keep it moving round for some time; in such cases I have held on to the arms and walked round on the shaft inside of the buckets until it would stop. I confess this was a dangerous operation and should not have been done. Sometimes we would have a man to hold the wheel from turning with the current, drift or ice, &c., until we were done.

There was an account in the newspaper, of a man having his head blown off by standing before the cylinder head of a locomotive engine. This is a dangerous place to stand, especially if the engine is old, as the nuts and threads from constant use and wear become slack, and in some cases almost stripped. This caution is particularly important when letting on high steam suddenly, especially if the load is heavy and the grade steep.

A man was walking on a large beam of timber to do some work, and whilst passing above the fly wheel, which was running at a rapid speed, he fell on it and was killed. It is likely that he became giddy by looking down at the wheel in rapid motion and lost his balance.

Many persons have been killed by standing before large grindstones making rapid revolutions, which have burst into fragments. No doubt one reason of bursting so frequently, is they were wedged up tight with dry wood, and then filled in with iron wedges, and water running constantly on the stone swells the wood, and this with the rapid motion would readily burst it. Care should be taken not to run a large stone with rapid motion; as the speed increases, the disproportion between the centripetal and centrifugal forces diminishes.* It would be possible to make a circular plate of cast iron, which possesses far more adhesive power than stone, revolve at such a rate that it would fly off in pieces. To prevent this result in grindstones, plates with screws are sometimes fastened to them. In this way they can be set quicker and truer. Still the fact mentioned shows this

* For the sake of common readers, we explain that the centripetal force is the attraction or power that holds the stone together. The centrifugal force is the power communicated by rotary motion which tends to throw off any substance from the circumference. Put water on a grindstone, and by a slow motion it can be kept on it, increase the speed and it flies off. When this takes place the centrifugal force, or tendency to fly off, overcomes the centripetal force or tendency to remain. And what takes place with the water it is easy to see will take place with the stone itself, if the speed is sufficiently increased.

will not give entire protection against danger from high speed.

It should also be considered that in proportion to the increase of the size of the stone must be the reduction of the quickness of its revolution. The danger must be estimated not by the number of revolutions in a given time, but by the rapidity of the motion of the stone's circumference. Suppose two stones, one of 3 and the other of 6 feet diameter, are revolving at the same rate. The circumference of the latter will move with double the speed of that of the former. If then the small stone is at its highest speed to be safe, the large one must fly to pieces.

Persons have been killed by being caught in gearing and belts. Great care should be taken, especially on the sides of two wheels running together, or on the side of the belt that runs down with the pulley; the one side draws in, and the other out, but there is danger on either side in case of being fastened to the gearing or belting. All persons about mills, factories, &c., should be careful not to wear long tail coats, large dresses, shawls, &c., as many persons in this way have lost there lives. I heard of a man working in an iron lathe, with a hand tool. The lathe was running very fast, and he had a handkerchief tied around his neck with long ends hanging down; while leaning over the lathe turning, the end or ends of the handkerchief were caught in the iron in the lathe. Immediately it began to wind up and drag him in, and no doubt would have killed him had it not been for some person at hand who unshipped the lathe. This will also apply to wood turners.

Care should be taken by the persons turning to have

their pieces well centered, so that they will not fly out of the lathe, a thing which frequently happens and is very dangerous, nor run from the centre whilst turning. To avoid this it is customary with a great many to first centre the piece true on the lathe, then take it out and drill a small hole in each end from $\frac{3}{8}$ to $\frac{5}{8}$ of an inch deep, and from $\frac{1}{8}$ to $\frac{1}{4}$ of an inch in diameter, depending on the size of the piece you are turning. The centre of the lathe then keeps to the centre of the small hole. The centre of the lathe always keeps drawing to the centre of the small hole, whereas when there is no hole drilled, the centre point being solid it cannot work its way into the piece you are turning, especially if it is very heavy. Its own weight, and the pressure on the point from the tool cutting it, keeps shifting it from side to side, and enlarging in this way the centre so that it is impossible to turn it true. I recollect one of the best workmen in Pittsburgh, when turning small spindles for cotton machinery, say from $\frac{1}{4}$ to $\frac{3}{8}$ diameter, had a lathe on purpose to drill every centre before turning.

CAUTION TO BOILER MAKERS AND ENGINEERS.

Boiler and engine makers should never allow any one to go inside a boiler, either for the purpose of holding on to the rivet heads whilst building the boiler or to clean it out, who is so large that he has to be squeezed through the man-hole. It is exceedingly dangerous. An instance of this happened at our boiler yard when we were building a locomotive boiler; a boy had to be forced through the man-hole in the steam dome to hold on to the rivets while fastening the steam dome to the boiler. When this was done he could not get out, having from some cause swelled while in. The boss boiler maker, James Booher, told me of the matter and asked me what to do; I told him to break the boiler head, which fortunately was made of cast iron; they cut the rivets out of the head and then broke it. If the head had been wrought iron, it would have been more dangerous, as it could not have been broken, but would have to be cut out, and whilst doing this there would be danger of smothering.

Another instance of the same kind happened at our boiler yard. The father of this same boy went inside of a twenty-four inch boiler to hold on to the rivets whilst putting on the boiler head. When the head was put in and fastened, he could not get out, being too large for the man-hole. The rivets had to be cut off and the boiler head taken out to release him. A smaller man was afterward sent in and the head put in again.

A fireman on the river went into a double flued boiler to clean it out. Being in liquor at the time, he got his leg between the flues and could not get it out; in trying to get it out he irritated it so that it swelled. Help was sent in to assist in getting it out, but it could not be done. The engineer told me that he took in some wedges and drove in between the flues and sprung them apart, and then had to bruise the leg and flesh in order to pull it out. It was fortunate that it was in the middle of the boiler, for if it had been at either end it would not have been an easy matter to spring the flues without flattening and destroying them, so that they would have to be taken out and repaired.

The following is taken from a newspaper:—"On Saturday of week before last, as several men were cleaning out two boilers at the coal works of the Ravine coal company, in Pittston, some one turned on the steam and hot water from the other boilers, scalding the men so that the flesh dropped from their bones. Four have since died."

It is also dangerous standing before fly wheels running at very fast speed, as they frequently fly to pieces, sometimes going out through the house and at other times through the roof, &c.

It is also dangerous standing before boiler heads that have the man plates screwed fast on the outside, especially when the nuts become slack from wear. There have been instances I believe of their blowing off; I heard of one some time ago. However, outside plates are now mostly out of date, and the inside plates used in their stead.

There are many other ways by which persons may be injured by machinery. I mention these few to put the unwary and unthinking on their guard; persons running engines and handling machinery had need to be wide awake and constantly on their guard. Never go to sleep on duty.

When acting as foreman at New Albany, Ind., I heard it said in the shop in which I was at work, that there was a fireman on board of a certain steamer went into one of the boilers to clean it out, and they pumped up the boilers and put out in haste, and never missed the man until under way; as to the particulars, I never heard much, as it was rather a delicate matter to say much about. The engineer, however, was then hired at $100 per month, which was as good then as $250 or $300 per month now, for the purpose of superintending the building of a large steamer, with five boilers, 43 inches diameter, to run in the Mobile trade. By particular request I made him a draft of the engine, for which he paid me my own price when the work was done, never once asking what would be the price beforehand.

Another instance: I have known the man for many years, and he used to build engines in Pittsburgh, he told me it himself time and again. When on board of some new steamer building at Pittsburgh, he was at work in one of the boilers, whether he was putting in bolts or what else I can't say, but I do not suppose his work was such as made much noise, because he told he was shut up and the man plate was put in the boiler; he was at the front end, and one of the gauge cocks happening to be out, he whistled through the gauge cock hole, when some person who was on the deck of the boat heard him, immediately gave the alarm and the man plate was taken off and he came out. I have no doubt but what he may have told the same story to hundreds. His name was John Scott, engine builder, Pittsburgh. He was well known here at that time, which is upward of twenty years ago. I mention these facts to put engineers and others on their guard. Never close your boilers until you are sure there is nobody in, but take the same care of the lives of those under your charge as you would wish them to take of yours if you were under them.

MISCELLANEOUS.

VARIOUS CAUSES FOR ENGINES SURGING, LABORING, &c.

Engines frequently surge when coming over the dead centre, and often the engineers are puzzled to find out the cause. I will state some of the causes. This takes place when there is too little clearance between the piston head and the cylinder heads, and when the pitman brasses are worn; in such cases the piston head strikes on the fast cylinder head, and sometimes the brasses after wearing will not key up tight on the wrists, and require chipping in the centre, to give clearance for drawing them up as it wears; and in all such cases as this there will not only be beating on the wrists, at both ends of the slides, but the piston head will strike on one or both cylinder heads. Frequently the main shaft is very long, and not being large and stiff in proportion to its length, and having a heavy fly wheel, it springs and causes the fly wheel to wabble and the shaft to tremble. When this is the case an engine never can be made to run smooth and easy. Others have their main shaft made entirely too short, just barely room to get the cam, fly wheel, band, pulley, cog wheel or crank on the end of it. It is hard for such engines to work easy; the side boxes on the main shaft must be kept all the time very tight, for if there is the least clearance it throws the crank out of square and causes the pitman to spring, and this will be in proportion to the length or shortness of the shaft. A shaft 8 feet long will be thrown out of square on the wrist only one-half as much as one 4 feet, and one 16 feet only one-fourth as much as the 4 feet. The main shaft ought to be at least from three to four times the length of the stroke of the engine.

Where the points of the piston head bolts and nuts have been battered up by striking on the loose cylinder head, clearance may be given in different ways. First, by putting in a thicker lead gasket on the loose cylinder head. Sometimes where the head was thick enough we would drill holes a quarter or half inch in it, for the point of the bolts and nuts to work into. Sometimes we would countersink the follower $\frac{1}{4}$ or $\frac{1}{2}$ inch, to receive the nuts of the follower's bolts; sometimes we would turn a little off one or both cylinder heads, as would be necessary. Sometimes we would turn some off the piston head, and sometimes the follower, and make it shallower. Sometimes we would make the nuts thinner and cut a little off the points of the bolts. And lastly, if you were hard put to, you could shorten the stroke by putting a new wrist in the crank, and turning the wrist on two different centres. Say you wanted to shorten the stroke half an inch or more, set the centre of the wrist a quarter of an inch below the centre of the hole in which it goes, then be particular in putting the mortise on the wrist to have the low side of the wrist next to the crank.

For example: I have often seen the point of the bolts and nuts battered up by striking on the cylinder head, where the clearance was scant. Suppose there was a quarter of an inch false motion at each end of the pitman in the brasses, then the pitman would allow the piston head to travel ¼ of an inch each way farther than the crank would allow, if the false motion was taken out of the pitman brasses by chipping them off, giving them draft and putting in backing behind the brasses. It is also necessary that the side boxes for the main shaft of the engine be kept close to the journals. Sometimes the packing gets slack for want of proper attention, and the follower in such cases will beat back and forward every revolution. Sometimes the piston heads get loose on the rod and beats back and forward; this is not likely to happen when the work is done as it should be. I was on board of a new steamer on her first trip out from Pittsburgh, and she had not made more than two miles down the river till she had to land, and remain until we took off the cylinder head, and drew out the piston rod and head and found it to be loose on the rod. I suppose the keys had been driven up with a hand hammer instead of a sledge. The cylinder was 16 inches diameter, 6 feet stroke; built at our shop. This was the fault of both the boss and the man who put it on: the boss first, for trusting a man to do this particular kind of work with whom he was not acquainted, being a new hand; it was the fault of the man for undertaking to do a thing he did not understand, as it requires to be done in the best manner by the best workman. Another cause is, frequently the wrist gets loose in the crank and requires to be keyed or taken out and bushed. Sometimes the crank may become loose on the shaft, having been put on too slack at the first. Another grand cause is letting the steam into the cylinder too soon, before the crank comes over the centre; and just in proportion to the amount let in too soon, in the same proportion will be the surging. This is destructive to an engine, causing it to labor most unnaturally and drag, being hardly able to move. It is also a bad plan to let it on too late, as it is a waste of steam and power to fill a portion of the cylinder with steam, without producing any effect on the crank. This is, however, a less evil than the former.

Another cause is, when the water is carried too high in the boilers, it does not leave a sufficiency of room in the boilers to hold dry steam. And also the want of a steam drum. Another cause is when the steam pipes on the boilers are too small, causing the boilers to foam, and thereby priming or filling the cylinder with water. Another cause is neglect on the part of the engineer to keep the cylinder cocks sufficiently open at all times to let out the water made by the condensed steam. Another cause, which some engineers may be perplexed with for a long time, and others may not be able to find out at all, is the heater drum inside may have corroded, so as to leak a portion of the water into the cylinder, and produce serious consequences. They may also be injured by the frost, and in order to find this out it would be necessary to stop and make an examination. Another cause is taking the steam from the end of a steam pipe; this is sure to draw water, especially if it is flush in the boilers. Another cause is, when the cylinder is a shade tighter on one end than the other. It is almost impossible to get a true cylinder; as the end of the boring head comes out last, it is likely to be the tightest on account of the cutters having partially lost their keen edge for cutting.

Another cause, especially when rope and hemp packing were used, is the piston head being suffered to get down, and rub on the bottom of the cylinder, and grunt and scrape it. When I used this kind of packing, before screwing the follower up hard, I raised it up as far as I could by putting in a wedge or knife, and then screwed it up tight, as the wear is mostly to be on the bottom side of the horizontal cylinders and packing.

Another cause of surging is, the nuts on the piston head bolts may be too slack and work back, and oftentimes come off; this causes surging, and if there is not clearance for the nut something is sure to break some where. Much damage has been caused in this way. Hence the necessity of using false followers to prevent the nuts from turning. Another cause of engines running rough and jarring and shaking the building is lopsided and drunken fly wheels, by not being properly balanced. With such fly wheels it is impossible for an engine to run regular, smooth or easy.

For example: put a stick of timber in a lathe and centre it a little to one side, and it will be very apt to jump out of the lathe, and if you should manage to hold it in by hard screwing, it will shake everything about it, so that it is dangerous to be near it. For this reason, in making cast iron pulleys, it is customary to rivet pieces on the heavy sides for the purpose of making them balance as near as possible; and sometimes to make them run true they turn the inside of the pulley close up to the arms. There is another cause which is sometimes exceedingly difficult to find out, as it is in some cases not to be seen, but it tells the story of defective workmanship by constant beating produced by false motion in the same. I allude to those shaft heads and flanges and cranks that were generally used in early days on steamers, and also stationary engines. They were usually bolted together with six or eight bolts, with jogs on the shaft head, and flange or crank, let into each other, and unless these jogs are a close fit with a shade draft screwed up hard and tight, they will work loose and chew the bolts and keep getting worse and worse. Some to avoid the labor of fitting, have put in cast steel keys, but if they are fitted up right by a master workman they are better without keys. Another cause is, when the fly wheel flange which is bored out goes on the shaft rather easy, one key in such cases will not be sufficient to hold, where it might possibly do if the flange was drawn on to the shaft with screws and clamps similar to car wheels. These flanges are generally put on by hand, and sometimes driven up with a battering ram. When putting them on this way, I get the distance the back of the fly wheel flange comes from the cam flange on the main shaft, and I have it left $\frac{1}{16}$ or $\frac{1}{8}$ of an inch larger than the main body of the shaft, tapering the large diameter for one inch back, down to nothing on the small diameter, and then it would be advisable to file a little off the back or corner of the back side of the flange, and then drive the flange up tight from the outside, and there will be little danger of the wheel sliding on the shaft either way. The extra size of the diameter on one side and the keys on the other, when well fitted and driven up, will be likely to hold it to its place without shifting. We had a 12 feet fly wheel on our engine shaft. The body of the shaft was about 7 inches in diameter. The fly wheel flange was slipped on by hand; it worked very well for a little while at first, but it got to sliding on the shaft to one side, and cutting the joist above; we kept still sliding it back as it slipped over. It kept chawing the key and seat, it also cut the shaft smaller and bored the flange larger, until we put in a bush of sheet iron all round, nearly ⅛ of an inch. We would have taken it down long ago, rather than be annoyed with it as we wêre, but the segments wære not only bolted together, but riveted hard and fast, so that it was rather too much of a job to undertake. I would therefore, in conclusion, recommend the above plan, and insist on putting in good large keys and seats, for I tell you it takes good fitting and solid keying to hold the flange firmly on the shaft without yielding, when the engine is running and the fly wheel under full headway, and then the engine all of a sudden stopped and the motion reversed. This will tell whether the fitting up has been well done or not. Another cause is, when the main shafts are too short; if there should be any yield it is harder on the crank, wrist and pitman, causing them to spring. Another cause is, when the shaft, pillar block and bed plates are made rather light; and lastly, when the shafts are made too long they will be liable to spring, especially if there is a heavy fly wheel in the centre, and not well balanced.

Another cause of engines laboring is, that frequently in casting the side pipes for the cylinder, they are made too long and at other times too short, and in such cases the pipes are often used in this way by dressing off the flanges projecting on the outside, square with each other, whilst at the same time perhaps one-half or more of the opening in the cylinder nozzle at each end may be closed, and this no doubt has often been the reason why engines have failed to work up to their power.

Another cause of surging and clattering in pitmans, strap joints, &c., is when the brass boxes are too small for the straps. Another cause is, when the pitman timbers do not fill the straps sufficiently tight at each end would allow the straps to spring up back and forward every time the piston goes out on the lower centre. Another cause is, when the bottom and side brasses fit too loose in the pillar block, and in addition the journal on the shaft being turned too wide to make a good fit. When machinery is thus carelessly fitted up, it is impossible to have a quiet, smooth working engine.

Another cause of engines laboring and dragging very hard, is the metallic packing having been screwed up too tight. When we first used it in our shop we experimented on it, to see how tight it would bear to be screwed up so as not to leak, and at the same time work free and easy. I tightened it up and set the engine to run for a short time, and then I bedded up the follower, and then tightened the nuts by turning them one-eighth of a turn round, which would be but one 64th part of an inch, supposing 8 threads to the inch, and then set the engine running again, and it would run very well for an hour or two at the rate of from 80 to 100 revolutions per minute; and all of a sudden it would begin to slacken its speed down to 30, 20 and 10 revolutions per minute, and at other times it would stick and stop dead. And when we would have steam up at its highest, I have had long levers rigged so as to pry on the fly wheel arms, with as many men as I could get around it, and at the same I have stood by with a full head of steam and the throttle valve handle in my hand to watch the engine when it would move, so as to stop it in time that none would be hurt. Our object was to get the piston out of the cylinder, and ease it a little by either scraping or sand papering it a little on the high places where it rubbed or made its mark. The least scraping imaginable sometimes will be sufficient to allow it to work free and easy. I would say here, of two evils choose the least, which is that it is better for the piston head to be a little slack than too tight, for two or three reasons. First, it will do more work. I heard once on a boat where it was too tight, and bent the piston rod something like a hook. I have also heard of its having to be taken off a boat when running, owing to its sticking, and hemp or rope worked in its place; and but a few miles from here, I heard of a singular instance on a stationary engine, of its having stopped all of a sudden and breaking the engine crank square off. This was no doubt owing to the headway and weight of the fly wheel being suddenly checked. The best remedy when the piston head gets fast in this way, is to cool the cylinder down outside and inside with water, and take it out and scrape it as described above.

Some engineers may wonder how the piston head could run one or two hours and then stop all of a sudden. I will give my views on this subject. The piston may be screwed up a slight shade too tight, and yet the engine will run at a fair speed with high steam, but in a short time rnnning, the friction caused by screwing the packing too tight, causes it gradually to heat hotter than the steam, and expand until it gets tighter and tighter and stops all of a sudden, and in some cases bends the piston rod or breaks the crank, &c., owing to circumstances. Some will wonder how its sudden stopping would bend the piston rod on a boat engine. I will explain this: Suppose the piston were suddenly to stick in the cylinder when the boat is under full headway, the motion given to the water wheels by the headway of the boat is what causes the piston rod to bend up double. Just the same as the headway of the fly wheel breaking off the crank, and the same principle that caused the steamer *Pocahontas* to break off both her main shafts suddenly, and at the same time to cause a streak of blue fire to come out of the stuffing box of the piston rod toward the cabin. This was caused by a small key dropping out of the puppet head attached to the valve on the exhaust side of the engine when the boat was under full headway, and the steam in the cylinder on this account could not escape and was compressed so as to produce the fearful results already stated. I have heard it said after this accident the gib and key were introduced into the puppet heads, so that the key might be made fast with a pin or nail; whether this is so or not I cannot say. Some used split keys, and others keys with rings in, but neither of these would do for a finished job. You no doubt have frequently taken notice of a small stream of water running on the piston rod, it is said for the purpose of keeping the packing around the rod from burning, as it is said that the steam burns it. I admit it may in part be the cause. I have no doubt that one great cause of its burning is the friction of the piston rod moving fore and aft in the packing, which being sometimes screwed up very hard, is of itself sufficient to set it on fire; this with the hot steam makes it very easily burnt. I have seen blankets frequently burnt to a cinder which were lapped around the steam pipes to prevent the condensation of steam.

CYLINDERS OUT OF TRUE.

Unless the cylinder is tolerably true, it is impossible for an engine to run well, and there are fewer true cylinders than most persons would imagine. I have always contended that the end of the cylinder last bored would be a shade less than the other, for this reason, that the edge of the cutters will become blunt as they advance. Some have told me that they will not, but if they do not lose any of their edge in cutting 6 or 8 feet, they will not in 6 or 8000 feet. Now if the cutters by use get dull, then the end last bored will be a shade less than the first. I mentioned this to an engine builder, and he told me he had seen the end bored last the largest. The cause of this is, it is probable that the two centres on which the boring barrel works were not exactly opposite to each other, and this would account for it, the same way that you turn a piece of iron tapering in the lathe, by shifting the lathe head to one side. It is not to be expected that a cylinder could be bored out true, where both centres of the lathe heads were not true to each other nor parallel to the sheers. We then conclude that the end last bored is the smallest of the two ends of the cylinder, and should be made the packing end, for this reason: if your cylinder should be tight packed when you give it the steam, and it once starts, it works with the greatest ease; but if the other end should be the tight end and the piston head tight packed, the moment the engine starts it runs up like a wedge, and sticks and will not work unless the packing is slacked. There is also danger of bursting the cylinder if very high steam were used in starting. I believe it is a first rate plan to drawbore cylinders by grinding them a few days with a stone and sand and water, or by using a circular piece of lead cast in the cylinder for this purpose, with a long handle to pull it fore and aft, and polish it with emery and oil, and in this way the tight end might be made larger. We have frequently drawbored cylinders with stone and sand, and with lead, emery and oil, and find it to be a great improvement to the boring; it answers the same purpose in the cylinder that draw filing was used for on the piston rods, valve stems, &c., or in other words, it runs the grain the same way as the friction, which otherwise would be crossways when bored or turned. I never thought that the boring of cylinders horizontal was a good plan, for the following reasons: especially the first cut when boring out the cylinder, the boring head wallows round and round in the cylinder, crowded up with sand and borings, which grinds the edge of the cutters, and makes them dull sooner than they would do if kept clean, and on this account they are liable to heat, and it is sometimes force work getting them through the first cut. I have thought that a bellows at the one end when boring, to give a constant blast, would be a good thing to blow back the sand and dirt as soon as cut. But it appears to me the best principle to construct a boring mill, would be to have the cylinder stand on end, and commence boring from above, then the dirt and cuttings fall out as soon as made, and the cutters would in this way retain their edge much longer; and there is less danger of the chips and iron cuttings getting between the wood in the boring head and the cylinder, which would spring the shaft and cause the cylinder to be bored more or less out of truth, as it is liable to do and is done on the former plan.

I am well acquainted with a man who put up steam boat engines, who told me that he put up forty cylinders in one season, and not one of them was perfect, but a shade tighter at one end than the other; notwithstanding this, I suppose they were true enough to have run the engine alone without any packing in the piston head.

HOW TO PUT A TRUE WRIST IN A CROOKED HOLE.

It sometimes happens in shrinking cranks on shafts, that the crank may not be quite hot enough, or the hole in it may be a shade too tight, and from this or some other cause you may not get it on quite as far as you intended; and in hammering it on it sometimes happens to be driven a little harder on one side than the other, thus causing the hole to be out of true, and throwing the wrist out of square. I knew an instance of this kind. The wrist could never be kept cool, it was always heating, and required constant oiling and nursing like a sick child. I was told one of the causes was that the wrist was not exactly true with the shaft, for the reasons already stated. It could not be got off without a great deal of labor and expense, besides being materially injured. I said when hearing of it, that I could easily put a true wrist in a crooked hole, by turning it on two different centres. One way of doing this is, first, to fit the wrist into the crank, then turn the shaft round and chip four square points on the wrist, parallel with the journals on the main shaft, and then centre the wrist to suit these points, and turn the wrist from these centres, being careful to put the wrist in the crank right, as it would fit only one way.

BALANCE GOVERNOR VALVE.

You find on page 244 a draft of a balance governor valve and throttle chamber, all cast together. This plan answers very well for small engines. C is the balance valve in the governor chamber. There are three different kinds of valves in the draft, A, B and C. The valve A is the best of the three for regulating most engines, on account of having four mitre openings cut out around the circle, below the top of each plug or valve. B is a round plug, filling each opening in the valve chamber on top; the plug is tapered off a little below, which gives a gradual opening when the valve commences rising. This valve is similar to the valve A, answering the same purpose and is easier made.

OVERSIZED FOLDOUT

COLOR ILLUSTRATION

was removed after page(s) 244
for in-house scanning

On 8·18 2000

The valve C is the same as the common puppet valve, having four wings below each valve to keep it from getting out of its place. This valve is superior to the others for rolling mills, &c., on account of its letting the steam on to the engine more suddenly than either of the other two.

TABLE OF MECHANICAL MOVEMENTS.

The movements illustrated on this page are for the conversion of circular motion into rectilinear motion.

Fig. 89. An eccentric generally used on the crank shaft for communicating the reciprocating rectilinear motion to the valves of steam engines, and sometimes used for pumping.

Fig. 90. A modification of the above; an elongated yoke being substituted for the circular strap, to obviate the necessity for any vibrating motion of the rod which works in fixed guides.

Fig. 91. Triangular eccentric, giving an intermittent reciprocating rectilinear motion, used in France for the valve motion of steam engines.

Fig. 92. Ordinary crank motion.

Fig. 93. Crank motion, with the crank-wrist working in a slotted yoke, thereby dispensing with the oscillating connecting-rod or pitman.

Fig. 94. Two circular plates revolving on the same centre. In one a spiral groove is cut; in the other a series of slots radiating from the centre. On turning one of these plates around its centre, the bolt shown near the bottom of the figure, and which passes through the spiral groove and radial slots, is caused to move toward or from the centre of the plates.

Fig. 95. On rotating the upright shaft, reciprocating rectilinear motion is imparted by the oblique disk to the upright rod resting upon its surface.

Fig. 96. A heart cam. Uniform traversing motion is imparted to the horizontal bar by the rotation of the heart-shaped cam. The dotted lines show the mode of striking out the curve of the cam. The length of traverse is divided into any number of parts; and from the centre a series of concentric circles are described through these points. The outside circle is then divided into double the number of these divisions, and lines drawn to the centre. The curve is then drawn through the intersections of the concentric circles and the radiating lines.

Fig. 97. This is a heart cam similar to Fig. 96, except that it is grooved.

Fig. 98. Irregular vibrating motion is produced by the rotation of the circular disk, in which is fixed a pin working in an endless groove cut in the vibrating arm.

Fig. 99. Spiral guide attached to the face of a disk; used for the feed motion of a drilling machine.

Fig. 100. Quick return motion, applicable to shaping machines.

Fig. 101. Rectilinear motion of horizontal bar, by means of vibrating slotted bar hung from the top.

Fig. 102. Common bolt and nut; rectilinear motion from circular motion.

OVERSIZED FOLDOUT

COLOR ILLUSTRATION

was removed after page(s) 246
for in-house scanning

On 8.18 2000

ENGINEERING TRICK.

When in Louisville, a shopmate of mine told me that when he was running engineer on the river, and standing his watch, he would alter the cam rod before the other engineer came on watch; this he did for the purpose of making better time than his partner, and of course when he came on he would set it right again, to let them see how much better he could run the engine.

CAUTION TO DISTILLERS OF OIL.

Persons having charge of oil stills about refineries, should be very particular in the winter to see that the water is drained off from the different pipes, tanks, and all other vessels about the premises that are liable to freeze, and do damage, when standing a few days, especially between Saturday and Monday. There was an oil refinery on the bank of the Allegheny river, near the Arsenal. After standing two days and two nights in extreme cold weather, one of the hands kindled fire under the oil still, and kept firing up for about the space of six hours, when the man-plate blew off the top of the still about 50 feet high in the air, and the burning oil flew up it was said about 200 feet high. The still held about 30 barrels, and it rained down the burning oil in large quantities. Two men that were standing alongside of the oil still were burnt to a crisp. This accident was caused from neglect of duty, for want of letting the water out of the low part of the pipe, in the crooked elbow that leads from the oil still to the condenser, which was filled with water and froze solid, and for want of vent, there was no other remedy but an explosion. The building was set on fire and partially destroyed. The boiler, breeching and chimney, with other things, were scattered. I mention this fact to show the necessity of all oil refineries having a set screw, or a small cock, which is far better, in the lowest part of the pipe, for the purpose of draining the water off the pipe, and keeping the passage clear in the winter season. And it would be a first rate plan, to have a safety valve on top of the still to guard against accidents of any kind. The pipe is also liable to be filled up sometimes with the dregs of the oil, &c.

RULES FOR SQUARING AND LINING OF SHAFTS.

RULE 1.—For squaring and lining of shafts, as used upon our steamers in early years, with one cylinder and four shafts—two main and two water wheel shafts. First—stretch a line through the centre of the cylinder timbers fore and aft with the boat; then fit a flat piece of board between the cylinder timbers, even with the top of the timbers and at the centre of the shafts; then make a centre point on this board for the tramble point at the centre of the shafts, and also on the line passing through the centre of the cylinder timbers and main wrist; then take any distance you please on the trambles—say 10 feet—and from the centre of the shaft; make a scribe or point from the shaft each way from the centre, 10 feet each; then from these two

~~OVERSIZED FOLDOUT~~

COLOR ILLUSTRATION

was removed after page(s) 248,
for in-house scanning

On 8/18/2000

points on the straight line in the centre of the cylinder timbers; place the trambles and describe two circles that will intersect each other on the timber which is to receive the pillar block on which the end of the main shaft is to rest; then stretch the line across the curves on these timbers, and this line for your shaft will be square with the centre line through the cylinder timbers. The next thing then before laying out for your pillar blocks, is to get the line for the shafts parallel, or at equal distances on both sides of the boat, with the sheer plank, and then the shafts would be level when the boat is in trim.

RULE 2.—How to square the shaft line to the cylinder lines by figures—6, 8 and 10, or any other numbers, more or less, in the same proportion. Draw the centre lines in the cylinder timbers, as in Rule 1, then make a mark on this line with a black lead pencil at the point where it is intended the centre of the shaft is to come; then measure 6 feet from this centre, each way on your line, and mark these points with a black lead pencil; then measure 8 feet each way from the centre point, out from the centre line, and then take a ten foot pole and try it to these points on the lines, and if they are more or less than the pole, bring the shaft line round at either end, keeping the line to the centre on the line fore and aft, and when you get two of these points to fit the length of the pole, the other two spaces will be the same length, and the lines will be square one with another. The centre line for the shafts will be equal, or parallel distances from the sheer plank, as in Rule 1, example for squaring of shafts. See plate.

N. B.—Before the shafts are put into the pillar

blocks, put a parallel straight edge across the two main pillar blocks on the top of the bottom brasses, and then some 2, 3 or 4 feet aft of the slides, put on another parallel straight edge across the top of the cylinder timbers, and see if these straight edges are out of twist on top; and if not, plane a narrow place across the top of the cylinder timbers until they are out of twist, and this place will be a guide, after the shafts are in their place, to put your slides and cylinder lugs true, and level with the line through the centre of the shaft.

RULE 3.—*How to line cylinders and square shafts for side-wheel boats, with double engines.* When the cylinder timbers for both engines are each one parallel from a line through the centre of the boat, fore and aft, you will then stretch two centre lines through the cylinder timbers parallel or equal distances with each other, then stretch the centre line for the shafts across these parallel lines where it is intended the centre of the shafts are to come, and then proceed to square the shaft line with the cylinder line according to Rule 1, as laid down on page 248, or according to Rule 2, as found on page 249.

Stern-wheel engines are squared in the same way as side-wheel boat engines are, when the timbers of the side-wheel boat are equal and parallel with each other, but not otherwise.

RULE 4.—*How to square shafts with cylinder timbers, when the timbers are not parallel with each other.* We would here remark, that it is a common thing on side-wheel boats with double engines, to have the cylinder timbers, at the water wheel, something like six inches narrower then they are at the cylinder, sometimes more and sometimes less, as it may happen. We are opposed to this, for the following reason: The water wheels being turned several degrees out of square from a line drawn through the centre of the boat, they will not pull straight ahead, but lose power in proportion to the number of degrees it is out of square.

Whether this be done intentionally, by the ship carpenter, or not, we cannot at present say. But there are some who allege that it is better to be a little out of square, saying that it throws the water in on the rudder, thereby causing a stronger current against the rudder-blade; and thus enable the pilot to steer the boat more easily. We have also heard that it was advantageous in another respect. The boat is narrower at the stern, and the water being displaced by the wheel a little out of square, it is said causes the water displaced by the boat to return more rapidly to fill the vacancy, and that this acts upon the stern or narrow part of the boat in the same manner that any pressure would upon the narrow part of a wedge, thus assisting to propel the boat.

Our opinion is, notwithstanding these arguments, that the cylinder timbers should be parallel and the water wheel square with a line through the centre of the boat; and then, if the rudder is constructed as it should be, the boat will be easily steered without any additional assistance from the water wheels.

But to square shafts with cylinder timbers that are not parallel with each other, a line must be drawn through each cylinder timber, and square each shaft from its own line, according to Rule 1, as laid down on page 248, or as Rule 2, page 249.

Notwithstanding these two shaft lines are not straight with each other, sideways across the boat, (the cause of which is the cylinder timbers not being parallel with each other,) yet they would be and are straight the other way, the line being equal distances from the sheer plank up. When re-lining shafts, after the boat has been running awhile, it may be that one or the other side of the boat has settled, sometimes an inch more or less. In lining the shafts in this case, it is not necessary that they be equal distances from the sheer plank, so that the centres of each shaft are at parallel distances from a line reaching across the boat which is parallel with the sheer planks; and the shaft can be squared by a line running through the cylinder. This can be done by making a small centre mark with a file or cold chisel on both sides of the wrist in its centre, and turning over and trying fore and aft on your line, and keying your pillar blocks one way or other until both these marks fit the line which passes through the cylinder.

For getting the shaft in line the other way, or up and down: Stretch a line across the boat, from the centre each way; that is, parallel from the sheer planks, straight on top, though not straight sideways. Let this line be some three, four or five feet above the top of the journals or caps; then take two small strips of wood, ½ or ⅜ inch square, and let there be a difference in the lengths of these strips equal to half the distance there is between the collar on the large journal and that of the smaller one; and then, if the long strip fits the collar on the small journal, and the short strip fits the collar on the large one, your shaft will be in line this way as well as the other. We suggest it as the easiest plan to measure from the tops of the collars, as it answers every purpose, and also saves the trouble of taking the caps off the tops of the pillar blocks, which would be a great deal of unnecessary trouble.

BALANCE VALVE IN FORCE PUMPS.

"You will here find the explanation of the balance valve, (as laid down on page 212,) which was intended to have been put in, but was neglected. In presenting a draft of this pump, we did not intend it as fit for practical use, but laid it down out of curiosity—thinking, perhaps, it might act as a stimulus in exciting others to introduce something superior to the common force pump now in general use. This pump will work as well as any other now used, and the valve being nearly balanced, it is that much less weight for the plunger to raise; it falls easier into the seat, and when raised by the plunger going down, strikes much easier on the force pump cap; because the surface of the valve operated on by the plunger is less in these kinds of valves than in the valves in common use. The resistance on the plunger from the boilers in this pump, is the same as in the force pump now used, and the only difference between the two at all, in working, would be the valve being nearly balanced, would be nearly the weight of itself less weight to be raised in throwing water into the boilers. To balance a valve is one thing, and to take the resistance caused by the pressure of the steam in the boilers, off the plunger, is another thing.

The balance valve in the force pump was not laid down here as intended for practical use; it is more complicated and costly than the present force pump; but we would ask the question, is it not possible for some one to introduce something superior to the present force pump?"

This passage is extracted from page 161 of the former edition of my book, published in 1853. Who knows but that the principle of the injector may have been suggested by reading these words? At all events it *is* here suggested. The draft of the pump is on page 108 of the old book, and the same is on page 212 of this edition.

WALLACE'S GOVERNOR.

On page 254 is a draft of a governor, having a double frog, (marked A,) which was invented by the author of this book in the year 1853. This is the most simple in its construction of any we have ever seen, and what we claim as our invention is the double frog. This governor requires no points, and needs but one bolt for supporting each of the levers to which the balls are suspended for vibrating. On this account the friction is much less than that of the common governor, whilst the work of fitting it up is about one-half or less than that of the common one. A is the double frog; the motion is given to the frog by the arm on which the governor balls are suspended, and from this same double frog A, the motion is given to the governor lever F, which connects and works the butterfly valve. B is the cast iron frame which is fastened to the upright shaft,

OVERSIZED FOLDOUT

COLOR ILLUSTRATION

was removed after page(s) 254
for in-house scanning

On 8·18 2000

and on this shaft the double frog A vibrates up and down. C is the governor ball; D is the governor pulley; E is one of the mitre wheels that works the upright shaft; F is the governor lever; G is the step in which the upright shaft revolves; H is an arm cast on each side of the frame, having in them a groove in which the arm on which the ball is suspended moves, and also allows it to rise to any height necessary, owing to the length of the arms.

STERN WHEEL STEAMERS WITH TWO WATER WHEELS.

There was a large stern wheel boat built in Pittsburgh, some years ago, having four cylinders and two water wheels. The object was, to round-to the boat quicker than could be done with two cylinders and one wheel. They used a double engine to drive each of the wheels, so that they could make the wheels turn in opposite directions at the same time. In this way they could round-to in less time, and in a narrower channel, than those boats having only one water wheel. This worked very well and answered the intended purpose, however there were but few of this kind of boats built. I will state some objections to their coming into general use. They are too weighty, and this, too, on the stern of the boat. They require a double set of engineers. The cost is a great deal more to fit a boat out in this way, and the friction is increased in proportion to the additional amount of machinery; and they are of no real advantage whatever, excepting making quicker turns than could be done with the common double engine and single water wheel. I saw in Cincinnati, about 25 years ago, one that had three engines and three water wheels, which were built by my boss Gudloe & Co., Cincinnati, for the steamer *Superior*. She was intended to be a very fast running boat, but proved to be a failure. She had, I think, six large double flued boilers on board, one 24 inch cylinder about 6 feet stroke, and a lever engine working two side water wheels. She had also in the stern, two 12 inch cylinders, 4 feet stroke slide valves, working a large water wheel, making in all three wheels. I always thought the main cause of the failure of the speed of this boat was, that the stern and side wheels did not pull together.

SPEED OF FLY WHEELS FOR GRIST MILLS, &c.

One of the failures in some grist mills is owing to the fly wheel being too light and running too slow, so that the speed of the outer circumference of the stones out traveled that of the fly wheel rim, so that it caused the stones to backlash, and the mill would never work to good advantage. There were two reasons for this: one was the diameter of the fly wheel was too small, and the other was, the speed of the engine was too slow. In order for a grist mill to grind to good advantage, the fly wheel rim should always take the lead of the stones, by running about twenty-five per centage faster than the rim of the stones; this used to be one of the secrets of getting up a good mill. I recollect of a person telling me of a certain mill that could not be made to work to do any good on account of the backlashing of the stones, and after enlarging the diameter of the fly wheel, so as to out travel the stones, in order to keep ahead of them, they were not troubled any more with backlashing. This shows the necessity of having all the parts of a mill in proportion with each other. You may have the same boilers and size of engines, and the same weight of metal or more in the small fly wheel that there is in the large one, and it may cost the same price, or even more than the one with the large fly wheel; and owing to the lack not of power but of speed, on account of the small diameter of the fly wheel, the former would hardly be worth taking as a gift, if you were to be bound to keep it running.

The product of the weight, diameter and number of revolutions per minute of the fly wheel, should exceed at least by about twenty-five per cent that of the weight, diameter and revolutions of the stones. The same rule will apply to grind-stones, counter fly wheels, or any other large wheel intended to revolve rapidly.

It is said that one horse will grind one bushel of wheat per hour, four horses four bushels per hour, eight horses eight bushels per hour, &c., &c., so that it would require an eight horse power engine to grind eight bushels per hour, twelve horse power engine to grind twelve bushels per hour, &c.

THE FORM OF AN ORDER FOR A STEAM ENGINE.

Persons in ordering steam engines are not sufficiently definite to be understood in regard to particulars;

and in handing in their orders, to receive proposals for the building of the same, as a general thing, they are too vague. They are sometimes written in the following manner:

"*Sir*—I wish to know your price for a 14 inch cylinder, 4 feet stroke, with two boilers, 36 inches in diameter, 28 feet long. Put up at M'Keesport.

"Please let me know your lowest. Yours in haste.

JAS. LOWRIE."

Now, persons answering this letter may each have his own way of building such machinery. One may make it as light as he can, while another may make it heavy. Much depends in this case upon the principle of the man who is employed to construct the engine, whether he will come up to the mark, or whether the sizes must be specified and their fulfillment exacted at the hands of the builder.

Now, the above order should be written thus:

"*Sir*—I wish to know your price, and terms of payment, for an engine of the following description: 14 inch cylinder, 4 feet stroke, side valve, good plain finish; main shaft about 13 or 14 feet between the journals; journals to be 8 inches in diameter, with bottom brasses; fly wheel 16 feet in diameter, rim 5000 lbs.; with two cylinder boilers, 36 inches in diameter and 28 feet long, made of $\frac{1}{4}$ inch iron; a governor and a cold water pump; well not more than 10 feet deep; we will want about twenty feet of well-pipe, 10 feet between cylinder timbers and boiler wall; to be ready by the middle of June, 1864."

ANSWER.

Terms as follows: half cash on contract, and the balance in two equal payments of ninety days each, with interest from date.

To persons purchasing steam engines to go to California, Mexico, Pike's Peak, or to any other place out of the reach of engine machine shops, I would suggest the propriety of taking along with them certain parts of the engine which will be needed, and most likely to give out first. Necessary extras.—One set or more of grate bars; extra liners for fire fronts; liners for furnace doors, and doors; man plates; boiler arches and bolts for same. Also, one set of gauge cocks; one check and blow-off valve, and seat for each; one pair cylinder cocks; one cock for force pump; one flange cock leading from cistern to the heater; one oil globe; one pair of brasses for crank end of pitman; one pair of brasses for the hot and one for the cold water pump, or more, if necessary; four pairs brasses for the pendulum and slide valve links; one pair or more for cam rod joints; one set of brasses for the cam frame to work in; one set of liners for the shoving head jaws; side boxes and bottom brasses for the pillar blocks. If the square cam frame is used, you will need two pieces of cam frame, and one cam of cast iron; metallic packing for cylinder; packing yarn; lead and ladle; gum; gasket paper; iron borings and lead gaskets for man and hand-hole plates; also, lead gaskets for force pump, and check and blow-off valve chamber caps. Also, a few extra joint bolts, of different sizes; three or four sharp picks, for cleaning the lime scales off the inside of the boilers and flues. Also, one or more chains to rub around the flues, to assist in cleaning them; sal ammoniac; a few cementing irons to make joints; also, one or two chipping hammers; three or four cold chisels, and two or three gauges; one sledge, one vice, one anvil, and one pair of bellows, with the necessary tools; callipers, tongs, &c.; fire irons—one poker, one rake, one crow foot, to haul out clinkers; one crooked poker, for clearing out ashes and clinkers between the grate bars from below; one or more shovels; one damper for each flue; brooms for sweeping out the flues; all necessary wrenches, with one or two extra monkey wrenches; oil cans, oil, tallow and beeswax, &c. &c. I throw out these suggestions for the benefit of the purchaser, to post him up and let him know what extra items will be necessary.

Men who understand their business know what extras will be needed, and those who do not know can find out by reading these suggestions. No doubt I have named more extras than will generally be wanted, and I also may have omitted some few. This depends a good deal upon the kind of an engine you get. Some will require more extras than others. I would always advise the purchaser to consult with the engine builder as to what amount of extras will be necessary, as every engine builder is likely to know, better than any one else, the weak parts of his engines, if there be any, and what will be most likely to wear or give out first, and require to be replaced anew. Another mistake I would correct. Persons who have gotten engines and are living at a distance, think that when any thing is wanted, all they have to do is to send for the articles, without giving any size or particulars whatever. And when you ask them for the particulars every way, they will answer by telling you the engine was made at your shop, &c., and you must have the patterns, not knowing, at the same time, that you may have a dozen or twenty different patterns, nearly all the same size, &c. I generally tell them I will not make any thing for them unless I have all the sizes, and am sure that I am right—if I make it, that it will be at their risk, and nŏt mine. I throw out these hints also, so that persŏns at a distance may not depend too much on the engine builder, but get beforehand such extras as will likely be necessary hereafter, &c. For example, a man, in writing for a pair of pitman brasses, may think it a very small matter, but there are a good many measures necessary: the diameter and length of the journal—also, the width of the pitman straps and the space between, and the probable thickness of the boxes—and a mistake or neglect of any one of these measures will be a sufficient cause for not making it. Hence the necessity, when sending an order for anything whatever, to give all the particulars. If for gauge cocks or cylinder cocks, send the size at the point and the number of threads to the inch; or, rub the bolt on a piece of paper, and it will show its own thread.

Where the engine is to be put up within a convenient distance of the machine shop, few extras will be needed, say a few grate bars, one pair pitman brasses, ditto brasses, brass liner for shoving head jaws, and a few link brasses—packing yarn, material for joints, and a few joint bolts, oil cans, &c. &c.

Persons about contracting for steam engines, and soliciting estimates from engine builders, should be exact in their descriptions of the power they require. To such persons these directions will be useful. Along with the horse power, get also the diameter of the cylinder and length of stroke; also, the kind of boiler, the diameter and length and thickness of the same. These are items of the greatest importance to know. There are other items, of less importance, which it would be to your interest to know—for instance, the diameter and length of the main shaft—also, the diameter and weight of the fly wheel, &c.; then, when you have got all your estimates in, comparing your notes or estimates one with the other, and then choose the largest cylinder and boiler that is rated at the lowest number of horse power, providing the builder is one whose work is known to give general satisfaction, and the prices are suitable.

HOW TO PUT UP AN ENGINE.

In setting up an engine, it is customary with many to put the centres of the cylinder slides and of the main shaft all in line with each other. If everything would remain as when first put up, this would be exactly right. The engine will then start from off each centre at equal distances from each end of the slides. But there is another thing to be taken into the account. Suppose the bottom brass of the pillar block to be one and a half inches thick, when new, and to wear down one inch, which would leave it half an inch thick; in this case, if the centres of the cylinder slides and shaft were in line when first put up, then the shaft would be one inch below the centre when the bottom brasses would be worn out: hence the necessity, when setting up a new engine, to have the centre of the main shaft as much above the centre of the slides and cylinder, as the half of the wear of the brasses would be when worn out, which would be half an inch. Then the centre of the shaft when the engine is first put up would be half an inch above the centre of the cylinder and slides, and half an inch below the same when the brasses are worn out. I am well aware that when the engine is on the after dead centre, and the shaft a half inch above the centre of the slides, the engine would come over easier from this centre than it would go out from the opposite centre; because, when the engine is on this inner dead centre, the shaft is half an inch above the centre, so that if the steam was given here on the centre, the engine would not move until the wrist in the crank was turned below the centre. The extra half inch is more than would be necessary if the engine was on the centre. This is the conclusion: the centre of the main shaft should always be above the centre of the slides and cylinder, equal to half the wear in the bottom brasses when worn out. When the engine is new it will require the piston, when going out on the lower centre, to be a little farther over on the slides than it would require on the other end, when coming over on the upper centre; and when the main shaft settles below the centre by wearing, it would then be the reverse at the other end of the slides. N. B. Some may say half an inch above and below the centre is a good deal, but these are the extreme points. The shaft is gradually approaching the centre as the brasses wear; when past the centre it sinks below it until it reaches the other extreme. This is the best that can be done.

There are other engines where the bottom brasses are not more than ¾ of an inch thick when new, so that the centre of the shaft in this case would not be more than ¼ of an inch above or below the centre of the cylinder and slides at any time, but most of the time it would be nearer, and at a certain time it would be exactly in the centre. There is no cure for this but what would be worse than the disease itself. It has been tried here on large rolling mill engines, to keep the shaft always up to the centre by having the bottom of the pillar blocks and bed plates planed up and fitted, and keys put between them to raise the blocks up as the shaft wears the brasses down, but they were very difficult to be kept in order this way, and I believe this plan has been abandoned. And on board of steam boats it would be impossible, on account of the wear of the brasses, to keep the shafts always in line, unless you would keep lowering your cylinder and slides on the timbers as the brasses wear, and let the shaft down, or else you would have to raise the pillar blocks up with gasket paper, or something else. The main thing is to keep the centre of the cylinder and slides exactly in line with each other, and always let the centre of the main shaft be one-half the thickness of the wear of the brasses above the centre of the cylinder and slides, when new.

I would add, that it would be an easy matter, if the bottom brasses were made flat on the bottom, and fitted between two pillars, to raise the brasses and put iron backing below them, same as is put in behind pitman brasses. This would only do where the bottom and top brasses are half circles, but it would not answer where side boxes are used, and they are generally used on large horizontal engines, so that the old plan I have alluded to, with all its inconveniences, is the very best that can be adopted. It has worked well—it still works well, and will ever continue to do the same. It is an old saying, let well enough alone.

A CHARGE TO OVERSEERS OF ESTABLISHMENTS USING STEAM POWER.

As damage is frequently done by the breaking of machinery, and the bursting of pipes, &c., and this mostly from neglect, I propose to give some directions both to engineers and overseers of establishments using steam. The very fact of the engineer knowing that the boss is posted up in this matter, will make him doubly careful to guard against accidents. Something of this kind appears to me to be necessary, to stir up both engineers and bosses to a sense of their duty. And if the boss is posted up on the matter, and the engineer not, and the boss should feel delicacy in telling him what was his duty, he could recommend him to get "WALLACE'S PRACTICAL ENGINEER," and read page 265 until he becomes acquainted with this part of his duty.

The following supposed conversation between the boss and the engineer, on Saturday evening just before quitting, will explain what I mean:

BOSS. "Stop, engineer. Have you let the water all out of the different parts of the engine—both ends of the cylinder, the heater, the hot and cold water pumps and pipes, cistern, steam chest, &c.? and have you raised the throttle valve a little, so that the steam may blow through the cylinder, and not burst the steam pipe nor throttle valve chambers? have you slacked up the fire under the boilers, &c.?"

ENGINEER. "No, sir, it is not cold, it is thawing; it is of no use, there is no danger, boss, not the least."

BOSS. "I did not ask you whether it was cold or

thawing, and I want you to go back and do as I bid you; I pay you for your work, and you have a right to obey my orders."

ENGINEER. "Well boss, if you say so, I suppose I will have to do as you say."

He goes back and does as the boss told him.

Monday morning, weather extremely cold.

BOSS. "Well engineer, is it thawing now or is it cold?"

ENGINEER. "Cold! bitter cold."

BOSS. "Was I not right in the directions I gave you on Saturday night?"

ENGINEER. "You were right, boss, who would have thought it! I never dreamt of such a change in the weather."

BOSS. "That is nothing new in this country. I have seen it frequently raining or thawing on Saturday evening, and on Sabbath morning or next day the wind would change and it would blow up to be desperately cold, so that by Monday morning everything would be frozen stiff. Now, engineer, I tell you there are numbers of mills around here, whose owners, for want of being posted up as we have been, and not using the precautionary measures we have done, are paying dearly for their negligence of duty to-day. One has burst a pump, others have broken a pendulum shaft, others a pump arm or pendulum, &c. This proves the proverbs to be true, 'an ounce of prevention is as good as a pound of cure,' and 'a stitch in time saves nine.' I have no doubt there is more damage done for want of thinking or considering, than from any other cause."

In cold weather, after the engine is stopped, the engineer should, before retiring, open the necessary cocks, to let the water out, so as to prevent damage by freezing, and also to take out the necessary set screws, for the same purpose. As engineers are in a hurry to be off as soon as possible after bell ringing, they do not care about taking time to take out the set screws, especially if the wrenches should be mislaid, whereas, had there been small cocks instead of set screws, they would stop and open them, as it could be done in an instant; and no engine can be said to be complete without stop cocks instead of set screws, &c. It would be much better to take an hour or two to thaw the pumps and pipes, if necessary, than to start up in a hurry and break down, and have to stop several days or weeks, as the case may be, besides contracting more or less of a bill. When persons are detained unexpectedly in this way, they are very apt to become excited and impatient, and on this account they sometimes do a large amount of damage, that would have been avoided had they kept cool and taken their time to see that everything was clear before starting.

In heating up an engine, especially in cold weather, it should be done very gradually, as there is great danger of breaking in frosty weather, by heating up suddenly, before the frost is entirely out of all parts of the engine. Engineers frequently, when starting the engines in frosty weather, are in too much of a hurry, before they are sure that the ice is all thawed out of the pumps, pipes, &c., and in this way they sometimes do a great deal of damage. I would recommend the plan of turning the fly wheel round once or twice by hand, before letting the steam on suddenly; and those engines that are too large to turn by hand, unship the pendulum and work it by hand, if there is any doubt about the ice being entirely thawed. I knew an instance, a short time ago, of a large engine where the force pump was frozen up. They had fire around it for some time, and supposed it was thawed. The engine was too large to turn by hand. They gave the engine the steam, and as it had almost come over the centre, it broke the pendulum. The engineer told me he thought that the break was occasioned by some pieces of ice falling down from the sides of the pump, under the plunger. This is why I spoke of turning the wheel round twice to make a more sure thing of it. I have trouble enough when I am careful, and I do not wish to add to my troubles by right down carelessness, and in addition to all this, contract a bill of unnecessary expenses.

CAUTION AGAINST FREEZING IN WINTER.

Frost, as well as heat, is one of the most powerful elements in nature, and it is not enough that great care should be taken that there is not a scarcity of water or an extra degree of heat, but that the boilers are not bursted by the frost. About the year 1849 we had the job of replacing a boiler head that had been bursted by the frost. This boiler was used at a pork house, and happening to be full of water, froze solid, and burst the head completely out, leaving the rim fast by the rivets to the boiler hull. How many other boilers have been burst in the same way, it is not for us to say, but every one knows that there is more or less damage done every year by the frost, such as the bursting of cylinders; followers breaking in the piston head, by the freezing of the packing; stuffing boxes on the fast cylinder head, from the same cause. The force pump and other stuffing boxes, are liable to burst from the same way when hard screwed up, with wet packing. (In extreme cold weather, it would be a good plan to slacken the nuts on the stuffing box bolts; and if the engine is very much exposed to the weather, it would be advisable to draw out the packing altogether.) Steam chest lids by the steam chest filling with water from the condensed steam; bursting of throttle valve chambers; bursting of force pumps, hollow plungers, breaking of pump arms, shafts and pendulum arms from the same cause. Also, side pipes, copper or iron steam and supply pipes, cold water pumps, check valve chambers, boiler stand pipes, mud and supply receivers, cold water cisterns, &c. Everything containing cold water is liable to burst. A short time ago we made a new cylinder to replace one that was split in two halves from end to end, having been froze solid with water in it; and whilst writing this book I was informed that the steamer *North Bend* burst her cylinder in the same way; it was 16 inches diameter, 6 feet stroke. She had been laying up at Wheeling during a spell of cold weather, and when they raised steam for the purpose of putting out, as soon as they let on the steam into the cylinder, to use as I heard it the engineer's own words, the cylinder opened out like a bean pod. We built this engine, and something like twenty years or more have passed away before I was made acquainted with this fact. I never dreamt of its having burst from this cause, the common report was that it was burst from foul play. The report was current that it was caused by water in the cylinder; but the true cause was for a long time kept concealed. I recollect of hearing of another cylinder of our build, making three in all having been burst by frost; and how many other cylinders have been burst in the same way, it is not for me to say, as no one knows the number. In some instances, it would be a good plan to take out the pump and cylinder cocks, and slack off the loose cylinder head, for the following reason: where the fires under the boilers are slacked up and the steam is a long time cooling down, and the cylinder exposed and the weather very cold, and the cocks and openings in the same being very small, no doubt the opening in the cocks would freeze solid, and thus the water made by condensed steam is retained in the cylinder, and is thus suffered to freeze up solid, and the result is that the cylinder will be most likely to burst. I mention these things to put the thoughtless and inconsiderate upon their guard.

These things which every one in the business knows occur almost by wholesale every year, are caused by the frost, and nineteen cases out of twenty could have been avoided by a little forethought. For example, by having the engine in a house well closed in from the inclemency of the weather, there would be but few nights so cold as to require letting the water off the pumps, cylinders, &c., except on Saturdays, where the engine stands over a day and has time to cool down.

It is almost a universal thing, during cold weather, for something to be broken on Monday, caused by freezing between Saturday and Monday; and what has happened may occur again, unless some precautionary measures are adopted. Now, we would recommend having the hollow plunger so tight as not to admit any water. (One of our most serious objections to the hollow plunger is their leaking at the bolt hole in the bottom.) Let the water out of the force and cold water pumps, and if the supply pipe to the boiler is below the force pump, have some way of letting the water out of it, and have a frost hole in the side of the steam chest, with a set screw, so that it may be taken out whenever there is danger from freezing; also the keys of large stop cocks, for water pipes from cisterns and other places where they may be used, should be taken out, as a very slight frost sometimes easily destroys both the keys and cocks. Many pendulum shafts and pump arms have been broken by starting the engines with more or less ice in the pumps. These things ought not to be allowed. A word to the wise is sufficient.

In conclusion, if small cocks were put into the different places for draining the water off the different parts of the engine instead of set screws, there is no doubt but that there would be fewer accidents occur than do, because an engineer could open a dozen cocks in less time than he would sometimes be in taking out one set screw; and where there is a number of set screws to take out, and perhaps different wrenches necessary to fit the same, in case of one or more of them being mislaid or taken away, as they often are; the engineer having no particular interest at stake, puts off in a hurry, neglecting to do what he considered as his duty to do and would have done had there been stop cocks used instead of set screws, and the result is, in this way there is a large amount of damage done every year, which is a continual tax upon the establishment, which might and should be avoided were the necessary precautions used.

GRATE BARS AND BEARERS.

There is scarcely any part about the construction of the steam engine more troublesome and more expensive to keep in repair and good order than the grate bars, on account of their burning out so soon, and their liability to fall out when the engine is in motion and all hands at work, and on this account there is a great deal of time and labor lost.

There is a great variety of grate bars in use; single, double and treble, varying in length from six down to two feet long. The sizes generally used are three, three and a half and four feet long. As a general thing they are straight on top, and some are made one or more inches rounding on top; one object of this was, when burning wood it was easier to shake up the fires, as the wood would roll on the bars, another object was to prevent them from bagging down in the middle. In plate C, on page 272 you have a side view of the grate bar A, which is a good bar for this reason: the back end is beveled for the purpose of keeping the ashes from settling in between the end of the grate bars and the back bar bearer, which would prevent the expansion of the grate bars when hot from forcing back the back grate bar bearer, as you will see on page 272.

But to make a more complete job, it might be beveled on both ends, as is shown on the front end of the grate

OVERSIZED FOLDOUT

COLOR ILLUSTRATION

was removed after page(s) 272,
for in-house scanning

On 8 · 18 2000

bar A, and on the back end of the grate bar E, and also on both ends of the grate bars F, G and H, or otherwise there would be danger from the expansion of the bars on account of the ashes crowding between the front end of the bars and bearer.

B is a very good bar; much better than the one above, because it has a short rib cast on the front end made to fit easy in a groove, which is cast on the front grate bar bearer; this holds the grate bars stationary at the front end, the back end of the bar rests on a plain flat piece of iron and is not moved by the expansion of the grate bars. The bridge wall may be built two or three or more inches back beyond the end of the grate bars, so as to allow a little space between the end of the grate bars and the bridge wall for the ashes, so that they may not be crowded so hard by the expansion of the grate bars, as to force the bridge wall back.

C, the back bearer, is also better on account of flanging down on the bridge wall, which makes it a more permanent job.

D is a side view of a single bar made from 6 to 8 inches wide, cast on its side, full of holes about two inches round, for the purpose of letting the air pass through to keep the bars cool and prevent them from springing. There have been a good many of these bars made, but they never have come into general use.

The grate bar D and bearers are the very best that have been got up. The front grate bar bearer is about 24 inches wide; in front of the fire front there is a 9 inch wall of fire brick, and beyond this wall about 5 inches, is a recess three inches deep to receive a fire brick lining 9 inches wide in a bed of fire clay or mortar. The object of keeping the grate bars so far back, is to save the cast iron liners and fire doors in the fire front, which so often burn out, and the air being excluded by the course of brick in the bearing bars, the fire will not be so hot nor hard on the liners and fire front as it would if the grate bars were close up to the liners, and admitted the air. It is also the intention when using these wide bearing bars, in front of the boiler, to pitch the coal or fuel back on the grate bars as much as possible, and not suffer the fuel to be crowded up close to the liners, which would be sure to burn them out. The back bearing bar is also made on an improved plan. The plate is made so as to receive a 9 inch bridge wall in front of the plate, which runs up on the back side of the wall as high as the top of the brick of the bridge wall. This holds the wall up, and there is a recess in this plate to receive the grate bars, and the back of the recess is intended to be built close up to the bridge wall, so as to hold it more securely to its place.

E is a draft of a grate bar which is marked *bad;* the front end is all right, yet the bar being square at the back end, and the bearing bar narrower, without any lower flange to lap over on the bridge wall, the ashes, when the bars shrink, settle in between the space, and when the bars expand by heating, it forces the bearer back nearly equal to the shrinkage every time they are heated, save what the ashes would compress, and every time they cool they fill up anew in the same way, and every time they are heated up they expand, and keep shoving back the bearing bar by degrees, until they shove it from under the grate bars, and this accounts for the frequent falling down of the grate bars. We ourselves

OVERSIZED FOLDOUT

COLOR ILLUSTRATION

was removed after page(s) 274
for in-house scanning

On 8·18 2000

have been very much annoyed in this way by the bars falling down when the hands were all at work, and the engine in full blast, and we would often have to stop in the middle of our work and haul out the fires, and put in the grate bars before we could go ahead again.

F is a very bad bar; there being no catch on the front end of the bars, nor recess in the bearers, they will fall out in one half the time of the above, as the ashes crowd in at both ends of the bars.

G is a worse plan, because the grate bar bearer is cast on the fire fronts, and on account of not having it lined with brick, it makes it disagreeably hot for the fireman, and the fire front burns out immediately, almost as soon as the grate bars.

H is the worst of all plans for the construction of grate bars and bearers; is the same in this as in C, it is cast on the fire front, which crowds the fire close to the casting and burns out the fire front, and the back end of the grate bar is laid on the bricks. A fire front and grate bars put up in this way will be sure always to give trouble, and be a constant bill of expense to keep in repair, besides the loss of time, disappointment of hands, customers, dead capital, &c.

I is a bar similar to the one in the other plate on page 272, with a single row of holes, the object of which was to prevent the bars from getting red hot, by allowing a circulation of cold air to pass through them. They are seldom used; they were tried more as an experiment than any thing else, but are not equal to the bars generally used.

J is a patent grate bar, which works on a pin at the back end. The bar is straight sideways, without any strips cast on the sides, so that they can be shoved from side to side at the front end, to let the clinkers fall through; then the bars are set as near as possible at their proper distance by the fireman. This kind of bar is used only where they burn stone coal. The pin is a new thing, but the plan of shifting the bars from side to side, is the same way as far back as I can recollect. They had side jogs cast on the back end and none on the front, and these were shifted in the same way the patent bars are, and for the very same purpose, with this difference: these having no pins in, greater care was necessary in spreading them apart and in bringing them together. I was informed by the head engineer of the steamer *Advance No.* 2, that their grate bars fell out about a dozen times during a short trip from Pittsburgh to Parkersburg and back, and twice during the trip they had to stop to haul out the fires to put up the bars. He told me that the back bearing bar was not made right, it should have had a flange cast on it to come down on the inside of the fire bed in the ash pit, and then have several long tie bolts reaching through it made fast to the fire front. I told him that would not do; the bars should be fast at one end and have room to come and go at the other, as you see on the grate bars C and E, page 272.

DOUBLE ACTING FORCE PUMP.

No. 1 presents a side view of a double acting force pump, which is sometimes used instead of two pumps, the common mode for steam engines which are not sup-

OVERSIZED FOLDOUT

COLOR ILLUSTRATION

was removed after page(s) 276
for in-house scanning

On 8.18 2000

plied by overhead water from water works or otherwise which require but one force pump. C is a double valve chamber. The cold water is drawn from the well through valve No. 2, and discharged through valve No. 3 into the cistern and reservoir. The double valve chamber D draws the hot water from the heater through the valve No. 4, and discharges it through the valve No. 5 into the boiler. In the construction of these pumps, it is necessary to have the upper valve chamber large enough to let the lower valves pass down through the upper ones. The depth of these lower valves and seats makes it very hard to get at the valves and seats to grind and keep them in repair. They are also very complicated; I have known of numbers of them being used and they did not give satisfaction, and in some instances, I believe, they have been displaced and others used in their stead.

NOMINAL HORSE POWER.

Of all the absurd terms to be met with in the vocabulary of mechanical arts, that of "nominal horse power" is perhaps the most absurd. Particular measures and weights bear, very properly, individual appellations, which, if not invariable in their meaning in a general sense, are so in particular instances. Thus, the term "pound," individually, does not, it is true, invariably denote one certain measure of the force of gravitation; different merchants employing it in various senses, according to the kind of trade they carry on. The pound of the jeweler is one thing; that of the corn merchant another. Yet the troy weight of the one can never be confounded with the avoirdupois weight of the other. The phrases "troy weight" and "apothecaries' weight" are understood throughout the length and breadth of the kingdom, and are rarely, if ever, confounded with each other. Measures of length are still more definite. A foot is equally a foot with the carpenter and the engineer, the worker in stone and the worker in iron, all over the kingdom. A two foot rule which can be used in London is equally serviceable in Manchester and Liverpool, Hull or Glasgow. Our engines are bought and sold at the rate of so much per nominal horse power; and it is certainly strange, considering the enormous sums which annually change hands in the trade, that there should be no fixed and definite meaning in the expression. Not only does it convey no idea whatever of the power of any steam engine, but it fails equally in expressing size. Were this all, its use might be pardonable; but, on examination, we find that nearly every centre of manufacturing industry attaches a special value to it, different to that which obtains elsewhere; a nominal horse power meaning one thing at Leeds, another thing at Glasgow, and something else at London; even different makers employing the phrase in distinctive senses, according to their individual proclivities.

During the first few years of his career as an engine builder, Watt adhered almost exclusively to one particular speed of piston per minute, only departing from it in exceptional cases, when engines were constructed out of the usual routine of the shops. He was not long in business, however, until he discovered that the term "horse power" conveyed too vague an idea to answer the purposes of a vastly extended trade. He accordingly instituted some experiments at one of the London breweries with the largest and strongest horses which he could obtain. A finely-turned brass pulley was affixed to the edge of a well; over this pulley a carefully made rope was run, one end descending the well, where it was attached to weights, altered as occasion required, while the other end was drawn forward by a horse, which thus raised the weight. From the results obtained from this, and some other experiments, Watt determined the power of a strong horse to be equal to a weight of 33,000 pounds, raised one foot in one minute; the horse being capable of maintaining this exertion for eight hours per day. This was the highest average obtained from the most powerful horses. Watt's first boilers were worked at an extremely low pressure, not more than 2 pounds or 3 pounds on the square inch above the atmosphere. His machinery was not very perfect; and the pressure on the pistons of his earlier engines seldom exceeded 10 pounds on the square inch. Newcomen's engines had an available pressure of not more than 7 pounds or 8 pounds on the inch. Those who bought from the Soho firm, could scarcely be induced to believe in the possibility of obtaining anything much over this; and as there was a doubt amongst the public, Watt gave them the benefit of it; and determining that his customers should receive even more than they bargained for, he magnanimously adopted the highest possible standard of horse power, and the lowest of steam pressure; and thus the Soho nominal horse power was measured by a piston moving at a speed of

128 feet per minute, under a pressure of but 7 pounds to the square inch. Other firms, however, quickly started into existence, who found it expedient to depart both from Watt's standards of speed and pressure, and in consequence different estimates of nominal horse power were adopted in different districts, and continue in force at the present moment. The standards adopted are, in many instances, simply ridiculous. Thus, at Leeds, a nominal horse power means 30 circular inches of piston area, without regard to either speed or pressure; while at Manchester 23 square inches are regarded as the proportion. The weight of a fly-wheel, or the thickness of a cylinder, might be selected as measures of the actual work performed with equal propriety. In Glasgow and London, pressure is employed as the standard; the mercantile value of a steam engine being calculated by an assumed pressure of 7½ pounds to the square inch at the former place, and 7 pounds at the latter, the regulation piston speeds being settled by empirical rules which bear little or no relation to practical results. Those adopted by the Admiralty may be selected as an example. The speed is supposed to vary with the stroke. With a 4 feet stroke the piston speed calculated on is 196 feet; with 5 feet stroke, 210 feet; with a 6 feet stroke, 228 feet; with a 7 feet stroke, 231 feet; with an 8 feet stroke, 240 feet per minute, and so on. It is almost needless to say that these velocities are seldom or never really adhered to. The average pressure maintained in the boilers of our Navy may be taken somewhere about 18 pounds to the square inch. If to this we add 12 pounds for vacuum, and deduct 4 pounds for wire-drawing and loss, the actual working

pressure per square inch of piston becomes nearly three times the nominal pressure. It is thus that the indicated power of marine and other engines exceeds the nominal many times. How many, depending, in a great degree, on the good faith of the firm contracting for the machinery and not at all on the stipulations of the contract! There are various instances in our Navy and mercantile marine where similar ships attain very different velocities with engines of the same nominal horse power, made by different firms; the speed depending not on the nominal but on the indicated power. Setting the general public aside, we thus find that the Government, by purchasing engines at the rate of so much per nominal horse power, place themselves completely in the hands of the manufacturers. The naval architect may calculate that 2,000 effective horse power is sufficient to drive a particular ship at a certain speed. Engines of 400 horse power nominal are ordered, in the expectation that they will work up to the required power. Whether they do or not rests with the makers. If they develop a force of 1,200 horses only, the designer of a ship is disappointed, but no blame can attach to the makers of the machinery. There are engines at this moment in the Navy giving out eight times their nominal power; many others only three; the first cost of the machinery being as nearly as possible the same in both cases. It is not strange, when we consider these things, that so many of our ships have failed to realize the speeds predicted for them.

A simple remedy exists for this state of affairs. Let the purchaser stipulate how many indicated horse power he requires, and pay for his engines by that standard.

Such a course would be found, in the long run, beneficial to all parties. Many firms are at present excluded from the Admiralty work because their reputation is not established; and the Government, having no check over them under existing arrangements of purchase and sale, fear to employ them, lest the indicated should not sufficiently exceed the nominal horse power. The sooner steam engines are bought and sold by real instead of ideal standards, the better. The words "horse power" are seldom or never used in connection with the locomotive; yet purchasers always get exactly what they want. Imaginary and arbitrary measures of either size, capacity, or power, are certain to lead the unwary and inexperienced astray, and are unsuitable to the advancement of the age.—*Eng. Mechanic's Magazine.*

The following sensible comments on the same subject are from the London *Engineer:*

"At present not less than six different rules are adopted in different places, and by different makers, nearly all giving different results; thus, strange as it may seem, in Glasgow an engine is not the same power that it is in Leeds or London Mr. Fairbairn calculates the power of his engines by "multiplying the area of the piston by 7 lbs. the square inch, and by 240, the speed of the piston in feet per minute." The Admiralty rule is, "multiply the square of the diameter of the piston in inches, by its velocity in feet per minute, which must be as follows: For a 4 feet stroke, 196 feet per minute; for a 5 feet stroke, 210 feet per minute; for 6 feet stroke, 222 feet; for 7 feet stroke, 231 feet; for 8 feet stroke, 240 feet per minute, and divide the result by 6,000." Boulton and Watt's formula is 33,000 lbs. raised 1 foot in a minute; but, strange as these rules may seem, they yield to the Leeds, Manchester and Glasgow rules, which are at the first place to allow sixteen circular inches, at the second ten square inches, and at the last ten circular inches of piston area per nominal horse power; these last rules at least show the most delightful simplicity if they have no other merit; but we might as well try to calculate the power of an engine from the diameter of the piston rod or the weight of the fly wheel. The *Persia's* engines, with 10 feet stroke and 101 inch cylinders, are called 818 horse power. While the *Warrior's*, with 112 inch cylinders, which, deducting the 41 inch trunk, are about equal to 103 inches, are call 1,250 horse power, though they have but 4 feet stroke; and we would not weary our readers by heaping up instances to prove what we believe is pretty well known, that the term "nominal horse power" is useless and unexpressive, and it is in vain to say that a standard is necessary when we are at this moment doing very well without one. No engineer can tell from the mere size alone, of an engine, what its power may be. All the purchaser requires to know are the actual dimensions of his engine and boiler, and the quality of the fuel he is about to employ, in order to calculate what amount of work it is capable of performing. It is thus that locomotives are bought and sold without the use of any such absurd term, the use of which must often lead to confusion in the mind of the purchaser, who is seldom very well up in these matters. Its use gives an opening to the fraudulent dealer. In an engineering point of view no such term is necessary, and the present multiplicity of arbitrary rules are quite unsuited to the commercial requirements of the age."

From the foregoing it appears that there is much uncertainty in ascertaining the power of engines. The following rule if adopted would be found perfectly satisfactory: Square the diameter in inches of the cylinder, and divide the product by 5, which gives the number of horse power. And for the benefit of those who do not understand figures, I will give a table of the horse power according to this rule. I wish you now to compare this table with the different tables I have laid down before you, and I have no doubt but that the majority will approve of this rule, for its great simplicity and correctness. &c.

EXAMPLE.—A cylinder 5 inches in diameter, how many horse power? 5×5 are 25; divided by 5, gives 5 horse power. Another: a cylinder 10 inches diameter, how many horse power? 10×10 are 100; divided by 5, gives 20 horse power. Another: A cylinder 20 inches in diameter, how many horse power? 20×20 are 400; divided by 5, gives 80 horse power, &c. In this rule it is not necessary to know the stroke of the engine, as the supposition is that all the pistons travel the same speed per minute.

Rule to find the number of men power in an engine.—Square the diameter of the cylinder and the product is the number required.

Cylinder is 5 inches diameter, 5
5
—
Divide this by 5, 5)25 men power,
—
gives the number of horse power, 5 horse power.

The strength of a horse is equal to that of five men.

I have given two selections on the subject of horse power, and also six cards from five different establishments, two of them from one establishment, having the number of revolutions per minute reduced of each engine, as you will see by looking at the two different tables on the cards, and of course the horse power in each engine is reduced accordingly in the same proportion. In all these tables the number of revolutions and horse power is mentioned, but nothing is said about the height of steam carried. You see a great difference in the power of the engines, in the different tables; for example, there is one 11 inch cylinder, 18 inch stroke, called 40 horse power. In the course of a few years the speed of the engine is reduced, and the power of the same engine is made out to be 25 horse power.

There is another table of New York engines; one cylinder is 11 inch bore, same as the above, and 22 inch stroke, called 15 horse power. How are we to account for this difference of the two engines? the smallest of the two being made out nearly three times as strong as the one having the same bore and 4 inches more stroke. I can understand it only in this way: when the one made out his calculation, he intended carrying 50 lbs. steam per square inch, whilst the other calculated on something like 150 lbs. steam; or else there must be a difference in the calculation of the speed of the two engines. There is no mention made whether these engines all work full stroke or cut off steam, and how much, so that we are left partly in the dark on the subject of the horse power; we cannot understand it with so much variation as we see in the different tables laid down before us. Unless we all work by one rule in the calculating of horse power we will come to incorrect conclusions. One man makes his rule very small, another makes his as large as possible, and another comes between the two, &c. Twelve inches is the length of the foot rule, I believe everywhere. It would be a strange rule that would measure 12 inches in Pittsburgh, and 20 inches in Philadelphia, and 30 inches in New York, &c., not only varying thus in the different cities, but in one and the same city.

For the benefit of those wishing to have a general rule to calculate horse power, so that the calculation, will come out nearly about the same everywhere, it will be necessary for all to calculate on the piston traveling a certain number of feet per minute; next, all to carry steam the same height, and all to work steam full stroke, or to cut off a certain amount, which ought to be stated, and to have the engines then to deduct a certain amount for friction. The presumption is that all the engines are to be finished complete and true, so that they will work to good advantage.

Nine square feet of boiler surface are said to be equal to one horse power; and one square foot of grate bar surface in the boiler furnace gives the same power.

TABLES OF HORSE POWERS, PRICES, &c.

Diameter of Cylinder.	Horse Power.	Diameter of Cylinder.	Horse Power.	Diameter of Cylinder.	Horse Power.
inches.		inches.		inches.	
1	$\frac{1}{5}$	26	$135\frac{1}{5}$	51	$520\frac{1}{5}$
2	$\frac{4}{5}$	27	$145\frac{4}{5}$	52	$540\frac{4}{5}$
3	$1\frac{4}{5}$	28	$156\frac{4}{5}$	53	$561\frac{1}{4}$
4	$3\frac{1}{5}$	29	$168\frac{1}{4}$	54	$583\frac{1}{5}$
5	5	30	180	55	605
6	$7\frac{1}{5}$	31	$192\frac{1}{5}$	56	$627\frac{1}{5}$
7	$9\frac{4}{5}$	32	$204\frac{4}{5}$	57	$649\frac{4}{5}$
8	$12\frac{4}{5}$	33	$217\frac{4}{5}$	58	$672\frac{4}{5}$
9	$16\frac{1}{5}$	34	$231\frac{1}{5}$	59	$696\frac{1}{5}$
10	20	35	247	60	720
11	$24\frac{1}{5}$	36	$259\frac{1}{5}$	70	980
12	$28\frac{4}{5}$	37	$273\frac{4}{5}$	71	$1008\frac{1}{5}$
13	$33\frac{4}{5}$	38	$288\frac{4}{5}$	72	$1036\frac{4}{5}$
14	$39\frac{1}{5}$	39	$304\frac{1}{5}$	73	$1069\frac{4}{5}$
15	45	40	320	74	$1095\frac{1}{5}$
16	$51\frac{1}{5}$	41	$336\frac{1}{5}$	75	1125
17	$57\frac{4}{5}$	42	$352\frac{4}{5}$	76	$1155\frac{1}{5}$
18	$64\frac{4}{5}$	43	$369\frac{4}{5}$	78	$1216\frac{4}{5}$
19	$72\frac{1}{5}$	44	$387\frac{1}{5}$	79	$1248\frac{1}{5}$
20	80	45	405	80	1280
21	$88\frac{1}{5}$	46	$423\frac{1}{5}$	81	$1312\frac{1}{5}$
32	$96\frac{4}{5}$	47	$441\frac{4}{5}$	82	$1344\frac{4}{5}$
23	$105\frac{4}{5}$	48	$460\frac{4}{5}$	83	$1337\frac{4}{5}$
24	$115\frac{1}{5}$	49	$480\frac{1}{5}$	84	$1411\frac{1}{5}$
25	125	50	500	85	1445

NOTE.—All these calculations are for a medium height of steam and speed.

OSCILLATING ENGINES.

A.—1.

Diameter of Bore of Cylinder.	Length of Stroke.	Revolutions per Minute.	Estimated Horse Power.	Price with Fire Front, Grate Bars, &c., and without Boiler or Pipes.	Price with Boiler and all complete, except Smoke Stack.	Price without Grate Bars, Fire Front, Governor, or anything but Engine.
in.	in.					
3½	7	300 to 325	4	$175	$225	$150
4½	9	260 to 300	6	225	300	200
5½	10	240 to 290	10	325	450	300
7	13	180 to 225	16	450	650	400
9	14	170 to 200	25	600	850	550
11	18	130 to 180	40	700	1150	650
13	18	130 to 180	56	900	1300	800
14	22	109 to 150	65	1100	1600	1000
16	24	109 to 150	85	1250	1800	1150

2.

Diameter of Bore of Cylinder.	Length of Stroke.	Revolutions per Minute.	Estimated Horse Power.	Price with Fire Front, Grate Bars, &c., and without Boiler or Pipes.	Price with Boiler and all complete, except Smoke Stack.	Price without Grate Bars, Fire Front, Governor, or anything but Engine.
in.	in.					
3½	7	200 to 225	2	$175	$225	$150
4½	9	175 to 200	4	225	300	200
5½	10	150 to 175	6	325	450	300
7	13	125 to 150	10	450	650	400
9	14	120 to 140	15	600	850	550
11	18	100 to 120	25	700	1100	650
13	18	90 to 110	40	900	1350	800
14	22	80 to 100	50	1100	1600	1000
16	24	65 to 75	65	1250	1800	1150

B.

Estimated Horse Power.	Diameter of Cylinder	Length of Stroke.	Number of Revolutions.	Price for Engine alone.	Price, including Fire Front, Grate Bars, without Boiler or Pipes.	Price, including Fire Front and Grate, Pipes, with Common Cylinder Boiler.	Price, including Fire Front, Bars, Pipes and Double Flue Boiler.	Price, including Front Bars, Pipes, Portable Boiler, Furnace in it.
2	4	8	200	$165	$180	$255	$275	$320
3	4½	8	200	185	200	275	300	360
5	5	10	180	225	245	375	400	475
5	6	8	200	225	245	375	400	475
6 to 7	6	12	150	325	350	500	535	650
10	7½	15	125	425	450	700	750	925
15	8½	18	110	525	550	850	900	1050
20	10	12	150	600	675	1125	1200	1425
25	10	24	75	650	720	1175	1350	
35	12	24	75	800	900	1350	1425	
45	14	28	60	900	1000	1550	1650	
55	16	32	50	1000	1100	1600	1800	
65	18	36	45	1100	1200	1750	1900	
75	20	40	40	1200	1300	1900	2050	
85	22	44	35	1300	1400	2100	2350	
100	25	50	30	1450	1800	2600	3200	

C.

Diameter of Cylinder.	Length of Stroke.	Price.	Diameter of Cylinder.	Length of Stroke.	Price.
inches.	inches.		inches.	inches.	
4	8	$150	12	24	$800
5	10	225	14	28	950
6	12	300	16	32	1150
7½	15	400	18	36	1400
8½	17	500	20	40	1650
10	12	600	22	44	2000
10	24	650	24	48	2300

D.

Diameter of Bore of Cylinder.	Length of Stroke.	Revolutions per Minute.	Estimated Horse Power.	Price with Fire Front, Grate Bars, &c., and without Boiler or Pipes.	Price with Boiler and all complete, except Smoke Stack.	Price without Grate Bars, Fire Front, Governor, or anything but Engine.
in.	in.					
4½	9	200	4 to 6	$225	$300	$200
5½	10	175	6 to 8	325	450	300
7	13	150	10 to 12	450	650	400
9	14	140	15 to 20	600	850	550
11	18	120	25 to 30	700	1100	650
13	18	110	40 to 45	900	1350	800
14	22	100	50 to 60	1100	1600	1000
16	24	75	65 to 75	1250	1800	1150

PORTABLE ENGINES.

A.

Horse Power.	Bore of Cylinder.	Stroke of Cylinder.	Weight of Engines.	Price complete.
	inches.	inches.	lbs.	
3	4	6	1800	$280
4	4½	10	2200	350
5	5	10	3000	425
7	6	12	3500	550
9	7	14	4000	685
12	8	16	4800	900

B.

NEW STYLE:

Horse Power.	Cash Price.	Estimated Weight.	Space occupied.	Diameter of Fly Wheel.	Face of Wheel.
		lbs.	feet.	inches.	inches.
1½	$175	1000	2x5	24	4
2½	275	1800	4x5	39	5½
3	325	2000	5x4	39	5½
4	400	2200	7x5	40	6
6	575	3000	7x5	44	7
8	735	4500	9x6⅓	48	8
10	880	5900	10x6½	60	8
12	1025	7000	14x6½	72	12
15	1300	9000	15x7	72	12
20	1700	10500	16x7	72	12

ANSWERS TO COMMON INQUIRIES.

1. The machinery is permanently attached to the boiler, and the engine may be removed entire from place to place, without deranging or injuring any part of it.

2. The boiler is locomotive, which is the best in use, generating from a third to a half more steam than others, with the same fire and water space, occupying less room, and adapted to both wood and coal.

3. The exhaust steam passes directly into the smoke pipe, by which all sparks from the fire are extinguished.

4. This engine is admirably suited to all kinds of mechanical and agricultural pursuits, where motive power is required.

5. An engine of four horse power, for example, will cut a cord of wood from the log in *ten minutes.* To run an engine of this size, it takes about one-eighth of a cord of good dry wood, and one hundred gallons of water per day. For a fifteen horse power, about one cord of wood and three hundred gallons of water per day.

6. Not only hard, but wood in all its forms may be used.

OLD STYLE.

Horse Power.	Cash Price.	Estimated Weight.	Space occupied.	Diameter of Fly Wheel.	Face of Wheel.
		lbs.	feet.	inches.	inches.
1½	$175	1000	2x5	24	4
2½	250	2000	4x5	39	5½
3	300	2200	5x4	39	5½
4	375	2500	7x5	40	6
6	550	3600	7x5	44	7
8	700	4800	9x6⅓	48	8
10	875	6000	10x6½	60	8
12	1050	7500	14x6½	72	12
15	1300	9000	15x7	72	12
20	1700	10500	16x7	72	12

The above list contains the price of engines complete, ready for smoke pipe and band. Smoke pipe furnished at ten cents per pound. The above prices include the expenses of boxing and shipping.

C.

WEIGHT AND DIMENSIONS.

Horse Power.	Weight.	Length.	Width.	Height.	Bore of Cylinder.	Length of Stroke.	Revolutions per Minu'e.	Diameter of Driving Pulley.	Width of Face.	
	lbs.	feet.	ft.	ft.	in.	in.		in.	in.	
12	7500	14	5	6	8	16	120	60	12	Cut off and Governor.
10	7000	14	5	6	8	16	100	60	12	" " "
8	5800	10½	5	6	8	14	110	48	12	" " "
6	4200	10	4	5½	7	14	120	48	9	" " "
4	2600	8½	3½	5	5⅝	12	140	42	6½	" " "
3	2000	6½	3½	5	5⅝	8	150	42	6½	" " "
2½	1600	6	3¼	4½	4½	8	150	30	6	L. Valve—Printers.
2	1000	5½	3	3½	3½	8	160	18	3½	S. Valve & Governor.
1½	900	5	3	3½	3½	8	160	18	3½	Lap " " "
1	700	4	2½	3	3	6	160	18	3½	Sqr. " " "

Horse Power.	Price.	For Blower.	Horse Power.	Price.	For Blower.
12	$985	$15	3	$262	$10
10	825	15	2½	212	8
8	665	15	2	167	8
6	480	15	1½	140	5
4	340	10	1	115	5

For extra finished engines: 12 horse power, $1100—10 do., $900—8 do., $740—6 do., $550.

PRICE OF ENGLISH PORTABLE ENGINES.

Extract from Ed. Cor. of the Ohio Cultivator of September 1, 1851, *dated London, August* 6, 1851.

In horse powers and threshing machines, also, our country is decidedly in advance of England; but unfortunately, there are no good specimens here on exhibition, to prove our assertion. We find that *steam power* is fast superseding horse power for threshing, grinding, cutting straw, &c., in this country; and this improvement, we doubt not, will soon be introduced by extensive farmers in our country.

Portable steam engines, of from four to six horse power, are here found more economical than horse power for threshing and other farm purposes. This would especially be the case in our country, where one engine and threshing machine could do the work of a neighborhood. These engines are constructed on a similar principle to that of a railway locomotive, only much lighter and simpler. They are mounted on four wheels like a wagon, with the tire of double width, and can easily be drawn from place to place by a pair of horses. The following table will show the weight, cost and consumption of coal per day (of ten hours), of the different size engines, as advertised by one firm, who have made and sold about *one hundred* engines during the past twelve months:

Horse Power.	Coal per day.	Weight.	Price.
3	3 cwt.	30 cwt.	$654 75
5	5 cwt.	50 cwt.	848 75
7	7 cwt.	60 cwt.	1042 75
9	9 cwt.	75 cwt.	1236 75

VERTICAL STEAM ENGINES.

Horse Power.	Bore of Cylinder. inches.	Length of Stroke. inches.	Price.
5	6½	16	$1000
10	9	22	1350
15	11	22	1600

The above prices do not include boiler or pipes. Locomotive, flue, or plain cylinder boiler, for ditto, furnished to order.

The pedestal of 5 horse engine is 3 feet by 2 inches by 2 feet 10 inches.

The band fly-wheel of ditto, is 5 feet 9 inches diameter, and weighs 1700 pounds.

The pedestal of 10 horse engine is 4 feet by 3 feet 5 inches.

The band fly-wheel of ditto, is 7 feet by 3 inches diameter, and weighs 2750 pounds.

The prices of engines in all the foregoing tables are as they were when currency was nearly equal to gold; now, (1864) they cost about three times as much.

RULE

TO FIND THE NUMBER OF REVOLUTIONS OF THE LAST DRIVEN WHEEL TO ONE REVOLUTION OF THE FIRST DRIVER.

Multiply the number of cogs of the driving wheels together, and the number of cogs of the driven wheels together. Divide the first product by the last, and the quotient will be the answer.

EXAMPLE.

1st driver, 100 cogs—2d, 74—3d, 40—4th, 80—5th, 60.
1st driven, 25 cogs—2d, 37—3d, 30—4th, 40—5th, 35.

```
   100 cogs.                 25 cogs.
    74 cogs.                 37 cogs.
  ------                    -----
  7400                      175
     40 cogs.               75
  ------                    -----
 296000                     925
      80 cogs.                30 cogs.
 --------                   -----
 23680000                   27750
        60 cogs.              40 cogs.
 ----------                 -------
 1420800000                 1110000
                                 35 cogs.
                            -------
                            5550000
                           3330000
                           --------
                           38850000
```

```
3885,0000 ) 142080,0000 ( 36 444/777 revs.
            11655
            -----
             25630
             23310
             -----
          5 ) 2220 ( 444/777
              3885
```

$36\frac{444}{777}$
1st driver, 100 revs. per min.

$3657\frac{1}{4}$ revolutions per minute.

$$\begin{array}{r} 444 \\ 100 \\ \hline 777\,)\,44400\,(\,57\frac{1}{7} \\ 3885 \\ \hline 5550 \\ 5439 \\ \hline 111\,)\frac{111}{777}(\,\frac{1}{7} \end{array}$$

NOTE.—In order to find the speed of the last driven wheel, the above quotient must be multiplied by the number of revolutions of the first driver per minute. In the above example the first driver makes 100 revolutions per minute, then $36\frac{444}{777} \times 100$ is $3657\frac{1}{7}$, which is the number per minute of the revolutions of the last driven wheel.

An idler must either be counted both driver and driven, or left out of the process altogether. The fifth driving wheel in the above example and the fourth driven are the same, and should be omitted.

$$100 \times 74 \times 60 \times 80 = 35520000$$
$$25 \times 37 \times 30 \times 35 = 971250$$

3552000 divided by $971250 = 36\frac{444}{777}$

The reason why the idler is omitted is, that it works on both sides, as will be seen in the plate; the idler is known also by the names of leader and carrier.

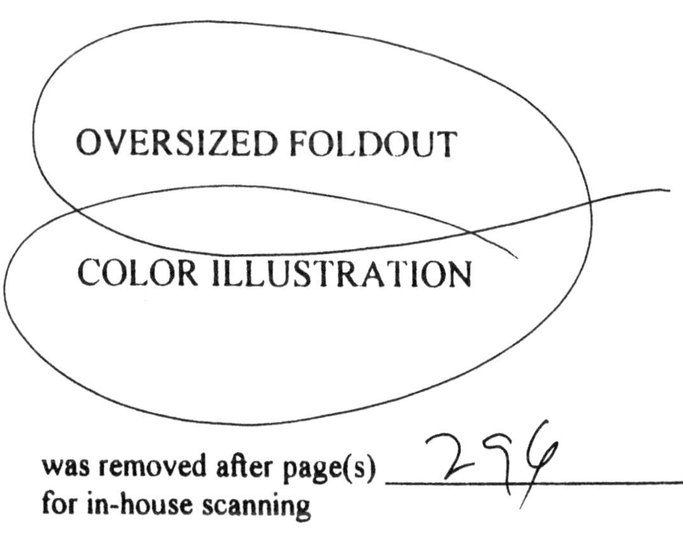

was removed after page(s) 296
for in-house scanning

On 8·18 2000

Table of Areas and Circumferences and Sides of Equal Squares.

Diam.	Area.	Circumference.	Side of Equal Square.	Diam.	Area.	Circumference.	Side of Equal Square.
				2½	4.908	7.854	2.2155
⅛	.0122	.3927	.1107	⅝	5.411	8.246	2.3262
¼	.0490	.7854	.2115	¾	5.939	8.639	2.4370
⅜	.1104	1.1781	.3223	⅞	6.491	9.032	2.5478
½	.1963	1.5708	.4331	3	7.068	9.424	2.6586
⅝	.3068	1.9635	.5438	⅛	7.669	9.817	2.7694
¾	.4417	2.3562	.6646	¼	8.295	10.210	2.8801
⅞	.6013	2.7489	.7754	⅜	8.946	10.602	2.9909
1	.7854	3.1416	.8862	½	9.621	10.995	3.1017
⅛	.9940	3.5343	.9969	⅝	10.320	11.388	3.2124
¼	1.2271	3.9270	1.0775	¾	11.044	11.781	3.3232
⅜	1.4848	4.3197	1.2185	⅞	11.793	12.173	3.4340
½	1.7671	4.7124	1.3293	4	12.566	12.566	3.5448
⅝	2.0739	5.1051	1.4401	⅛	13.364	12.959	3.6555
¾	2.4052	5.4978	1.5508	¼	14.186	13.351	3.7663
⅞	2.7611	5.8905	1.6616	⅜	15.033	13.744	3.8771
2	3.1416	6.2832	1.7724	½	15.904	14.137	3.9880
⅛	3.5465	6.6759	1.8831	⅝	16.800	14.529	4.0987
¼	3.9760	7.0686	1.9939	¾	17.720	14.922	4.2095
⅜	4.4302	7.4613	2.1047	⅞	18.665	15.315	4.3202

Diam.	Area.	Circumference.	Side of Equal Square.	Diam.	Area.	Circumference.	Side of Equal Square.
5	19.635	15.708	4.4310	7½	44.178	23.562	6.6465
⅛	20.629	16.100	4.5417	⅝	45.663	23.954	6.7573
¼	21.647	16.493	4.6525	¾	47.173	24.347	6.8681
⅜	22.690	16.886	4.7633	⅞	48.707	24.740	6.9789
½	23.758	17.278	4.8741	8	50,265	25.132	7.0897
⅝	24.850	17.671	4.9848	⅛	51.848	25.515	7.2005
¾	25.967	18.064	5.0956	¼	53.456	25.918	7.3112
⅞	27.108	18.457	5.2064	⅜	55.088	26.310	7.4220
6	28.274	18.849	5.3172	½	56.745	26.703	7.5328
⅛	29 464	19.242	5.4280	⅝	58.426	27.096	7.6436
¼	30,679	19.635	5.5388	¾	60.132	27.489	7.7544
⅜	31.919	20.027	5.6495	⅞	61.862	27.881	7.8651
½	33.183	20.420	5.7603	9	63.617	28.274	7.9760
⅝	34.471	20.813	5.8711	⅛	65.396	28.667	8.0866
¾	35.784	21.205	5.9819	¼	67.200	29.059	8.1974
⅞	37.122	21.598	6.0927	⅜	69.029	29.452	8.3081
7	38.484	21.991	6.2034	½	70.882	29.845	8.4190
⅛	39.871	22.383	6.3142	⅝	72.759	30.237	8.5297
¼	41.282	22.776	6.4350	¾	74.662	30.630	8.6405
⅜	42.718	23.169	6.5358	⅞	76.588	31.023	8.7513

Diam.	Area.	Circumference.	Side of Equal Square.	Diam.	Area.	Circumference.	Side of Equal Square.
10	78.53	31.41	8.86	15	176.71	47.12	13.29
¼	82.51	32.20	9.08	¼	182.65	47.90	13.51
½	86.59	32.98	9.30	½	188.69	48.69	13.73
¾	90.76	33.77	9.52	¾	194.82	49.48	13.95
11	95.03	34.55	9.74	16	201.06	50.26	14.17
¼	99.40	35.34	9.97	¼	207.39	51.05	14.40
¼	103.86	36.12	10.19	½	213.82	51.83	14.62
¾	108.43	36.91	10.41	¾	220.35	52.62	14.84
12	113.09	37.69	10.63	17	226.98	53.40	15.06
¼	117.85	38.48	10.85	¼	233.70	54.19	15.28
½	122.71	39.26	11.07	½	240.52	54.97	15.50
¾	127.67	40.05	11.29	¾	247.44	55.76	15.73
13	132.73	40.84	11.52	18	264.46	56.54	15.95
¼	137.88	41.62	11.74	¼	266.58	57.33	16.17
½	143.13	42.41	11.96	½	268.80	58.11	16.39
¾	148.48	43.19	12.18	¾	276.11	58.90	16.61
14	153.93	43.98	12.40	19	283.52	59.69	16.83
¼	159.48	44.76	12.62	¼	291.03	60.47	17.05
½	165.12	45.55	12.85	½	298.64	61.26	17.28
¾	170.87	46.33	13.07	¾	306.35	62.04	17.50

Diam.	Area.	Circumference.	Side of Equal Square.	Diam.	Area.	Circumference.	Side of Equal Square.
20	314.15	62.83	17.72	25	490.87	78.53	22.15
¼	322.06	63.61	17.94	¼	500.74	79.32	22.37
½	330.06	64.40	18.16	½	510.70	80.11	22 59
¾	338.16	65.18	18.38	¾	520.76	80.89	22.82
21	346.36	65.97	18.61	26	530.92	81.68	23.04
¼	354.63	66.75	18.83	¼	541.18	82.46	23.26
½	363.05	67.54	19.05	½	551.54	83.25	23.48
¾	371.54	68.32	19.27	¾	562.00	84.03	23.70
22	380.13	69 11	19.49	27	572.55	84.82	23.92
¼	388 82	69.90	19.71	¼	583.20	85.60	24.14
½	397.60	70.68	19.94	½	593.95	86.39	24.37
¾	406.49	71.47	20.16	¾	604.80	87.17	24.59
23	415.47	72.25	20.38	28	615.75	87.96	24.81
¼	424.55	73.04	20.60	¼	626.79	88.74	25.03
½	433.73	73.82	20.82	½	637.92	89.53	25.25
¾	443.01	74.61	21.04	¾	649.18	90.32	25.47
24	452.38	75.39	21.26	29	660.51	91.10	25.70
¼	461.86	76.18	21.49	¼	671.95	91.89	25.92
½	471.43	76 96	21.71	½	683.49	92.67	26.14
¾	481.10	77.75	21.93	¾	695.12	93.46	26.36

Diam.	Area.	Circumference.	Side of Equal Square.	Diam.	Area.	Circumference.	Side of Equal Square.
30	706.85	94.24	26.58	35	962.11	109.95	31.01
¼	718.68	95.03	26.80	¼	975.90	110.74	31.23
½	730.61	95.81	27.02	½	989.79	111.52	31.46
¾	742.64	96.60	27.25	¾	1103.78	112.31	31.68
31	754.76	97.38	27.47	36	1017.87	113.09	31.90
¼	766.99	98.17	27.69	¼	1032.06	113.88	32.12
½	779.31	98.96	27.91	½	1046.34	114.66	32.34
¾	791.73	99.74	28.13	¾	1060.72	115.45	32.56
32	804.24	100.53	28.35	37	1075.21	116.23	32.79
¼	816.86	101.31	28.58	¼	1089.78	117.02	33.01
½	829.57	102.10	28.80	½	1104.46	117.80	33.23
¾	842.38	102.88	29.02	¾	1119.24	118.59	33.45
33	855.29	103.67	29.24	38	1134.11	119.38	33.67
¼	868.30	104.45	29.46	¼	1149.08	120.16	33.89
½	881.41	105.24	29.68	½	1164.15	120.95	34.11
¾	894.61	106.02	29.91	¾	1179.32	121.73	34.34
34	907.92	106.81	30.13	39	1194.59	122.52	34.56
¼	921.32	107.59	30.35	¼	1209.95	123.30	34.78
½	934.82	108.38	30.57	½	1225.41	124.09	35.00
¾	948.41	109.17	30.79	¾	1240.97	124.87	35.22

Diam.	Area.	Circumference.	Side of Equal Square.	Diam.	Area.	Circumference.	Side of Equal Square.
40	1256.63	125.66	35.44	45	1590.43	141.37	39.88
¼	1272.39	126.44	35.67	¼	1608.15	142.15	40.10
½	1288.24	127.23	35.89	½	1625.97	142.94	40.32
¾	1304.20	128.01	36.11	¾	1643.88	143.72	40.54
41	1320.02	128.80	36.33	46	1661.90	144.51	40.76
¼	1336.40	129.59	36.55	¼	1680.01	145.29	40.98
½	1352.65	130.37	36.77	½	1698.22	146.08	41.20
¾	1368.99	131.16	36.99	¾	1716.53	146.86	41.43
42	1385.44	131.94	37.22	47	1734.94	147.65	41.65
¼	1401.98	132.73	37.44	¼	1753.45	148.44	41.87
½	1418.62	133.51	37.66	½	1772.05	149.22	42.09
¾	1435.36	134.30	37.88	¾	1790.75	150.01	42.31
43	1452 20	135.08	38.10	48	1809.55	150.79	42.53
¼	1469.13	135.87	38.32	¼	1828.45	151.58	42.76
½	1486.16	136.65	38.55	½	1847.45	152.36	42.98
¾	1503.30	137.44	38.77	¾	1866.54	153.15	43.20
44	1520.53	138.23	38.99	49	1885.74	153.93	43.42
¼	1537.85	139.01	39.21	¼	1905.83	154.72	43.64
½	1556.28	139.80	39.43	½	1924.42	155.50	43.86
¾	1572.80	140.58	39.65	¾	1943.90	156.29	44.08

Diam.	Area.	Circumference.	Side of Equal Square.	Diam.	Area.	Circumference.	Side of Equal Square.
50	1963.49	157.07	44.31	55	2375.82	172.78	48.74
¼	1983.17	157.96	44.53	¼	2397.47	173.57	48.96
½	2002.96	158.65	44.75	½	2419.22	174.35	49.18
¾	2022.84	159.43	44.97	¾	2441.06	175.14	49.40
51	2042.82	160.22	45.19	56	2463.00	175.92	49.62
¼	2062.89	161.00	45.41	¼	2485.04	167.71	49.85
½	2083.07	161.79	45.64	½	2507.18	177.49	50.07
¾	2103.34	162.57	45 86	¾	2520.42	178.28	50.29
52	2123.71	163.36	46.08	57	2551.75	179.07	50.51
¼	2144.18	164.14	46.30	¼	2574.19	179.85	50.73
½	2164.75	164.93	46.52	½	2596.72	180.64	50.95
¾	2185.41	165.71	46.74	¾	2619.35	181.42	51.17
53	2206.18	166.50	46.97	58	2642.07	182.21	51.40
¼	2227.04	167.28	47.19	¼	2664.90	182.99	51.62
½	2248.00	168.07	47.41	½	2687.82	183.78	51.84
¾	2269.06	168.86	47.63	¾	2710.85	184.56	52.06
54	2290.22	169.64	47.85	59	2733.97	185.35	52.28
¼	2311.47	170.43	48.07	¼	2757.18	186.13	52.50
½	2332.82	171.21	48.29	½	2780.50	186.92	52.73
¾	2354.28	172.00	48.52	¾	2803.92	187.71	52.95

Diam.	Area.	Circumference.	Side of Equal Square.	Diam	Area.	Circumference.	Side of Equal Square.
60	2827.43	188.49	53.17	65	3318.30	204.20	57 60
¼	2851.04	189.28	53.39	¼	3343 88	204 98	57.82
½	2874.75	190.06	53.61	½	3369.55	205.77	58.04
¾	2898.56	190.85	53.83	¾	3395.23	206.55	58.26
61	2922.46	191.63	54.05	66	3421.19	207.34	58.49
¼	2946.47	192.42	54.28	¼	3447.16	208.13	58.71
½	2970.57	193.20	54.50	½	3473.22	208.91	58.93
¾	2994.77	193.99	54.72	¾	3499.39	209.70	59.15
62	3019.07	194.77	54.94	67	3525.65	210.48	59.37
¼	3043.46	195.56	55.16	¼	3552.01	211.27	59.59
½	3067.96	196.34	55.38	½	3578.47	212.05	59.82
¾	3092.55	197.13	55.61	¾	3605.02	212.84	60.04
63	3117.24	197.92	55.83	68	3631.68	213.62	60.26
¼	3142.03	198.70	56.05	¼	3658.43	212.41	60.48
½	3166.92	199.49	56.27	½	3685.28	215.19	60.70
¾	3191.90	200.27	56.49	¾	3712.23	215.98	60.92
64	3216.99	201.06	56.71	69	3739.28	216.76	61.14
¼	3242.17	201.84	56.94	¼	3766.42	217.55	61.37
½	3267.45	202.63	57.16	½	3793.66	218.34	61.59
¾	3292.83	203.41	57.38	¾	3821.01	219.12	61.81

GOVERNORS OR REGULATORS.

No part of the steam engine has proved to be more of a failure than the governor. Latterly, however, they are making great improvements in this part of the engine. The principal cause of failure was the speed of the governor, which was either too fast or too slow. Another cause was defective butterfly valves, which are seldom if ever made tight. In a few instances these valves have done very well. Another cause was that the balls were frequently made too light, &c., and had to be weighted with lead or something else.

The following extract is from an English work by Robert Brunton:

"GOVERNOR, OR DOUBLE PENDULUM.—If the revolution be the same, whatever be the length of the arms, the balls will revolve in the same plane, and the distance of that plane from the point of suspension, is equal to the length of a pendulum, the vibrations of which will be double the revolutions of the balls. For example; suppose the distance between the point of suspension and plane of revolution be 36 inches, the vibrations that a pendulum of 36 inches will make per minute, is $= \frac{375}{\sqrt{36}} = 62$ vibrations, and $\frac{62}{2} = 31$ revolutions per minute the balls ought to make."

Another example from Mr. Thomson, formerly an engine builder in Pittsburgh, but now superintendent of the city gas works:

"A common pendulum will make two vibrations in

the same time that the balls of a conical pendulum on a steam governor of the same length from the centre of suspension to the centre of oscillation, will perform one revolution. Therefore to ascertain the proper length of the rods of a governor, that is required to make a given number of revolutions per minute, by the foregoing rule, find the length of a pendulum that will vibrate twice for every revolution required of the governor, and it will be the proper length for the rods of the governor."

The following is from a work on the steam engine, by James Renwick, LL. D.:

"The action of the fly, in producing regularity of motion, reaches only to the inequalities that take place in the motion of the piston, during a single stroke. Should the flow of steam increase, the mean motion of the fly wheel will be accelerated, and should the flow be diminished, the fly-wheel will uniformly be retarded. Neither does it control any change in the motion of the machinery, driven by the steam, unless that change be periodic. But it frequently happens that the quantity of steam, supplied by the boiler, fluctuates. Some regulator is, therefore, necessary, which shall control the prime mover itself. For this purpose, a governor is adapted to the steam engine. This is also required in cases where the quantity of work to be performed is fluctuating, as is the case in many branches of manufactures, where a part of the machinery may be suddenly stopped, or may be as suddenly connected with the engine. The governor is an apparatus that is sometimes called a conical pendulum. Two heavy balls are suspended by bars to the opposite sides of a vertical axis. This axis is set in motion by the engine; as it turns, the balls of the governor acquire a centrifugal force, which may be sufficient to overcome their weight, and cause them to diverge and fly off, performing in their course a larger circle than before. As the balls fly off, they act, through the intervention of a system of levers, upon a valve that is situated in the steam pipe. This, which is called the throttle-valve, has the form of a circular disk of metal, exactly filling up the pipe, when placed across it. It turns upon pivots placed at the opposite ends of one of its diameters, and may thus, either present its edge to the steam that passes along the pipe, in which case it hardly resists its course; or may assume any intermediate position, until it close the pipe altogether. When the balls of the governor revolve with so little velocity that the centrifugal force cannot overcome their weight, the levers place the throttle valve in the position that presents its edge to the steam; when the velocity becomes great enough to throw out the balls to their utmost limit, this valve is thrown across the pipe, and shuts the passage completely; with intermediate positions of the valves, the passage is more or less open, according to the rotary velocity of the governor.

"The governor is driven by a strap that passes over a drum on the axis of the crank, or by wheels and pinions, deriving their motion from the same part of the engine."

Either of these two plans will do. In order to increase the speed of an engine governor to any rate you may please, all that is necessary is to have a counter shaft with a nest of 2, 3 or more pulleys, and a corresponding set of pulleys on the governor shaft, and if the engine is running on the slow speed, and you wish to increase it, when putting on the blast all that is necessary is to shift the belt of the small pulley on the governor shaft on to the larger; this reduces the speed of the governor, and opens the valve and runs the engine faster, and in this way you can have any speed on the engine you please, or as many different speeds as you have different pulleys. In order that a governor work well it should be very sensitive, and work with as little friction as possible; the arms on which the balls are suspended should be about 30 degrees when down, and allowed to rise 10 degrees, and not more than 15, which would be an angle of 45 degrees when up.

I will conclude by giving you a practical rule to get the proper speed for the governor. Put a temporary crank on the governor shaft, and turn it round by hand until it raises the frog or balls exactly half way up, and count the number of revolutions per minute; this will give the right speed for the governor: or if you prefer you can put on a temporary pulley on the governor shaft, and run it with a belt from some other pulley in the shop, and in this way you would have a more regular motion than by hand.

TABLE OF THE WEIGHT OF CAST IRON PIPES.

Bore.	Thick.	Long.	Weight.			Bore.	Thick.	Long.	Weight.			Bore.	Thick.	Long.	Weight.		
1	$\frac{1}{4}$	3 ft.6	0	0	12	$6\frac{1}{2}$	$\frac{5}{8}$	9	3	2	21	$11\frac{1}{2}$	$\frac{3}{4}$	9	7	2	8
	$\frac{3}{8}$	3 ft.6	0	0	21		$\frac{3}{4}$	9	4	1	21		1	9	10	1	2
$1\frac{1}{2}$	$\frac{1}{4}$	4 ft.6	0	0	21		1	9	6	0	14	12	$\frac{1}{2}$	9	5	0	24
	$\frac{3}{8}$	4 ft.6	0	1	4	7	$\frac{3}{8}$	9	2	1	7		$\frac{5}{8}$	9	6	2	8
2	$\frac{1}{4}$	6	0	1	8		$\frac{1}{2}$	9	3	0	7		$\frac{3}{4}$	9	7	3	20
	$\frac{3}{8}$	6	0	2	0		$\frac{5}{8}$	9	3	3	20		1	9	10	3	0
$2\frac{1}{2}$	$\frac{1}{4}$	6	0	1	16		$\frac{3}{4}$	9	4	3	5	$12\frac{1}{2}$	$\frac{1}{2}$	6	5	1	16
	$\frac{3}{8}$	6	0	2	10		1	9	6	2	4		$\frac{5}{8}$	9	6	3	9
	$\frac{1}{2}$	6	0	3	10	$7\frac{1}{2}$	$\frac{3}{8}$	9	2	2	4		$\frac{3}{4}$	9	8	1	0
3	$\frac{1}{4}$	9	0	2	20		$\frac{1}{2}$	9	3	1	6		1	9	11	0	21
	$\frac{3}{8}$	9	1	0	6		$\frac{5}{8}$	9	4	0	22	13	$\frac{1}{2}$	9	5	2	20
	$\frac{1}{2}$	9	1	1	12		$\frac{3}{4}$	9	5	0	10		$\frac{5}{8}$	9	7	0	14
	$\frac{5}{8}$	9	1	3	6		1	9	7	0	0		$\frac{3}{4}$	9	8	2	7
	$\frac{3}{4}$	9	2	1	0	8	$\frac{1}{2}$	9	3	2	4		1	9	11	2	12
$3\frac{1}{2}$	$\frac{1}{4}$	9	0	3	0		$\frac{5}{8}$	9	4	1	25	$13\frac{1}{2}$	$\frac{1}{2}$	9	5	3	7
	$\frac{3}{8}$	9	1	0	21		$\frac{3}{4}$	9	5	1	18		$\frac{5}{8}$	9	7	1	12
	$\frac{1}{2}$	9	1	2	14		1	9	7	1	16		$\frac{3}{4}$	9	8	3	16
	$\frac{5}{8}$	9	2	0	8	$8\frac{1}{2}$	$\frac{1}{2}$	9	3	3	2		1	9	11	3	24
	$\frac{3}{4}$	9	2	2	0		$\frac{5}{8}$	9	4	2	26	14	$\frac{1}{2}$	9	6	0	4
4	$\frac{3}{8}$	9	1	1	10		$\frac{3}{4}$	9	5	2	22		$\frac{5}{8}$	9	7	2	16
	$\frac{1}{2}$	9	1	3	12		1	9	7	3	8		$\frac{3}{4}$	9	9	1	0
	$\frac{5}{8}$	9	2	2	12	9	$\frac{1}{2}$	9	4	0	0		1	9	12	1	14
	$\frac{3}{4}$	9	2	3	21		$\frac{5}{8}$	9	5	0	4	$14\frac{1}{2}$	$\frac{1}{2}$	9	6	0	24
$4\frac{1}{2}$	$\frac{3}{8}$	9	1	2	2		$\frac{3}{4}$	9	6	0	2		$\frac{5}{8}$	9	7	3	14
	$\frac{1}{2}$	9	2	0	4		1	9	8	0	26		$\frac{3}{4}$	9	9	2	2
	$\frac{5}{8}$	9	2	2	14	$9\frac{1}{2}$	$\frac{1}{2}$	9	4	0	18		1	9	12	3	6
	$\frac{3}{4}$	9	3	0	21		$\frac{5}{8}$	9	5	1	0	15	$\frac{1}{2}$	9	6	1	21
5	$\frac{3}{8}$	9	1	2	22		$\frac{3}{4}$	9	6	1	6		$\frac{5}{8}$	9	8	0	14
	$\frac{1}{2}$	9	2	1	10		1	9	8	2	20		$\frac{3}{4}$	9	9	3	7
	$\frac{5}{8}$	9	2	3	17	10	$\frac{1}{2}$	9	4	1	10		1	9	13	0	26
	$\frac{3}{4}$	9	3	1	24		$\frac{5}{8}$	9	5	1	26		$1\frac{1}{4}$	9	16	3	5
$5\frac{1}{2}$	$\frac{3}{8}$	9	1	3	10		$\frac{3}{4}$	9	6	2	14	$15\frac{1}{2}$	$\frac{1}{2}$	9	6	2	14
	$\frac{1}{2}$	9	2	2	0		1	9	9	0	8		$\frac{5}{8}$	9	8	1	14
	$\frac{5}{8}$	9	3	0	18	$10\frac{1}{2}$	$\frac{1}{2}$	9	4	2	14		$\frac{3}{4}$	9	10	0	10
	$\frac{3}{4}$	9	3	3	7		$\frac{5}{8}$	9	5	3	7		1	9	13	2	17
	1	9	5	0	12		$\frac{3}{4}$	9	7	0	0		$1\frac{1}{4}$	9	17	1	6
6	$\frac{3}{8}$	9	2	0	0		1	9	9	2	0	16	$\frac{1}{2}$	9	7	0	22
	$\frac{1}{2}$	9	2	2	21	11	$\frac{1}{2}$	9	4	3	14		$\frac{5}{8}$	9	8	3	7
	$\frac{5}{8}$	9	3	1	17		$\frac{5}{8}$	9	6	0	11		$\frac{3}{4}$	9	10	1	20
	$\frac{3}{4}$	9	4	0	16		$\frac{3}{4}$	9	7	1	7		1	9	14	0	8
	1	9	5	2	20		1	9	9	3	20		$1\frac{1}{4}$	9	17	3	14
$6\frac{1}{2}$	$\frac{3}{8}$	9	2	0	16	$11\frac{1}{2}$	$\frac{1}{2}$	9	5	0	7		$1\frac{1}{2}$	9	21	3	4
	$\frac{1}{2}$	9	2	3	20		$\frac{5}{8}$	9	6	1	12		2	9	29	3	21

The foregoing table of the weight of cast iron pipes, gives the length of pipe according to the diameter of bore, as generally used in practice.

Diameter of bore in inches.
Thickness of metal in inches.
Length of pipe in feet.

It is found to be of great use in making estimates of pipes:—for instance, it is required to know the weight of a range of pipes 225 feet long, $7\frac{1}{2}$ inches diameter of bore, and metal $\frac{5}{8}$ths of an inch thick.

9) 225

25 pipes in the whole length.

One pipe weighs 4 . 0 . 22, which, multiplied by 25, is equal to 104 . 3 . 18, or 5 tons, 4 cwt. 3 quarters, 18 lbs. weight of the whole range.

TABLE OF THE VELOCITY OF MOTION.

The following is a table of the velocity of Motion, for boring cast iron cylinders, pumps, &c., and heavy turning, with fixed cutters.

It will be observed, that the surface bored is constantly the same, 78.54 feet per minute; this velocity is found to be the most advantageous: a velocity greater than this, not only takes the temper out of the cutters, but also causing more heat, expands the metal: and if the machine stops but for a few seconds, a mark is left from the contraction of the metal.

Turning has a velocity double to that of boring.

TABLE.

BORING.		TURNING.	
Inches Diameter.	Revolutions of Bar per minute.	Inches Diameter.	Revolutions of Shaft per minute.
1	25.	1	50.
2	12.5	2	25.
3	8.33	3	16.67
4	6.25	4	12.50
5	5.	5	10.
6	4.16	6	8.32
7	3.57	7	7.15
8	3.125	8	6.25
9	2.77	9	5.55
10	2.5	10	5.
15	1.66	15	3.33
20	1.25	20	2.50
25	1.	25	2.
30	0.833	30	1.667
35	0.714	35	1.430
40	0.625	40	1.250
45	0.56	45	1.12
50	0.5	50	1.
60	0.417	60	0.834
70	0.358	70	0.716
80	0.313	80	0.626
90	0.278	90	0.556
100	0.25	100	0.50

N. B.—The progression of the cutters may be $\frac{1}{16}$ of an inch for the first cut, and for the last $\frac{1}{24}$.

If hand tools are employed in turning, the velocity may be considerably increased.

A SUIT THAT WILL NEVER WEAR OUT.

Rev. Daniel Burgess, a dissenting minister of London, in the seventeenth century, preaching on the robe of righteousness, said: "If any of you would have a good and cheap suit, you will go to Monmouth street; if you want a suit for life, you will go to the court of chancery; but if you wish a suit which will last to eternity, you must go to the Lord Jesus Christ, and put on his robe of righteousness."

TABLES OF THE WEIGHT OF MALLEABLE AND CAST IRON PLATES, BARS, &c.

TABLE *of the Weight of a square foot of Cast and Malleable Iron, Copper and Lead, from* 1-16*th to* 1 *inch thick.*

Thick.	Cast Iron.		Mall. Iron.		Copper.		Lead.	
	lbs.	oz.	lbs.	oz.	lbs.	oz.	lbs.	oz.
1 Sixteenth.	2	6.6	2	7.8	2	15	3	11
2 "	4	13.3	4	15.6	5	14	7	6
3 "	7	4.	7	7.4	8	13	11	1
4 "	9	10.6	9	15.2	11	12	14	12
5 "	12	1.3	12	7.1	14	11	18	7
6 "	14	8.	14	14.9	17	10	22	2
7 "	16	14.7	17	6.7	20	9	25	13
8 "	19	5.3	19	14.5	23	8	29	8
9 "	21	12.	22	6.3	26	7	33	3
10 "	24	2.7	24	14.2	29	6	36	14
11 "	26	9.3	27	6.	32	5	40	9
12 "	29	0.	29	13.8	35	4	44	4
13 "	31	6.7	32	5.6	38	3	47	15
14 "	33	13.4	34	13.4	41	2	51	10
15 "	36	4.	37	5.3	44	1	55	5
1 inch.	38	10.7	39	13.1	47	0	59	0

TABLE *of the Weight of a Lineal Foot of Malleable and Cast Iron Bars, from 6-16ths to 3 inches square.*

Sixteenths on the side.	Area in Square Sixteenths	MALL. IRON. Ounces.	CAST IRON. Ounces weight.	ROUND RODS. The 1-16ths on the side is the diameter of Rod. Ounces weight.
6	36	7.4736		5.83
7	49	10.1724		7.99
8	64	13.2864	12.8960	10.43
9	81	16.8156		13.20
10	100	20.7600		16.30
11	121	25.1196		19.72
12	144	29.8944	29.0160	23.47
13	169	35.0844		27.53
14	196	40.6896		31.94
15	225	46.7100		36.44
1 inch.	256	53.1456	51.5840	41.50
1	289	59.9964		46.80
2	324	67.2624		52.47
3	361	74.9436		58.46
4	400	83.0400	80.6000	64.81
5	441	91.5516		71.41
6	484	100.4784		78.37
7	529	109.8204		85.66
8	576	119.5774	116.0640	93.27
9	625	129.7500		101.21
10	676	140.3376		109.46
11	729	151.3404		118.05
12	784	162.7584	157.9760	126.95
13	841	174.5916		136.19
14	900	186.8400		145.74
15	961	199.5036		155.62
2 inches.	1024	212.5824	206.3360	165.82
1	1089	226.0764		176.34
2	1156	239.9856		187.19
3	1225	254.3100		198.36
4	1296	269.0496	261.1440	209.86
5	1369	284.2044		221.68
6	1444	299.7744		233.83
7	1521	315.7596		246.30
8	1600	332.1600	322.4000	259.09
9	1681	348.9756		272.20
10	1764	366.2064		285.64
11	1849	383.8524		299.41
12	1936	401.9136	390.1040	313.49
13	2025	420.3900		327.91
14	2116	439.2816		342.64
15	2209	458.5884		357.70
3 inches.	2304	478.3104	464.2560	373.09

CUTTING OFF STEAM.

The plate opposite is designed to show why steam cannot be cut off equal at each end of the slides. The dotted line A is drawn through the centre of the shafts. The curved line E is described on the centre of the wrist of the shoving head, with a radius equal to the length of the pitman, and through the centre of the shaft. There is also a circle described on the centre of the shaft, with a radius equal to the distance from the centre of the shaft to the centre of the crank wrist. Now, it will be seen, that the time occupied by the piston in the last half of its outward travel and the first half of its inward travel, is just the time it takes the crank to pass from where the dotted curve cuts the circle going out to the point where it cuts it coming in. The difference beween this and the time occupied in the last half of the inward, and the first half of the outward travel, is just the sum of the difference between the dotted and the curved lines on the two sides of the centre of the shaft. Hence it is that steam cannot be cut off equal at each end of the slides. Might not this be the reason of some engines escaping more steam and puffing louder at one end than the other? In proportion as the length of the pitman is increased, the variation will be lessened; and, on the other hand, as the pitman is shortened, the variation will be increased, as will be seen in the plate by the curved line F, described on the centre C. The difference of variation in the curve is equal to the difference between the points respectively where the dotted lines E and F cut the circle and the point where it is cut

OVERSIZED ~~FOLDOUT~~

COLOR ILLUSTRATION

was removed after page(s) 314
for in-house scanning

On 8·18 2000

by the straight line A. Hence, a pitman half length will make double the variation as in the plate. If a rack and pinion were used instead of a crank the motion would be equal.

COMBUSTIBLE MATERIALS.

In an interesting paper on fires and fire insurance, published in the January number of the London Quarterly Review, it is asserted, on the authority of Mr. Brainwood, as his belief, that by long exposure to heat, not much exceeding that of boiling water, or 212 degrees, timber is brought into such a condition that it will fire without the application of light. The time during which this dessication goes on until it ends in spontaneous combustion, is, he thinks, from eight to ten years; so that a fire may be hatching on a man's premises during the whole of his lease, without making any sign. The small circulating pipes which convey hot water through a building, have been known to have set fire to wood, even when the temperature of the water is not over 300 degrees. Builders should inform themselves of these facts, and never place pipes conveying heated air or water near the wood work of a building.

In the year 1863 there were 1404 fires in the city of London, only 39 of which resulted in the total destruction of the buildings. For the whole number of fires there are 112 alleged different causes: 227 originated from candles, 117 from flues, 26 from matches, 107 from sparks, 100 from gas, 24 from hot ashes, 31 from smoking tobacco, 41 from airing linen, 39 from children playing with fire and matches. During the same year there were 361 fires in New York and 300 in Paris.

HOW TO PUT ON COALS.—It seems there is an art in this apparently simple operation, and the process now recommended is: "Before you throw on coals, pull all the fire to the front of the grate, fill up the cavity at the back with the cinders or ashes which will be found under the grate, then throw on the coals. The gas evolved in the process of roasting the coals will be absorbed by the cinders, which will render them in an increased degree combustible. The smoke will thus be burnt, and a fine glowing smokeless fire will be the result."

EXPLOSION OF NAPHTHA.—At an inquest lately held in England, a grocer testified that while he was pouring coal oil from a barrel into another vessel, a lighted candle being within three feet, he saw a small blue flame run along the outside of the barrel to the bung hole. Of what followed he was ignorant. But it appears that a terrible explosion ensued, for the grocer was pitched up into the street insensible; his house was set on fire, the upper apartments quickly filled with a dense black smoke, by which three of his children were suffocated, while his wife and three other little ones barely escaped with their lives. This explosive stuff was found to be a very light coal oil, or naphtha, the vapor from which is highly explosive.

DANGEROUS CHARACTER OF BULK PETROLEUM.—The *Oil City Register*, in alluding to a recent fire, states that petroleum, in bulk, is very dangerous after being recently agitated. Any movement of a large quantity brings up the benzole, which is the lightest quality of it, to the top and into the atmosphere. This is an inflammable gas. The slightest contact with a flame sets it off in a flash. Bulk oil impregnates the atmosphere, on the contact of a flame of any kind it ignites and explodes.

SPONTANEOUS COMBUSTION.—A curious case of spontaneous combustion was discovered a week or so ago in the barn on the premises of Daniel Althouse, deceased, in Eastern Township, Berks County. The hay in the mow was found to be in a charred state, from which it was evident that it had taken fire by spontaneous combustion, but for want of air had afterward been extinguished without any damage. Cases of spontaneous combustion where hay is put away not properly cured, are not unfrequent.

The Indiana *Sentinel* says: A case of spontaneous combustion is said to have occurred west of the canal yesterday. A woman was found in a waste house almost burned to a crisp, and as there was no evidence of fire having been near her, and she was known to have indulged freely in the use of alcoholic drinks, the supposition is that she was consumed by the flame thus generated.

TO DETECT EXPLOSIVE COAL OIL.—Many disasters being already occasioned from the use of explosive coal oil, the following receipt for ascertaining whether or not the article is explosive, may not be out of place: Pour a small quantity into a saucer, and bring a lighted match slowly down to it. If explosive, the oil will blaze and flash up almost like powder; if not explosive, it will not burn at all. The latter only is safe for use.

BURNING FLUID.—According to the record kept by Mr. E. Merriam, there were, during the year ending September 1st, 1853, some thirty-three fatal and disastrous explosions of burning fluid and kindred preparations, mostly in the cities of New York, Brooklyn, Williamsburg and vicinity, in which nineteen persons were killed, twenty-three persons fatally or severely injured, three persons slightly wounded, and some three or four buildings fired. The preparations alluded to are burning fluid, camphene, spirit gas, rosin oil, &c.

SCENES ON BOARD A FROZEN SHIP.

A whaling vessel which sailed from London in the year 1840, found in the Polar sea a ship embedded in the ice, with sails furled, and no signs of life on board. The captain and some of the crew descending into the cabin, found curled upon the floor a large Newfoundland dog, apparently asleep, but when they touched it, they found the animal was dead and frozen as hard as a stone. In the cabin was a young lady seated at a table, her eyes open, as if gazing at the intruders in that desolate place. She was a corpse! and had been frozen in an apparently resigned and religious attitude. Beside her was a young man, who it appeared, was the commander of the brig, and brother to the lady. He was sitting at the table dead, and before him was a sheet of paper, on which was written, "Our cook has endeavored since yesterday morning to strike a light, but in vain; all is now over." In another part of the cabin stood the cook with the flint and tinder in hand, frozen, in the vain endeavor to strike fire that could alone save them. The terrors of the seamen hurried the captain from the spot, who took with him the log-book as the sole memento of the ill-fated ship. It appeared that she also was from

London, and had been frozen in that place over fourteen years.

SITTING ON SAFETY VALVES.

It seems that an ignorant fellow in England recently adopted the old trick of engineers on the Mississippi river—sitting on the safety valve lever so as to increase the steam pressure. This is what happened: "The deceased actually sat upon the safety valve, and insisted upon retaining his seat, although warned that his sitting there was a source of great danger. The boiler exploded, and Hirst was thrown a distance of at least 100 yards, and fell dead in a field. The end of the boiler was driven out, and the main portion of the boiler itself was forced in the air a height of 100 feet at least, and fell at a distance of 150 feet from its place. Mr. Inett, the engineer, was buried beneath the bricks and *debris*, and sustained serious injuries, as did also Mr. Walker's groom, one of his farm servants, and two of the laborers who were engaged there. One of them was found insensible under the hot bricks in one corner of the engine-shed and fearfully scalded. Mr. Walker himself and two women who had just arrived to assist in the threshing had very narrow escapes." All from the recklessness and stupidity of one man.

ANTHONY HARKNESS.

Anthony Harkness, a wealthy and useful citizen of Cincinnati, died recently of cancer in the head. He was born in Rhode Island, in 1793; came to Cincinnati, a poor journeyman mechanic, in 1820; built one of the first machine shops for making steam engines and sugar mills, and was the pioneer manufacturer of locomotives in that city; joined with Jacob Strader and Samuel Fosdick, in 1844, in erecting the Franklin Cotton Factory; and has as length passed away at the age of sixty-five, leaving half a million of dollars and an unblemished name to his surviving wife and three children. The Cincinnati *Gazette* says:

He was, in the first place, an honest man. He never for a moment lost the confidence of any one who had occasion to transact business with him. Everything connected with this feature of his character was of the true metal. There was no trickery or deceit about him —not a particle. His word was ever as good as his bond, and what he promised he meant to, and always did, if possible, perform. If a man ordered an engine, or a sugar mill, he would fare as well without a contract as with one. He always did what he believed to be right between man and man, regardless of circumstances or consequences. He scorned to take advantage of any one who might be, by accident or otherwise, placed in his power. Thus he acquired a reputation that was in itself a fortune. His business never diminished, but steadily increased, and never was the aphorism, "honesty is the best policy," more fully exemplified, than in the successful career of Anthony Harkness.

OVERSIZED FOLDOUT

3 COLOR ILLUSTRATIONS

was removed after page(s) 322
for in-house scanning

On 8·18 2000

CUTTING OFF STEAM ON THE SLIDES.

THE object of the draft on page 321 is to show why the steam cannot be cut off at equal distances from both ends of the slides, and also to show how much it is less at one end than at the other. For example, see plate No. 1, page 321. When the crank is square up, in the centre between the two dead points, the centre of the shoving head has not reached the centre of the slides by the distance equal to the space between the curved line E and the straight line A, through the centre of the main shaft, as will be seen on plate on page 314, and also on plate No. 3, page 323, by the space between the straight line D through the main shaft, and the curved line E. So that using a half stroke cam, as you see in the plate No. 1, the steam will always be cut off before reaching the centre of the slide as shown in the draft from A to B at the shoving head, which distance is always equal to the difference between the curved and straight lines D and E, on the crank wrist, plate No. 3.

The variation is the same with all cut off cams, whether cutting off at $\frac{1}{2}$ stroke, $\frac{5}{8}$, $\frac{3}{4}$ or $\frac{7}{8}$. This variation is not in the cam, which always cuts off true to the crank; but it does not cut off at $\frac{1}{2}$ stroke on the slides, because the centre of the shoving head is not on the centre of the slides when the crank is square up or square down, as is seen in plates Nos. 1 and 2. The difference with all cut off cams, whether $\frac{5}{8}$, $\frac{3}{4}$ or $\frac{7}{8}$, will be the same on both ends; that is, they cut off as much more at the one end as they cut off less at the other, equal to the distance between the curved and straight lines on plate No. 3. The cause lies in the one end of the pitman being made to run in a straight line on the slides by being attached to the shoving head whilst the other end rises and falls with the crank, producing an angle with the pitman from the horizontal centre line and a curve from the perpendicular line through the centre of the main shaft, and this is the reason, when the crank is in the centre between the dead points, that the steam is cut off equal to the distance of the centre of the crank-wrist from the straight line through the main shaft more than half stroke in coming in and as much less than half stroke going out.

PLATE No. 1. When the crank is square up, the steam is cut off before coming to the centre of the slides from the end A, equal to the distance between the curved and straight lines on the crank, in plate No. 3.

PLATE No. 2. When the crank is square down, the steam is not cut off till it has passed the centre of the slides, equal to the distance between the curved and straight lines in plate No. 3.

This draft is to show that when the centre of the shoving head is in the centre of the slides the centre of the crank-wrist is not square up or square down, but is on a curved line described by the pitman A and C.

The object of the draft on page 322 is to show that the steam cannot be cut off at equal distances from both ends of the slides, and also to show how much it is less at one end than at the other.

For example, see plate No. 1, page 321, when the crank is square up in the centre, between the two dead points, the centre of the shoving head has not reached the centre of the slides by the distance equal to the space between the curved line E and the straight line A, through the centre of the main shaft, as will be seen on plate No. 1, page 321, and also on plate No. 3, page 323, by the space between the straight line D, through the main shaft, and the curved line E. So that using a half stroke cam, as you see in the plate No. 1, the steam will always be cut off before reaching the centre of the slides, as shown in the draft from A to B at the shoving head, which distance is always equal to the difference between the curved and straight lines D, on the crank-wrist, plate No. 3. The variation is the same with all cut off cams, whether cutting off at $\frac{1}{2}$ stroke, $\frac{5}{8}$, $\frac{3}{4}$ or $\frac{7}{8}$. This variation is not in the cam, it always cuts off true to the crank, but it does not cut off at half stroke on the slides, because the centre of the shoving head is not in the centre of the slides when the crank is square up or square down, as is seen in plates Nos. 1 and 2. The difference with all cut off cams, whether $\frac{1}{2}$, $\frac{5}{8}$, $\frac{3}{4}$ or $\frac{7}{8}$, will be the same on both ends; that is, they cut off as much more at the one end as they cut off less at the other, equal to the distance between the curved and straight lines D, on plate No. 3.

HOW TO LAY OUT A SLIDE VALVE CAM,

LINE BY LINE SEPARATELY.

First, in the centre of the circle A, you lay out the first circle, which is the inside of the eye of the cam; second, you describe the second circle, which line gives the width or sufficient amount of metal for the heel of the cam; you next get the distance in circle B, for the first movement of the cam, which will be done according to the rule on page 180. Get the distance from the end of the valve B, page 142, to the back of the opening, as it stands on the draft, &c. Read the rule mentioned, and at the same time see the draft on page 142, for example; after having got this distance, then draw the circle No. 3, which is the cut off circle for the lean side of the cam.

To get the second movement, take the distance from the other end of the valve to the back of the other letting on opening, as laid down in the draft on page 142, &c. The valve laid down in the draft at the end B requires $\frac{3}{16}$ of an inch for the first movement and $\frac{5}{16}$ for the second. After getting these two circles, the one for the first and the other for the second outside of the heel of the cam, you next step off the width of the nose of the cam at equal distances from the perpendicular line, plate C. If you wish to cut off at about half stroke, the cam will be nearly sharp on the point, and if at five-eighths it will be three or four inches wide on the nose. Read the balance of rule on page 181.

Next, you describe the circle No. 6 from the right hand centre of the nose of the cam. This completes the first movement.

From the centre in the left hand side of the nose of the cam, you describe the circle No. 7, plate D, which gives the right hand circle for the heel of the cam.

With the same distance on point No. 7, you describe circle 8, which forms the left hand side of the nose of the cam. This completes the lean side of the cam. No. 9 circle, plate E, is got by placing one point of the

OVERSIZED FOLDOUT

COLOR ILLUSTRATION

was removed after page(s) 324
for in-house scanning

On 8·18 2000

compass in the centre of the cut off point, or first movement on the left hand side, and this gives the circle 9.

No. 10, you place the compass in the centre of the eye of the cam and describe the circle 10 on the right hand side, which is made to fit into the circle 9, which makes the cam just as wide across the horizontal line as it is on the upright line from the nose to the heel of the cam, and thus it is made to fill the yoke completely all around.

No. 11 is the cam F complete, the same as No. 10, with a horizontal line through the centre of the cam.

No. 12 is the cam as laid down in No. 11, with a horizontal line through the centre of the cam, and the upper half circle is stepped off into eight equal parts, and the two diagonal lines 12 and 12 run out from the centre through the cam, where the two circles leading down from the nose on the right and the left intersect the two circles which form the lean and the full side of the cam, and the proportion of the half circle cut off from the diagonal lines down to the horizontal line through the centre, shows one part on the lean, and two parts on the full sides, making three parts in all cut off, and five parts remaining on, which shows $\frac{3}{8}$ of the steam to be cut off and $\frac{5}{8}$ remaining on, which makes it a $\frac{5}{8}$ cam.

DIRECTIONS FOR PUTTING UP STEAM ENGINES.

Engines that are bedded down on a cast iron bed plate, are frequently bolted on a brick foundation, built to suit them, and made fast by tie-bolts built in the wall, to suit the holes in the bed plate. On the lower end of the bolts are large iron plates to keep the bolts from pulling up through the wall. Sometimes the lower ends of the bolts are made fast by keys, others have nuts, and others a square head with a square recess in the cast iron washers, to keep the bolts from turning when screwing them up. Others bolt the bed down on a rough stone foundation, while some who prefer an extra and permanent job, put the bed plate down on cut stone. For temporary use, especially for boring and pumping oil wells, they will answer every purpose by being made fast to heavy timbers, which are secured to other heavy cross timbers or mud-sills partly sunk in the ground. Engines fastened on wooden frames are put down in the same way as those mentioned above; and sometimes they are made fast by bolting the engine timbers to the mud-sills or otherwise. If the timbers are sufficiently deep and heavy, cut a recess in each of the cross timbers, three or four inches deep, and let the cylinder timbers drop into the same, and be made fast by wooden keys. In all cases the engine should be put down level crossways on the top of the slides and through the centre of the main shaft, in case one journal of the main shaft should be larger in diameter than the other; but as a general thing they are put up level fore and aft. The variation either way would make no particular difference, but in all cases, the valve chambers of the pumps should be plumb, especially where the brass valves and seats are used, so that the valves, after having been raised when working, will fall more easily into their seat than they would if on an incline.

MEDIUM FREIGHT WEIGHT OF OIL ENGINES AND BOILERS, ALL COMPLETE.

One six inch cylinder, eighteen inches stroke, on timbers, with one thirty inch boiler, two ten inch flues of three-sixteenth iron, twelve feet long including chimney, brichen and boiler castings, all complete, about 5,200 ℔s.; and on a cast iron bed plate, the same weight. One seven inch cylinder, eighteen inches stroke, with one thirty-two inch boiler, fourteen feet long, two ten inch flues, three-sixteenth iron, all complete, as above, 5,400 ℔s.; on a cast iron bed plate, about the same weight, 5,400 ℔s. One seven inch cylinder, fourteen inches stroke, with one thirty-two inch boiler, fourteen feet long, two flues of three-sixteenth iron, with the engine all complete, about 5,400 ℔s. One cylinder, eight inches bore, fourteen inches stroke, fitted up on a cast iron bed plate, with one thirty-two inch boiler, sixteen feet long, with two flues, three-sixteenth iron, all complete, about 5,600 ℔s. One seven inch cylinder, twenty inches stroke, with one thirty-two inch boiler, sixteen feet long, with two ten inch flues, three-sixteenth iron, all complete, about 6,300 ℔s., on a cast iron bed plate. One eight inch cylinder, twenty inches stroke, with one thirty-two inch boiler, eighteen feet long, two ten inch flues, three-sixteenth iron, with a cast iron bed plate, about 6,600 ℔s.

On all these engines mentioned, the crank that drives the walking beam or bell crank, which is used for boring and pumping, is made fast on the outer end of the main shaft. These engines generally run from thirty to forty revolutions per minute when boring, and from forty to sixty when pumping.

There are engines used much smaller than those mentioned, in some cases as small, I believe, as four inch diameter of cylinder and eight inches stroke, and five by ten and six by twelve; but these engines run very fast, and the speed is reduced by using a counter-shaft in proportion to the size of the engine and the depth of the well.

Some are using the counter-shaft with the large engine, the object of which is to get the well farther off from the boiler furnace, so as to prevent danger by explosion in case the gas takes fire by coming in contact with the boiler furnace or stack, as has frequently been the case when the boiler has been too close to the well.

But the counter-shaft is indispensably necessary for the small engines, in order to get a sufficiency of power by running the engines very fast, which is not necessary for this purpose on the larger engines; and when they are used for the large engines, it is in order to get the boiler and stack away off some thirty or forty feet from the well. This can be done in another way without using the counter-shaft, as follows: instead of setting the boiler alongside of the engine, as is the usual custom, set the back end of the boiler some five or six feet off from the end of the cylinder. This will place the front end of the boiler or smoke-stack the whole length of the boiler, engine and walking-beam from the well, which for a fourteen feet boiler, and twenty inch stroke engine, the well would be about sixty feet off from the boiler furnace door and chimney, which as a general thing would be out of the reach of all danger of taking fire by coming in contact with large quantities of combustible gas.

MILNER'S CUT-OFF VALVE GEAR.

We think it proper to insert in this place a description of Milner's Cut-off Cam Valve Gear, patented July 30th, 1850. The improvement consists in working the steam valves by the combined action of two D cams: I is the loose cam, with a segmental slot, and index plate on it; the yoke of this cam is attached to the upper end of the oscillating bar N, by the connecting link O, and the lower end of said bar is attached to the yoke of the fixed cam, in the same manner. The steam valves are operated from the centre of the oscillating bar by the inside rod V. The fixed cam operates the exhaust valves as usual in other engines, and being attached by its yoke to the lower end of the oscillating bar, also opens the steam valves, as soon as the engine arrives at the point at which the engineer has set the loose cam I, to cut off steam; it moves back the upper end of oscillating bar N, and cuts off steam. By slacking the screw and moving the loose cam to the figure at which it is desirable to cut off steam, it can be cut off at from one-eighth to seven-eighths of the stroke with precision, enabling the engineer always to use all the steam he can make at any given pressure, and also to cut off at such a point, as to be able to keep steam without throttling it; and as it is well known that boats on the Mississippi, with a load, and a head wind, cannot work off all their steam with these fixed cut-offs, nor supply steam to allow full strokes, they are obliged to lay to, or add pressure to their boilers to make headway. This invention, then, will add to the safety of boats and passengers; for, by changing the cut-off, they can use all their steam and go ahead. Also, when running with fair wind, light load and favorable tides, they cannot make steam enough, they are obliged to throttle it, and lose much of its elastic force.

This invention will be advantageous for light draught boats, and also for ships on a long voyage, requiring less weight of boiler and fuel for a given power. Example: A boat now running with two cylinders of fifteen inch diameter, and two boilers double flued, forty inches, and cutting off steam at three-fourths of the stroke, would run quite as fast with one boiler, if the cylinders were twenty and a half inches, and steam cut off at one-fifth of the stroke. Again: the two boilers would supply cylinders of twenty-nine and a half inches, cut off at one-fifth stroke, and would very nearly double the power, with very little additional weight, and no more fuel.

Again: this improvement recommends itself to engineers and steamboat owners by its simplicity and easy construction; also by its durability. Cut-off cams for half-stroke even, are soon worn out, and are a continual cost to engines, whereas these D cams will answer the purpose to cut off at any point, and are not subject to wear out as the pointed cams are; they can also be so altered as to suit any change of fuel, from good to bad and *vice versa*; or in case of a want of fuel, to use what they have to the best advantage. See plate on page 198.

PUPPET-VALVE CAMS.

You draw the first circle the size of the eye of the cam, within which is the letter A. Next draw the second circle, which should always be half an inch or more larger in diameter than the cam flange, so as to keep the cam yoke clear of the cam flange on the main shaft. When, however, the cams are made fast to the shaft by keys or set screws in a flange, cast on the side of the cam, around the eye, the second circle may be smaller, so as to allow only metal enough to make the cam sufficiently strong at the small part of the eye. In order to draw the third circle, it will be necessary to know the amount of throw requisite for the cam to raise the valves the proper height. With this distance, draw part of the outer circle for the nose of the cam, marked third circle. Then take half the distance between the outside of the second and third circle, which is lengthways of the cam, and describe the fourth circle, which makes the breadth and length of the cam equal, as in cam B.

In the next operation, you take equal distances from the centre of the nose of the cam, marked points fifth. This is where the difficulty lies with a great many engineers, to know what width to make the nose of the cam. As this is the place from which the cam is to receive its shape, so as to make it cut off steam quick or slow, as may be wanted, it will be necessary to have some idea of the difference between a cut-off and full stroke cam. It will be observed that all cut-off cams are narrower at the nose than across the centre, some more and others less, as you will see by looking at the half stroke cut-off cams A, B, C, D, E and F, on page 190. As a general thing, the proportions of the throw of our cams are about one sixth the diameter of the whole cam. For instance: a cam twenty-four inches in diameter, would have four inches throw. All cams of similar proportions, having a sharp nose, or nearly so, would cut off at about nearly half stroke, as you will see on page 190, A and D. Cams of this proportion, having sharp noses, cannot be made to cut off any less nor let on any more than half stroke, because the amount of throw is about equal to one-sixth of the whole diameter of the cam. But as there are exceptions to general rules, you will see by looking at the cut-off cam B, on page 178, that it is sharp in the nose, and similar to the two cams A and D, on page 190; but here lies the difference: while the throw of the cams A and D is equal to one-sixth of the whole diameter, the throw of the cut-off cam B, on page 178, is but one-thirteenth of the diameter of the cam, and on this account it cuts off at three-eighths of the stroke of the piston. And on the same principle of enlarging the size of the cam, and reducing the throw in the same proportion, you can cut off steam as close as you please, say one-sixteenth, one-thirty-second, one-sixty-fourth or less, if you choose; and, on the other hand, by reducing the diameter of the cam, and enlarging the throw, say to one-fourth or one-third of the diameter of the cam, you can cut off steam five-eighths, three-fourths or seven-eighths with a sharp nose cam, as you will see on opposite page. But to make it more plain and easy, we will take another view of the matter. All full stroke cams are wider across the nose than through

OVERSIZED FOLDOUT

2 COLOR ILLUSTRATIONS

was removed after page(s) 334
for in-house scanning

On 8·18 2000

the centre of the eye of the cam, and less at the heel and below the centre than through the centre, or, in other words, all full stroke cams are wide on the nose and narrow at the heel, and all cut-off cams are the reverse, sharp on the nose and broad at the heel, as you will see by looking at the cams on page 194.

In the next operation, you take the diameter of the cam, and place one point of the compass in the right hand centre point, marked 5, on the nose of the cam, and draw the left hand circle, marked 6, forming the left hand side heel of the cam, as seen in cam C.

In the next operation, you draw the right hand heel of the cam from the left hand centre, 5, in the same way which is marked 7, as in cam D. You then draw a circle from the right hand point, in the heel of the cam, on the circle 7, which describes the left hand circle and side of the nose of the cam, marked circle 8, and then, in the same way, from the opposite point on the circle, on the left hand side of the heel of the cam, you form the other side of the nose, on the right hand side of the cam E, marked 9. This gives a full view of a cut-off cam, as drawn, all complete. Above the centre it is stepped off into eight equal spaces. In cam F, you draw two lines, C and H, from the centre out to the circumference of the cam, through the points where the circle leading down from the right and left hand side of the nose intersects the cut off part of the circle of the cam; and from the points of intersection downward to the horizontal centre line, you see the amount of steam cut off; and from these points above the diagonal lines, you see the amount of steam let on.

In the last operation, the upper half circle is stepped

off into any number of equal parts you please, say eight, twelve, sixteen, thirty-two, &c., for the purpose of ascertaining the exact amount of steam cut off from the engine, and to know how much is let on. The upper half circle is stepped off into eight equal parts, and there is one and a half parts on the right and left hand side cut-off, which makes three parts off and five parts on, which makes a five-eighth cam; that is, the steam is let on the piston head five-eighths of the way, and cut off while it runs the other three-eighths.

GENERAL RULES FOR BUILDING BOILER FURNACES AND STACKS FOR THE OIL REGIONS.

I propose to give the following directions, by observing which almost any bricklayer, stone mason, or other handy person, can, without the assistance of an engineer, set the boilers.

First: For double-flued boilers, that are generally supplied on top with a check-valve chamber, the foundation may be made of stone, especially if brick is scarce. The stone work ought always to be a few inches below the bottom of the grate bars, for if it is too close, the heat of the fire will be apt to crack the stone work. For a boiler thirty inches in diameter and fourteen feet long, the space between the two brick walls should be thirty-six inches clear, leaving three inches space on each side between the boiler and the brick walls, for the action of the fire and heat upon the boiler. When flued boilers are used, there should be nine or ten inches space clear between the back boiler head and the end wall, to allow room for the heat and smoke to return back through the boiler flues into the chimney or stack. The back wall at the end of the boiler is built up about as high as the top of the flues, and the space between the end of the boiler and back wall is then covered with an iron plate or brick tile, and the joints filled up with plaster, so as to exclude the air. The sides of the boiler should be closed in even with the tops of the flues, in order to make the boiler safe, and prevent it from being burnt, in case the water should, from any cause, be suffered to get too low. If a first class engineer was employed to run the engine, the brick work might be closed in with safety at the lower gauge cock, which ought to be from three to four or more inches above the tops of the flues, but not less, and thus give more fire surface; but as very common hands are mostly used for running these engines, the first plan would be the safest, and make nearly as much steam as the latter. The bridge wall is built at the back end of the grate bars, for the purpose of keeping the fire up in the furnace on the grate bars. Sometimes it is built square up at the end of the bars, within about four inches from the bottom of the boiler, so as to let the flame and smoke pass off close to the bottom of the boiler; others build the bridge wall a few inches back from the end of the grate bars, and taper it back a little toward the top. In this way it is less in danger of being thrown down by shaking up the fires, &c. It is also customary to leave an opening or door about the middle of the boiler wall, for cleaning out the ashes and dirt from under the same. The top of this opening should be even with the bottom of the boiler; and if the space beneath the boiler has not been filled up, it would in this case be better to have the bottom of the opening or door even with the outside ground floor, so that it would be much easier to clean out, from under the boiler. In such cases, it is customary to turn an arch of brick, or to build over the opening on top of a few iron bars; then the opening is filled up with a single lining of brick, which has to be taken down and built up every time you clean out under the boilers. Others leave an opening, in the outside, even with the ground floor, so as to make it easier to clean out the ashes; but in case a stand-pipe was to be used, underneath the boiler, for it to rest on, and at the same time to answer for supplying on one side and blowing out at the other, then the boiler wall could not be closed in at the back end until the joint was made between the bottom of the boiler and the flange on the stand-pipe, which would require to be done by one who understood it. These joints are sometimes run in with lead; or three or four thicknesses of sheet lead, well coated between the sheets with white lead, would answer, and require less labor. Others use a rust cement, made of iron borings driven in with a calking iron; and others a cement made of iron borings and red lead, or mixed together with white lead, will answer where the red cannot be had.

The end of the boiler where the water is to be blown off should be one inch lower than the other, so as to run the water clean off when cleaning out the boilers.

If a cylinder boiler is used, the same directions for building the boiler walls will answer as for the flued boilers, with the exception that the stack for the cylinder boilers will require to be at the back end of the boiler, and there should be an offset in the back end of the stack, for covering the space between the end of the boiler and the stack with brick or iron plates, to allow for the expansion and contraction of the boiler at the back end. For particulars see the draft of a side view of a boiler on page 70, and read the rule there laid down.

Some leave two openings in the walls, for cleaning out under the boilers, one in the end of the stack, and one on one side of the boiler wall, and if the boilers are large, there might be one on each side of the boiler walls, besides one in the end of the stack. The top of these openings should not be higher than the bottom of the boiler. If the space under the boiler is not filled in back of the bridge wall, the bottom of these doors might be even with the ground floor, then the dirt would be much easier cleaned out. Cast iron frames and doors would save the labor of pulling down and building up the brick-work every time you would have occasion to clean out under the boilers.

TABLE

SHOWING THE DIAMETER, AREA AND CONTENTS OF OIL TANKS.

This calculation is made for tanks one foot high, and their contents are given in barrels of forty gallons each. A cubic foot is estimated to hold seven and a half gallons. A barrel contains five and one-third cubic feet.

TABLE.

Number of different sized oil tanks.	Diameter of tanks in feet.	Superficial area of the bottom of each tank in feet.	Number of barrels in each tank, one foot high.	Different sized tanks.	Diameter in feet.	Superficial area of the bottom of each tank.	Number of barrels in each oil tank, one foot high.
1	6	28.25	5 3/10	22	21	346.36	64 7/8
2	6½	33 17	6 3/16	23	22	380.13	71¼
3	7	38.05	7¼	24	23	415.47	77 9/10
4	7½	44.15	8¼	25	24	452 39	84 5/8
5	8	50.25	9 2/5	26	25	490.87	92 1/25
6	8½	56.71	10 5/8	27	26	530.09	99½
7	9	63.06	11 9/10	28	30	706.86	132½
8	9½	70.34	13 7/8	29	35	962.11	180 2/5
9	10	78.54	14¾	30	40	1256.06	235½
10	10½	86.59	16¼	31	45	1590.04	298 1/50
11	11	95.00	18 1/16	32	50	1963.05	368 1/6
12	11½	103.86	19½	33	55	2375.08	445 2/5
13	12	113.00	21 1/6	34	60	2827.04	530 1/7
14	13	132.75	24¾	35	65	3318.03	622 2/11
15	14	153.93	28 7/8	36	70	3848.04	721 1/16
16	15	176.71	33 1/8	37	75	4417.08	828 3/8
17	16	201.00	37¾	38	80	5026.05	942 2/5
18	17	227.00	42½	39	85	5674.05	1064
19	18	254.00	47¾	40	90	6361.07	1192 1/12
20	19	283.05	53 1/8	41	95	7088.23	1329
21	20	314.16	59	42	100	7854.00	1472 1/12

The above is the usual method; there are, however, two hundred and thirty-one cubic inches in each gallon, consequently seven and a half gallons would make four and a half inches more than a cubic foot, in an exact calculation.

The Pennsylvania freight weight of a barrel of benzole, including the barrel, and allowing forty gallons to

OVERSIZED FOLDOUT

COLOR ILLUSTRATION

was removed after page(s) 340
for in-house scanning

On 8.18 2000

each barrel, is 300 lbs.; refined oil, 330 lbs.; crude oil, 340 lbs.; and residuum or tar, from 340 to 365 lbs. Empty barrels are generally rated at 70 lbs. each, but when the staves and heads are extra thick, they weigh 75 lbs.

MEDIUM SPEED OF ENGINES WHEN BORING AND PUMPING.

The medium speed of engines is from thirty to forty revolutions per minute when boring, and from forty to sixty revolutions when pumping. The crank for boring and pumping is generally attached to the outer end of the engine shaft, and connected with one end of the walking beam, the other end of which is used for boring and pumping. The two cranks should be on the dead centres at once, so that the moment the engine begins to take the steam, the pump box is at half stroke in the chamber.

Table showing what depth the different sizes of engines are capable of boring and pumping.

Inches diameter of boiler.	Feet length of boiler.	Number of flues in boiler.	Thickness of boiler.	Inches diameter of cylinder.	Length of stroke of cylinder in inches.	
32	14	2	$\frac{3}{16}$	6	14 to 18	from 5 to 700 feet.
32	16	2	$\frac{3}{16}$	7	14 to 20	from 7 to 900 feet.
32	18	2	$\frac{3}{16}$	8	14 to 20	from 9 to 1200 feet.
36	20	2	$\frac{3}{16}$	9	20 to 24	from 12 to 1600 feet.

Small engines geared up to drive counter shafts.

Inches diameter of Boiler.	Feet length of boiler.	Number of flues in boiler.	Thickness of boiler.	Inches diameter of cylinder.	Length of stroke of cylinder in inches.	
32	14	2	$\frac{3}{16}$	$4\frac{1}{4}$	8 to 12	The diameter of the cylinders in this table is about one-half the square inches of those in the foregoing table.
32	16	2	$\frac{3}{16}$	$5\frac{1}{2}$	10 to 15	
32	18	2	$\frac{3}{16}$	$5\frac{3}{4}$	10 to 15	
36	20	2	$\frac{3}{16}$	$6\frac{1}{2}$	12 to 18	

The high speed of these engines is reduced by the counter shaft and cog wheels, or belts and pulleys, so as to give from thirty to forty strokes for boring and from forty to sixty for pumping. In this way much smaller engines are used for boring and pumping, although the amount of boiler in both cases would require to be the same to do the same amount of work in the same time. I mention this for the benefit of those who may have small engines for which they have no other use. In all cases where new engines are to be purchased, it is the better plan to have them without the counter shaft and belts, as the less gearing the better; and get the engines sufficiemtly large at first. I am informed by a person engaged in boring oil wells, that the average price of boring, say from six hundred to eight hundred feet deep, including the engine, boring tools and all the fixtures and labor, is from six to seven dollars per foot, so that those engaging in the business can know what it costs to put down one well. A second well could be put down cheaper than the first, &c.

IMPLEMENTS USED IN DRILLING.

As "oil" is the absorbing topic at present, the following description will be read with interest:

The "derrick" consists of four upright poles, from thirty to thirty-five feet high, made to form a square at the base of six to eight feet, while at the top (the poles slanting) the square is reduced to about five feet. On the top of the derrick, directly over the well, is a wheel around which runs an inch rope, used for hoisting the tools out of the well whenever their removal becomes necessary from accident or the accumulation of sand.

The "windlass" attached to the derrick, about three feet from the ground, affords an excellent leverage in hoisting the tools from the well, which weigh, when screwed together for boring, from three to five hundred pounds.

The "spring pole" is made of a straight hickory tree, about thirty-five feet in length, one end fastened in the ground, while the middle is braced up with a stout upright post, and the other end extends directly over the well, to which the rope is attached that sustains the auger stem and drill. A foot board is nailed on the end of the spring pole, upon which a man stands when boring, supported in his position by a strip running from side to side of the derrick, three feet above the pole, which answers for a hand-hold; a tread board, forming an inclined plane of twelve inches, is also fastened to the same end of the pole, which keeps one man constantly busy with one foot, while alongside of the well the borer sits on a stool; it is his business to twist the rope at every rebound of the pole, in order that the drill may strike the rock crossways alternately.

The boring tools consist of a round iron auger stem, twenty feet long and two inches thick, and five bits, two feet long, the same thickness as the stem, which are made so that they can be readily screwed on the stem at pleasure. The first bit (or more properly drill) used, is chisel shaped, and makes the hole, which is two inches wide. The other four (generally styled "reamers," and made bell shaped, two being three, and two four inches wide,) are intended to enlarge the well and smooth off the rough edges of the rock.

The operation in boring consists simply of an up and down motion, with a fall of the drill of from one to three feet.

The "sand pump" is composed of a copper tube, five feet in length and two inches in diameter, with a leather valve at the bottom, which opens as the pump descends in the water, and shuts as it is hauled up. The tubing is made in sections twenty feet long, of cast iron or copper, fastened together by means of brass screws.

The "seed bag" is intended to prevent water from running into the well; it is made of leather, cut to fit tight around the outside of the tubing, perhaps a foot above the oil; the bag, three-fourths of a yard in depth, is filled with flax seed, and the top tied loosely around the tube. In this manner the tube is lowered into the well, the water in a few minutes swelling the seed to such a bulk that the space between the tube and the walls of the well is entirely closed, and rendered water-proof. The pump inside of the tubing has two valves, which work alternately, the lower one being shut while the upper one is open.

COBBLING UP STEAM BOILERS.

Respecting the practice of "mending" steam boilers, as a cobbler would an old shoe, the London *Mechanics Magazine* says: "None except those persons who have resided for a lengthened period in our mining and manufacturing districts, can conceive of the reckless disregard of human life displayed in the employment of steam power. Boilers are patched in the rudest manner while they hold together. We have seen a plain cylindrical boiler of 4 feet in diameter and some 30 feet long, carrying 60 pounds steam, with three patches over the furnace side walls, each consisting of a plate more than a square foot in area, covering a rent the result of corrosion. These patches were not riveted on. Each was fixed in its place by a single ¾ inch bolt, tapped into a flat bar 2½ inch by ½ inch, and a couple of feet long, placed outside the shell, the plate being placed inside and held up in its place by the pressure of the steam, the joint being made tight by red lead and a bit of canvas. This kind of patch is common all through Staffordshire, and is used because the plates will not bear riveting from wear. We have seen the boiler-maker, ere now, send his hammer through the so-called sound plate, by accidentally striking it, instead of the rivet, which he wished to close. We might accumulate a volume of such instances were it necessary. Those who employ steam power should recollect that the duration of a boiler is far from being a mere question of time. It depends on so many circumstances, that it is impossible to say what may be its condition without frequent and careful inspection by those who can form a proper opinion; and we may conclude this article by pointing out that every man who makes use of steam power is guilty of criminal negligence, if he disregards the means of safety which inspection alone can place ready to his hand."

CONCERNING STEAM BOILERS.

We have in previous numbers of the *Scientific American* frequently called the attention of engineers and manufacturers to the condition of their steam boilers; for we have felt, and still feel, that in too many cases they are neglected and overlooked. If there is any department where false economy is out of place, it is certainly about a steam boiler; and by this we mean a disposition to let repairs go until a more convenient season, or as a person once said in our hearing, "till it gets so that it is worth mending;" this is false economy. The tailor's proverb about "the stitch in time" is eminently true of steam and the apparatus driven by, or the vessels containing it. All the leaky rivets (if any) should be driven tight, slack braces set up to their duty, seams caulked where they require it, ashes kept away from water-drip when it falls on the sheets, clinkers prevented from forming on grate bars (where anything like decent coal is provided, no excuse should be received by manufacturers for this neglect), safety valves overhauled and put in working condition (too many of them are mere percussion caps, so to speak), flues swept at least once a week, ashes and soot kept out of the smoke box; every ounce of it is a non-conductor that robs the boiler of its rightful heat.

OVERSIZED FOLDOUT

COLOR ILLUSTRATION

was removed after page(s) 346
for in-house scanning

On 8-18 2000

SECOND ENLARGEMENT OF SECOND EDITION
For 1872.

THE

Practical Engineer,

ILLUSTRATED WITH VALUABLE PLATES, SHOWING THE CRANK ON THE TOP COMING OVER. WHEN IT REACHES THE CENTRE PERPENDICULAR LINE, IT CUTS OFF STEAM LESS THAN HALF STROKE ON THE SLIDES, AND WHEN THE CRANK IS BELOW IT CUTS OFF MORE THAN HALF STROKE, JUST AS MUCH AS THE OTHER LACKED.

ALSO,

A PLATE OF THREE DIFFERENT SETTS OF PULLEYS—SHOWING THREE DIFFERENT MODES OF CALCULATING THE SPEED OF SAME. &c.

BY

JOHN WALLACE,

ENGINE BUILDER.

Orders with money enclosed sent to JOHN WALLACE, No. 319 Liberty Street, or to my residence, No. 363 Wylie Street, Pittsburgh, will receive immediate attention. The Books will be sent by Mail or Express, as persons ordering them may direct. Be careful to back your letters thus:

JOHN WALLACE,
ENGINE BUILDER,
No. 319 LIBERTY STREET, PITTSBURGH, PA.

Pittsburgh:
A. A. Anderson & Sons, Book and Job Printers, 67 and 69 Fifth Avenue.
1872.

RULES FOR CALCULATING

THE

SPEED OF DRUMS OR PULLIES.

PROBLEM I.

The Diameters of the Driver and the Driven being given, to find the number of revolutions of the Driven:

RULE: Multiply the diameter of the Driver (A) by its number of revolutions, and divide the product by the diameter of the Driven (B); the quotient will be the number of revolutions of the driven.

EXAMPLE.

Multiply the diam of driver (A.) 8 feet,
By its No. of revolutions, 100
—–800

And divide the product by the No.
of feet diameter of the driven, B. 4—200
Answer—No. of revolutions of the driven.

PROBLEM II.

The diameter and revolutions of the Driver and the revolutions of the Driven being given, to find the diameter of the Driven.

RULE: Multiply the diameter of the Driver (C) by its number of revolutions, and divide the product by the number of revolutions of the Driven (D); the quotient will be its diameter.

EXAMPLE.

Diameter of Driver C, is 7 feet,
and runs 100 revol's per minute,

Divided by No. of revolutions of Driven, D. 300) 700 (

Answer: $2\frac{1}{3}$ ft. dia. Driven (D)

PROBLEM III.

To ascertain the size of the Driver.

RULE: Multiply the diameter of the Driven (F) by the number of revolutions you wish it to make, and divide the product by the revolutions of the driver (E); the quotient will be the size of the Driver.

EXAMPLE.

Driven F, is 2 feet diameter,
and runs 1200 revolutions per minute,

No. of revolutions of driver, E, is 200) 2400 (12 ft. diam. of Driver.
200
400

A VIEW OF TWO HALF STROKE CAMS—ONE COMING IN AND THE OTHER GOING OUT—With Plates.

On page is plate No. 1, with a side view of a half stroke Cam, showing the relative position of the Cam and Crank to each other; also the Pitman Journal of the Shoving Head with the Slide and centre line through the same. The Cam cuts off steam at half stroke on the Crank, and less than half stroke on the Slides (when coming in, as shown on the draft, Plate No. 1,) equal to the vibration or distance from the curve to the perpendicular straight line running through the centre of the main shaft to the curved line (G).

Perhaps most engineers at first would suppose that if the steam is cut off at half stroke on the crank, that it is also cut off at half stroke on the slides, and if at three-fourths on the crank, three-fourths on the slides also. But this is impossible, as shown on the draft, on account of the pitman when raised at one end only equal to the throw of the crank above the centre of the main shaft, the pitman is thrown on an acute angle with the centre line of the shaft, cylinder and slides, and on this account will not reach from one perpendicular line to the other. The steam is cut off on the crank, exactly half-way between the two dead points at half stroke of the crank; but on the slides it is cut off at less than half stroke when the pitman (H H) is coming in—equal to the vibration of the pitman from the straight line when the centre of the other end of the pitman is on the centre of the slides. See Plate No. 1.

In Plate No. 2, the steam is cut off on the slides equal to the vibration, more than half stroke, when the pitman (I I) is going out; so that it cuts off on Plate No. 2, as much more steam than half stroke, as is shown on Plate No. 1 to be cut off less than half stroke. Thus you see on Plates Nos. 1 and 2, the steam is cut off on the two cranks at half stroke, whilst on the slides (see Plate No. 1) the steam is cut off before the shoving-head comes to the centre of the slides; whilst on Plate No. 2, you see the steam is not cut off until the centre of the shoving-head has passed the centre of the slides.

You see on the two Plates, Nos. 1 and 2, the steam is cut off exactly at the same place on the slides, at the line (A A), the angle of both pitmans being equal distances from the centre of the slides towards the main shaft.

The crank on plate No. 1 is at half stroke before it reaches the curved line (G).

The crank on plate No. 2 has to pass the curved line (J J) to reach half stroke.

In giving a back motion to the engine, the centre of crank on plate No. 1 would have to pass the curved line (G G) to reach the centre perpendicular (D D) line; and on plate No. 2, the centre of the crank No. 2 would reach the centre before it reaches the perpendicular line (DD). Reversing the motion would cut off less than half stroke on plates Nos. 1 and 2, and more than half stroke on plate No. 2, and *vice versa*.

OVERSIZED FOLDOUT

COLOR ILLUSTRATION

was removed after page(s) 7 9 ads
for in-house scanning

On 8·18 2000

You have these two plates separately on pages but I thought it would be much better improvement and more easily understood to have them together, as shown on page

HOW TO FIND THE DEAD CENTRE OF AN ENGINE, &c.

One plan is to use a straight edge (A) on the inside face of the pitman strap, (B)—(Page see plate), and turn the wheel until you get the centre on the shaft (C) equal distances between the two faces of the pitman straps, (B and D).

Another mode is to get a strip that will reach from the deck to the centre of pitman—as near as you can guess—then turn the crank above and below the dead centre, until you see the jaws of the shoving-head move a quarter or half inch on the slides, above and below, each way, and make a mark on the pitman when it is above and below, somewhere aft of the slides, to suit the length of the strip; and make a centre mark on the pitman between these two points, and turn the wheel until the centre between these two points corresponds to the length of the strip, which will give you the dead centre of the crank.

Fast running engines require larger openings to let the steam in and out of the cylinders than slow running engines.

OPENINGS IN PIPES FOR COLD WATER PUMPS.

It is a rule with some to have the inside diameter of the feed or suction pipe equal to one half the inside diameter of the pump; this is large enough for common pumps used about steam engines. One-third size will do very well where the motion of the pump is slow. I have known a pump 4 inches in diameter, about 10 to 12-inch stroke, have a pipe only 1 inch in diameter, the pump running about thirty revolutions to the minute and worked very well considering. But it was too small.

The size of the pipe depends something on the speed of the pump. The pipes for the pumps of water works engines are exceptions to this rule; they are often made larger inside than the pumps. No doubt one reason for this is to prevent them from drawing up sand and gravel, which would be very injurious to the pump, cutting out the packing, piston rods, valves, &c.

SOME PRACTICAL SUGGESTIONS IN REFERENCE TO THE MANAGEMENT OF ENGINES, &c.

Question—Can you cut off steam on a Puppet Valve Lever Engine, with an Eccentric Cam?

Answer—No. You can no more cut off steam on a Lever Engine with an Eccentric Cam, than you can cut off stęam from an engine with a short full stroke slide valve; because an Eccentric Cam is always of itself a full stroke cam, and gives no stoppage or rest to the cam yoke to cut off steam, as the regular puppet valve cut off cam does.

Question—How is it then, that quite a number of lever engines, having puppet valves, use eccentric, or full stroke cams, and yet the steam is by some means cut off from the cylinder?

Answer—The steam is cut off, but not by the cam. It is cut off by the knocker being peculiarly shaped for that purpose, and is properly a cut-off knocker, (See a draft of the cut off knocker (A) on page , fig. 1.) This knocker is shaped differently from those generally used for the cut-off cams. They are made nearly all straight on top where they touch the points of the lever (B), and if worked with a full stroke cam, the instant one lever is down the other would commence to rise; and they might be called full stroke knockers. But not so with this knocker. One end drops down just in proportion to the amount of steam you want to cut off. In this case the cam requires to be set considerably ahead, so as to bring the knocker up to the lever, so as to open the valve as soon as the engine begins to move on the slide; and just in proportion as the lever droops the cam has to be set ahead to bring the point of the drooping knocker up to the lever to take the steam as the engine approaches the centre; and just in the same proportion as the one arm of the knocker droops, or falls down below the bottom of the lever and below the top of the other arm on the same knocker—in the same proportion will the steam be cut off. And in proportion as you bring the top of the knockers up to a straight line, or to the bottom of the levers in the same proportion, you let on more steam; and if you bring the tops of the knockers on both sides of the rock shaft up to the bottom of the levers when they are down, and the engine on the dead centre, the knockers will work full stroke.

A SHORT AND CORRECT RULE FOR FINDING AND PUTTING THE ENGINE CRANK ON THE DEAD CENTRE.

It is not necessary to put the engine on the dead centre to find the dead centre of the crank, as is the general custom among engineers. The rule is as follows: Turn the fly or water wheel, above and below the dead centre, repeatedly, until you get the jaw of the shoving head on the slides, at a point where it does not move on them—notwithstanding you may turn the wheel a little above or below the dead centre.

To find the dead centre in this way, it requires a considerable amount of extra labor and time, and is by no means necessary. Turn the wheel round until the outside of the jaw of the shoving head moves one-half inch to an inch from the wearing mark it leaves on the end of the slides, then make a mark on the end of the slide, outside of the jaw—or inside, if the slide is too short—then turn the wheel round, so as to move the shoving-head jaw from the mark made on the slide—say $\frac{1}{2}$, $\frac{3}{4}$, or 1 inch—more or less, as you please, from the mark; then take a strip and measure from the top of the deck, plank or timber, up to the centre of the wrist in the crank, and make a mark on the same. Then turn the wheel in the opposite direction until the outside of the jaw of the shoving-head reaches the same mark, near to the end of the slide. Then make another mark on the strip to correspond with the centre of the wrist—one above and one below; then take the distance between these two centres, on the strip, and turn the wheel round until the centre of the wrist corresponds to the centre mark on the strip between these two points. This gives the correct dead centre of the engine, which it is necessary to get in order to setting the cams correctly, so as to give and exhaust the steam to and from the engine at the proper time, in order that it may work up to its full power.

CLASSIFICATION AND GRADING OF ENGINEERS—HOW SHOULD IT BE DONE?—SOME REASONS IN SUPPORT OF IT.

Question—How should Engineers be graded?

Answer—Into three different classes.

There should be the *First Class*—of first-rate head engineers—No. 1 First Engineer.

There should also be a *Second Class*—of first engineers—No. 2 First Engineer.

There should also be a *Third Class*—of first engineers—No. 3 First Engineer.

There should also be the same number of grades of Second Engineers, and of Strikers—No. 1, No. 2, and No. 3 Second Engineers, to suit the three different grades of Steamboats and Engines—No. 1, No. 2 and No. 3.

The three different grades are as follows: Good—Better—Best.

A man might make a good first engineer on a No. 3 boat, who would not be so good on a No. 2 boat; and a man might make a good engineer on a No. 2 boat, but would not be so good on a No. 1 boat.

I think it would be better and more satisfactory for the employers and engineers both to have steamboats and engineers thus graded, and the wages to correspond with the different grades of boats. And if any amongst the lower grades of engineers on the lower classes of boats are possessed of genius and talent it will soon be discovered, and the way is open for advancement and promotion to those who are fit subjects for it. I think it would be a better and more satisfactory plan for drilling and bringing out more expeditiously, young and aspiring engineers, to be masters of their profession.

There should also be at least three different grades of prices for the three different grades of engineers; for it is unreasonable and wrong for an engineer to ask as much for running a second and third class boat, as for running a first class boat. This is another reason why I think there should be three grades of first and second engineers.

Another reason is, that any sensible engineer can see and know that small and inferior boats are not able to pay one-half of the wages that large No. 1 and No. 2 class of boats are able to pay. For example, some large boats carry from one to two thousand tons, and some about three thousand—and passengers in proportion—whilst some of the smaller boats do not carry more than one, two and three hundred tons—some more and some less—and passengers in proportion. The larger boats generally make their trips in much less time than small boats; so that the larger boats may make from five to ten times as much in a trip as the smaller boats. And hence they can afford to pay better wages.

Another reason why less wages are paid on smaller boats is, that they can make more time than large boats, which are obliged to lie up a good part of the season for want of water, &c.

NOTE.—To go more minutely into the particular grades of boats. there might be three classes of No. 1 boats, three classes of No. 2 boats, and the same number of classes No. 3 boats, making in all nine different grades of boats; and no doubt it is the same with the engineers. But to be governed by this rule at present, would give too much trouble. Almost every boy knows that there are three different grades of No 1, No. 2 and No. 3—first, second and third class of boats, as well as No. 1, No. 2 and No. 3, first class No. 1 and second class No. 2 engineers—just the same as there are first, second and third class mechanics in all the different branches; as well as clerks, preachers, lawyers, doctors, &c., &c.

The generality of employers who engage men, are not competent of themselves to judge between the three different grades of men. and are as likely to give a third class man as much, and sometimes more, than he is willing to give to a first class man, especially if he is a good talker and can blow his own horn very well. It takes a diamond to cut a diamond, and it takes a workman to tell who is a good workman. So it takes a good engineer to be competent to tell a good engineer from a bad one. It is true as a tree is known by its fruit, so a good engineer may be known from a bad one by persons knowing very little about machinery, by the way in which the engine is kept running, and the boat making speed, &c.

But still, as I have said before, a good engineer is more competent than any one else to judge of the difference between a good and bad engineer.

HOW TO DETERMINE THE HORSE POWER OF AN ENGINE—SIZE OF GOVERNOR-PIPE, &c.

On page see a note on getting the horse power of an engine, it reads thus :—

Square the diameter of the cylinder and divide by 5, with medium steam and speed. I suppose this rule would take better if I had stated the amount of steam required to be used, and speed of engine requisite, according to this rule, which I will state.—Steam, 100 ℔s. per square inch, and the travel of the piston to be 300 feet per minute.

EXAMPLE—What number of horse power would there be in an engine 16 inches diameter, 3 feet stroke?

Diameter of cylinder 16 inches,
16 squared,

96
16

5)256

½)51 1-5 Horse Power.

25 6-20

An engine same size, carrying but 50 ℔s. steam, would be one half this power; 75 ℔s., three-fourths, and the power would vary in proportion as the speed of the piston or height of steam is varied from the rule above.

A rule that will generally apply in deciding as to the

size of governor required, is to divide the diameter in inches, of cylinder, by 4, the result gives the size suitable.

To obtain the full power of the engine, the steam pipe should be not less than one-fourth of the diameter of the cylinder, with stop valve and governor openings to correspond.

EXAMPLE—If the cylinder is 12 inches diameter, then the steam pipe, governor and stop valve should have a 3-inch opening; and if 16 inches diameter, a 4-inch opening would be required; and if 20 inches, a 5-inch opening would be required. According to this rule, the area of the diameter of the steam pipe in square inches, is one-sixteenth of that of the cylinder.

Diameter of Steam Pipe.	Square Inches.	Diameter of Cylinder.	Square inches in Cylinder.
3	7,608	12	113.09
4	12,566	16	201.06
5	19,635	20	314.15

EXAMPLE—A steam pipe containing one square inch, would supply a cylinder, containing 16 square inches in diameter.

One square inch steam pipe would require a round steam pipe full $1\frac{1}{8}$ inches diameter to give 3—9,940.

$$3,\frac{9940}{1000}$$

The cylinder then would be $4\frac{5}{8}$ diameter gives 16,800.

$$16,\frac{8,00}{10,00}$$

HOW TO SET BOILERS.

In order to set boilers on a level when the boat is in trim, fore and aft, some persons measure from the kelson up, allowing for the thickness of the deck plank, and thus make the boilers level or parallel with the kelson, fore and aft. The most simple and correct way, however, after the boat is equally trimmed, is to place a little clay in each end of the boiler flues and then put some water into them. Should the boat be a little more draft at the head or stern, of course a proportionate allowance should be made.

A great part of mankind employ their first years to make their last miserable.

"A prudent man forseeth the evil and hideth himself: but the simple pass on and are punished."

He who serveth none but himself is a slave to a fool.

www.ingramcontent.com/pod-product-compliance
Lightning Source LLC
LaVergne TN
LVHW020555110826
845149LV00002B/282

9781418188337